A
TIME
OF
ONE'S
OWN

Catherine
Grant

A TIME OF ONE'S OWN

Histories of Feminism in
Contemporary Art

Duke University Press   *Durham and London*   2022

© 2022 DUKE UNIVERSITY PRESS.
All rights reserved
Designed by Courtney Leigh Richardson
Project Editor: Bird Williams
Typeset in Garamond Premier Pro and Helvetica Neue LT Std
 by Copperline Book Services

Library of Congress Cataloging-in-Publication Data
Names: Grant, Catherine (Catherine Mary), author.
Title: A time of one's own : histories of feminism in contemporary art /
Catherine Grant.
Description: Durham : Duke University Press, 2022. | Includes
bibliographical references and index.
Identifiers: LCCN 2021057125 (print) | LCCN 2021057126 (ebook)
ISBN 9781478016205 (hardcover)
ISBN 9781478018841 (paperback)
ISBN 9781478023470 (ebook)
Subjects: LCSH: Feminism and art. | Feminism in art. | Homosexuality
and art. | Art—Political aspects. | Feminist theory. | Queer theory. | BISAC:
ART / History / General | ART / Women Artists
Classification: LCC N72.F45 G74 2022 (print) | LCC N72.F45 (ebook) |
DDC 704/.0420905—dc23/eng/20220526
LC record available at https://lccn.loc.gov/2021057125
LC ebook record available at https://lccn.loc.gov/2021057126

Cover art: Mary Kelly, *WLM Demo Remix*, 2005, still, 1.30 minute film loop.
Collection Centre for Contemporary Art, Warsaw. Courtesy of the artist
and Pippy Houldsworth Gallery.

For my friends

Contents

Acknowledgments

This book has taken a long time to write, and there are many people to thank. While I was working on it, a number of important friendships developed, particularly through shared enthusiasms around feminism and its histories in art. Friends who have helped with all kinds of support, from reading recommendations to sharp critiques, include Fiona Anderson, Judy Batalion, Sam Bibby, James Boaden, Sarah James, Dominic Johnson, Sam McBean, Ella Mills, Ros Murray, Tahani Nadim, Kate Random Love, Elsa Richardson, Dot Price, Jeannine Tang, and Francesco Ventrella. Two writing groups have sustained me through the writing of this book. At Goldsmiths, I've drawn on the imagination and insight of Ros Gray, Laura Guy, Ian Hunt, Susan Kelly, Kristen Kreider, Nadja Milner-Larsen, and Wood Roberdeau. While Kristen, Laura, and Nadja have now left Goldsmiths, their work continues to inform my thinking, and many conversations with them have prompted ideas found in these pages. In Hilary Robinson's writing group, I have had the honor of drawing on the feminist expertise of Flick Allen, Lina Džuverović, Althea Greenan, Alexandra Kokoli, Ceren Özpınar, Lara Perry, Helena Reckitt, Lucy Reynolds, Jo Stockham, and Amy Tobin. Althea Greenan, as curator of the Women's Art Library, has been a friend for more than twenty years, and her insights into feminist friendships, collaborations, and conflicts across generations have always been of huge value.

The first piece of writing was done as part of the "Writing Art History" project at the Courtauld Institute of Art, London. My sincerest thanks go to Patricia Rubin and the members of the writing group, who supported and interrogated the earliest ideas found here. My students at the Slade, the Courtauld Institute of Art, and Goldsmiths were incredibly helpful as I worked out ideas around the legacies of feminism in contemporary art and proposed my expanded concept of reenactment through Brecht and Woolf. Some have now gone on to do groundbreaking scholarship, and I'm honored to call a number of them friends—in particular, Jen Boyd, Giulia Damiani, Flora Dunster, Clarissa Jacobs, Louisa Lee, Kostas Stasinopoulos, and Amy Tobin. Flora requires special thanks for introducing me to a couple of key works in the book and for fantastic research assistance. She also introduced me to Erin Liu, whom I thank for collating the bibliography from all manner of files and papers. Lisa Castagner is an important artist in her own right but was generous enough to take photographs of my office and bookshelves to visualize what I'd been trying to get down on paper. Mignon Nixon, my PhD supervisor, inspired me greatly with her subtle, humorous, and detailed feminist scholarship and pedagogy. Her mention of Virginia Woolf's advice to women in *Three Guineas* made me return to Woolf's work on feminism, politics, and creativity for what would be an incredibly fruitful line of investigation.

This book maps a network of artists, curators, writers, archivists, and activists who have engaged with feminism and its histories. I thank them all, particularly those who were interviewed for this book or who entered into email conversation about their work: Ego Ahaiwe Sowinski, Pauline Boudry and Renate Lorenz, Ginger Brooks Takahashi, Oriana Fox, Clare Gasson, Rose Gibbs, Faye Green, Laura Guy, Emma Hedditch, Nazmia Jamal, Mary Kelly, Catherine Long, Samia Malik, Allyson Mitchell, Laura Mulvey, Every Ocean Hughes, Ochi Reyes, Lucy Reynolds, Michelle Williams Gamaker, and Rehana Zaman. I also thank all of the artists who have given me images of their work to reproduce in this book. I've drawn on the research assistance and expert advice of archivists, librarians, curators, and gallerists, many of whom have been very generous in sharing resources and ideas. I've already mentioned Althea Greenan at the Women's Art Library, who was invaluable, as were her colleagues Lesley Ruthven and Jessa Mockridge. Alongside this fabulous collection I have relied on volunteers at the Lesbian Herstory Archives, Brooklyn, New York; Kelly Wooten, Research Services and Collection Development Librarian, Sallie Bingham Center for Women's History and Culture, Durham, North Carolina; Anna Piggott, Feminist Library, London; Helen MacDonald, Glasgow Women's Library; Simon Gowing, Melanie García, and Roberta Cotterli at Tanya Leighton, Berlin; Emily Pethick, Rijksakademie, Amsterdam; Kadeem Oak and Lizzy Whirrity, Cubitt Gallery, London; Freddie Radford, Pippy Houldsworth Gallery, London; Alex Bennett, Hollybush Gardens, London; Kalale Dalton; Sam Roeck, Eisenman Studio; Cecilia Widenheim, Malmö Konstmuseum; and Lena Malm, Iaspis, Stockholm.

I presented early versions of many chapters in this book at conferences and seminars, and I thank all of the organizers and participants for thought-provoking conversations. Particularly important moments include "The Granddaughters' Generation," a celebration at University College London on the occasion of Linda Nochlin's eightieth birthday, organized by Jo Applin and Francesca Berry; the Her Noise symposium at the Tate Modern, organized by Irene Revell; the Feminist Object(ive)s symposium, University of York, organized by Victoria Horne and Amy Tobin; "Recollecting Forward: Feminist Futures in Art Practice, Theory and History," at the Association of Art Historians Annual Conference, Royal College of Art, London, organized by Joanne Heath and Alexandra Kokoli; "Flying: An Interdisciplinary Conference on Kate Millet" at Birkbeck, University of London, organized by Sam McBean; the "Anachronism" symposium at Queen Mary, University of London, organized by Ros Murray; the "We (Not I)" workshop at Raven Row, London, organized by Melissa Gordon; and "Gleaning from Mary Kelly," Institute of Contemporary Arts, London, organized by Mignon Nixon. Irene Revell's curation has been inspirational, particularly her work with Electra and Clare Louise Staunton at Flat Time House. The editors of journals and books that published early versions of some chapters helped immensely to sharpen my thinking as it progressed. Special thanks to Jo Applin and Francesca Berry at the *Oxford Art Journal*, where early versions of chapters 1 and 3 were published; Lara Perry and Victoria Horne, editors of *Feminist Art History Now*, where some of the ideas found in chapters 2 and 3 were tried out in a different form; and Cait McKinney and Allyson Mitchell, editors of *Inside Killjoy's Kastle: Dykey Ghosts, Feminist Monsters, and Other Lesbian Hauntings*, where a shorter version of chapter 2 appeared. Early on, this research was supported by a travel grant from the Terra Foundation and a number of Research Support Awards from the Art Department at Goldsmiths, for which I'm very thankful. I also thank Gavin Butt and Stephen Johnstone, who have both been important mentors during my time at Goldsmiths.

My family have been mostly bemused by my writing on fannish attachments and feminism but have been supportive and proud nonetheless. My mum, dad, sisters, and brother have all encouraged the bookish enthusiasms that fuel much of what follows. My partner, Francis Summers, has been there throughout, sharing many ideas and moments of excitement as well as the looped and disrupted temporalities of parenting. Our children, Maud and Ezra, and my stepdaughter, Betty, have stretched out the time of writing this book, but now that it's done, I'm grateful, as it made me think deeply about what I wanted from writing and how having a time of one's own is a profoundly political endeavor. Thank you to Annie Lubinsky for taking the manuscript through the final stages with such care, Courtney Leigh Richardson for the beautiful cover, and Jane Horton for the index. Finally, a sincere thank you to Ken Wissoker and Joshua Gutterman Tranen at Duke University Press, and to the anonymous readers of the manuscript, for pushing my ideas forward into the form you read here.

Introduction
Anachronizing Feminism

This book began with a zine hanging in a gallery as part of a modest exhibition about self-publishing in 2004. The zine's cover was a simple combination of the title in gold lettering, "LTTR," and a photograph depicting a woman wearing a strap-on and a mask of David Wojnarowicz, an artist whose career had been dedicated to representing queer life and death (figures 1.1–1.2).[1] Flicking through the pages of the zine (this was a small show in which the publications were available to touch as well as creating an installation in the space) I saw something I had been looking for, something that I recognized: a feminism that was queer, satirical, performative, angry, heartfelt, and funny.[2] This was not feminism taught as an institutional set of texts, rules, or politics. This was a feminism that was remade from icons and ideas of previous moments; remade for a community that was queer and rebellious; that mixed what was needed from feminism as well as from queer, trans, anti-capitalist, and postcolonial sources. On reading that LTTR stood for (among other things) "Lesbians to the Rescue," I laughed. However, the zine was serious about the need to take up the possibilities of feminism and remake them for the contemporary moment, something I also had felt was central to what I wanted to do as an art historian and a writer. At the back of the zine was a call for submissions for the second issue. This otherwise unremarkable call for participation spoke to me, as I wanted to take part in the community LTTR was shaping across its pages. As I flicked through

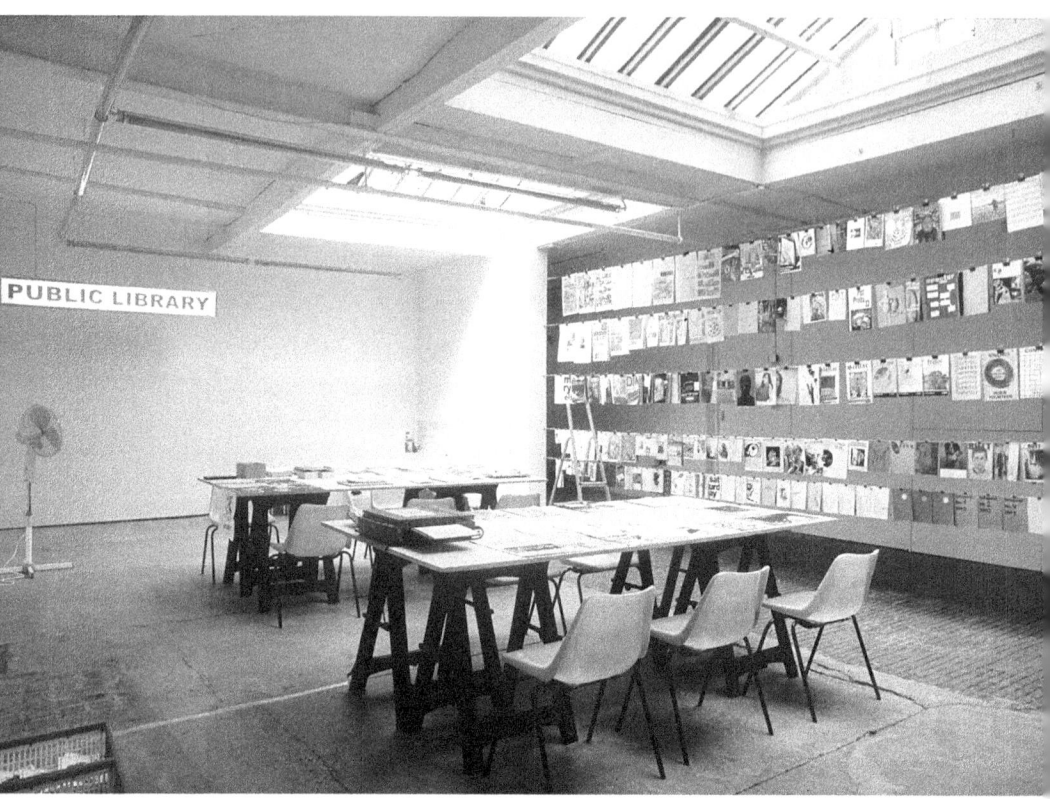

FIGURE I.I. Installation shot of "Public Library," part of the first Publish and Be Damned zine fair, curated by Emily Pethick and Kit Hammonds, designed by Pablo Léon de la Barra, Cubitt Gallery, London, 2004. The first issue of *LTTR* is just visible in the second row of zines. Courtesy of Cubitt Artists.

the list of contributors, I recognized connections with friends and groups in London, although the zine was based in New York. The threads of a queer feminist constellation materialized on the page, with connections felt across time and space.

The zine format is one that offers space for the reader to become a participant and encourages a blend of writing and image making that does not necessarily pay attention to historical conventions or disciplinary boundaries of the topic at hand. In this first issue of *LTTR*, the historical material reanimated ranges from an Artemesia Gentileschi painting to Valerie Solanas's *SCUM Manifesto*, alongside theoretical texts on trans politics; performative objects, including a bookmark based on a phrase used by Civil War reenactors; personal reflections; performance documentation; and a photograph that would be used

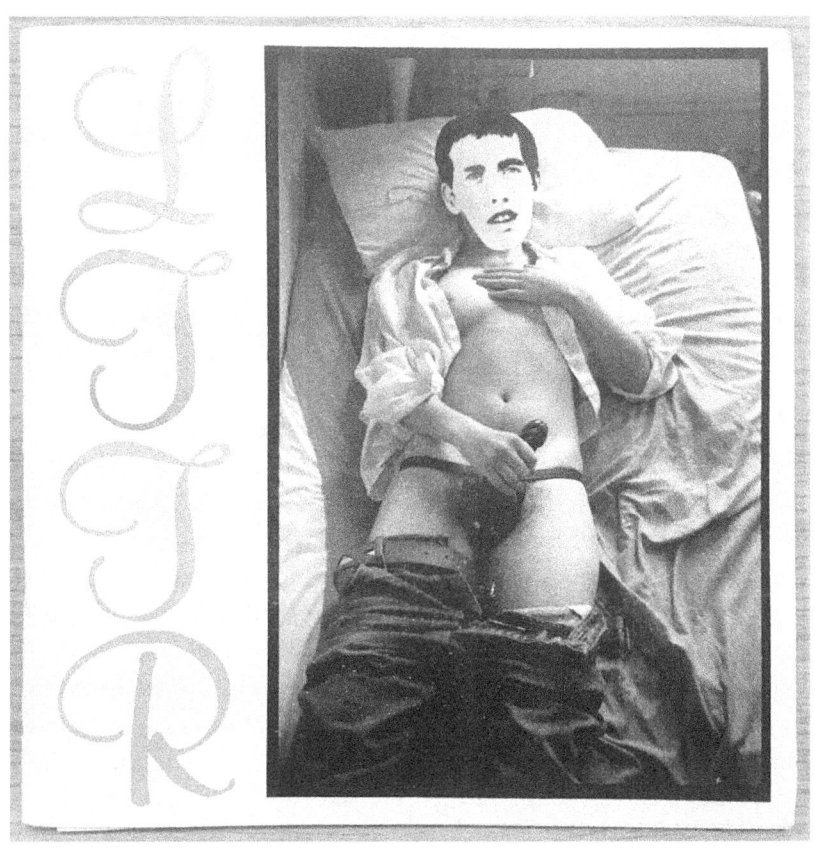

FIGURE I.2. *LTTR*, no. 1, September 2002. Cover image: Every Ocean Hughes, *Untitled (David Wojnarowicz Project)*, 2002. Photograph by Catherine Grant. Courtesy of the artist.

in J. D. Samson's 2003 *Lesbian Calendar*. There are no demarcations among historical modes of feminism or any clear definition of what might constitute artistic practices influenced by feminism. Instead, there is a messy, productive, and assertive relationship to a range of politics that center feminism but do not end there. The zine embraces historical material in a manner that refuses the narratives of "postfeminism" or "bad girls" in art that dominated the 1990s.[3] Instead the publication could be placed as an artistic reimagining of riot grrrl and queer punk scenes that emerged in the early 1990s and were still going strong in the early 2000s—based on music, do-it-yourself (DIY) production, and local community formation—sidestepping the concerns of an art world that had mostly relegated feminism to a historical movement.[4]

Since the publication of the first issue of *LTTR* (in 2002) there has been a groundswell of explicit references to feminism in contemporary art. This book asks how and why artists and other cultural practitioners have engaged with histories of feminism since the early 2000s. I argue that what joins many contemporary artistic approaches to feminism's histories can be understood as strategies of fannish reading and rewriting, with all the excesses of affect that the figure of the fan implies, which I contextualize and develop within an expanded concept of reenactment. My starting point for theorizing reenactment as it is found in these affective encounters is as a form of embodied quotation that takes archival material as a script to be taken up, re-performed, rehearsed, and revised. To understand the process of revision that can take place through the respeaking of a text or the rehearsal of a gesture, I propose that artists, curators, and writers have staged conversations both with groups in the present and imaginatively with figures and ideas from the past. Covering artworks from 2002 to 2017, this book maps a revival of feminism in contemporary art that is not an unquestioning celebration or nostalgia.[5] Instead, it takes up the creative, and political, implications of disrupted temporalities to activate "a time of one's own." Each chapter explores how the critical return and revision of feminist ideas in art have led to proposals and discussions as to what feminism means in the contemporary moment and what else it might need to draw on. Like *LTTR*, the chapters return to a range of material that is various and sometimes surprising, including feminist artworks, political actions, literary texts, iconic figures, TV shows, influential artists, obscure events, and archival objects. Across the chapters, a mostly Anglo-American set of references is returned to for what they offer in the present, a series of relationships that, I argue, can be articulated as forms of fannish, autodidactic, collective learning from history.

The argument that threads through the book is that, for many artists and writers influenced by feminism, the present moment can be understood only through an intense, embodied engagement with history. Their forms of learning from history reinhabit and reimagine feminism's pasts, often through a combination of archival research and personal experience. These moments of connection are ones I recognize in my own encounters with feminism as both a contemporary politics and a rich historical resource. This project began as I attempted to write alongside these contemporary art practices, to give words to my own sense of feminism's disruptive, looping temporalities and my place within them. While I say this book begins in the early 2000s, in fact its beginnings are multiple, stretching back across my own passionate attachments to histories of feminism found outside of and within art. In each chapter, I work through elements of how artists and other cultural producers are creating moments through which to engage with feminism's histories. In this introduction, I situate the strategies of reenactment that are employed in these practices through the idea of *anachronizing*. The importance of anachronism in thinking about history and the contemporary moment has been developed by a number of theorists. It is threaded through queer theories of temporality and is key to politicized thinking about history.[6] Here, the particular stakes of anachronizing feminism are grounded by encounters that take place within the artworks themselves and the experience of the viewer as well as by the potential for learning that occurs.[7] *To anachronize* is a verb that foregrounds the strangeness of moments of time coming together. This anachronizing brings out the specificity (and possible malleability) of our contemporary moment as well as a reflection of what might be useful from feminism's past. The word *anachronize* itself sounds made up but resides in the dictionary, although it is described as a verb that is rare. The definition given is "to confound time" or "to put into a wrong chronological position; to transfer to a different time."[8] Feminism itself has been seen as an anachronism, but rather than seeing this as a problem, I use it as a starting point into the layers of time and experiences that are brought together in attempts to imagine a feminist future. To "confound time" is to imagine time differently, and in the artistic practices I highlight, this often occurs through visceral and affective encounters. This book explores how artists have done this to bring feminism's histories back to life in the present, transforming them as they do so. As Juliet Mitchell has proposed, feminism is not a failed revolution but the "longest revolution."[9] As someone who has found feminism through its histories, I have included my own anachronistic experiences within the real and imagined feminist communities that are in this book, narrating an intentionally incomplete history of feminism's pasts reimagined in recent artistic practices.

This book charts a period in which ideas from queer theory about disrupted temporalities and archival affects have been taken up within artistic practices that foreground feminist histories.[10] Rather than a progression from feminist to queer, I explore the productive conversations that have taken place between them as well as the meditations within feminism on the possibilities of thinking politically across time. Joining these conversations with a focus on embodied relationships with material histories, this book draws on thinking across disciplines from performance studies to feminist theory.[11] The background to these theoretical developments has comprised numerous grassroots initiatives that have reworked feminist politics in the present as well as a resurgence of intersectional feminist imagining across academic and popular writing that draws on queer and trans theory, Black feminism, and anti-capitalist politics.[12] In this introduction I explore how these developments in feminist art, activism, and thinking have commonalities with discussions about how to define *the contemporary* in art history and philosophy, and I propose models through which to think about these returns as politically and affectively motivated scenes of learning: contemporary versions of consciousness-raising across and through history.

FANS AND FEMINIST COMMUNITIES

My first theorization of these relationships between the past and the present was to propose that artists such as those found in *LTTR*, as well as myself and other writers and curators, are "fans of feminism." I started working on this idea after noticing an increase in references to feminism's histories by contemporary artists alongside renewed discussions of feminism in contemporary art. This moment is marked by the exhibition *WACK! Art and the Feminist Revolution* (2007), which amplified the growing interest in feminist art, politics, and ideas across generations of artists, writers, and curators.[13] The energy, community building, pleasure, and queerness of much of this contemporary engagement with feminist histories was something I saw as a form of fandom to which I related, rather than seeing myself as a "daughter" or "granddaughter" of previous feminist moments.

The figure of the fan is one way to get around the problem of how to conceptualize relationships across time, which has been subjected to fierce debate within feminist discourse. The fan is not gendered or imagined in a familial structure. As I explore in chapter 1, as early as 1986 B. Ruby Rich was defining a generational shift within feminism, saying: "Feminism has become a mother figure, and what we are seeing is a daughter's revolt."[14] More than thirty years later, there is still a pull toward the familial and the maternal when thinking about lineage in feminist art.[15] The figure of the fan challenges this and begins temporally disruptive conversations across time that understand there is a differential across historical moments but refuse to see that as a linear progression. To be a fan is to have a close attachment to the fan object, one that has been influentially theorized as an attachment that is antagonistic as well as admiring.[16] To be a fan is also often to be in dialogue, taking part in a community that is driven by a shared fascination and a desire to learn.[17]

The community around LTTR has grown into a transnational queer network. It started small, a group of friends based in New York.[18] Since the first issue of *LTTR* was published in 2002, the group has become well known within contemporary art and is now seen as setting a key example in developing queer feminist approaches to art practice and writing.[19] The term *queer feminist* was not yet in popular circulation in the early 2000s, and LTTR referred to itself as a "feminist genderqueer collective."[20] Until the mid-2010s, most combinations of *feminist* and *queer* acknowledged the tensions among various non-heteronormative versions of feminism, including lesbian feminist, trans, and queer perspectives. Many of the artists in this book are having queer conversations with feminism or feminist conversations with queer history, often interrogating the possibilities for a queered feminism that does not police boundaries of identities, politics, and communities. In this book I am interested in how queerness has been part of feminism all along, how lesbian and non-heteronormative histories are central to feminism, rather than in seeing "queer feminism" as a new phenomenon. When I first came across LTTR, its use of the word *lesbian* transgressed what was seen as "relevant" within contemporary art; it read as an anachronism at a time when *queer* dominated as a term and put *lesbian* into play with a range of trans, feminist, and otherwise queer perspectives on sexuality and identity. As Every Ocean Hughes puts it: "We're here to reconstitute a new team under an old threat. . . . [T]his lesbian we speak of, I find him as ambiguous in nature as in verse. I find her over and over again."[21] Also key was the group's forceful self-organizing in the face of an art world that was still dominated by artists sold on their own uniqueness and individuality through a powerful gallery system. In contrast, LTTR drew on DIY networks, putting out a project aimed at fellow queers and feminists (while also staging the problems of working in close-knit communities). Across the chapters of the book I chart a series of projects that are often working on the periphery of the commercial art world, although some of the artists have become well known, and I explore tensions between levels of art-world success and privilege alongside more familiar tensions around generational identity.

Across the course of the book, there is not a straightforward progression through time; instead, there is a swerving motion that charts a course between queer feminist practices from the early 2000s and the conversations with the Women's Liberation Movement across North America and Western Europe, through archival research that delves into decades (and sometimes centuries) of feminism's histories, to conversations that stretch from the 1980s to the 2010s about the possibilities of intersectional feminist and queer politics. This swerving motion (which I think of as a series of returns) is also found in the location of the artists and cultural practitioners. It articulates a transnational network of feminist artists, writers, and curators that stretches across North America, the United Kingdom, and Western Europe. This includes cultural practitioners working in London, where I write, as well as in New York, Los Angeles, and Berlin, all well-known centers for contemporary art. They are joined by those working in cities that include Newcastle, Glasgow, and Preston in the United Kingdom; Stockholm; Oslo; Vienna; and Toronto. The projects explored here are not the result of my intrepid exploration but, rather, connections across these locations, a spiderweb of transnational feminist and artistic networks. My encounter with *LTTR* in a small exhibition in London is an example of this. The selection of artists' publications shown in an artist-run gallery was the product of friendships across the Atlantic as well as curatorial research.

Similarly, across the course of the chapters I have not smoothed out the different moments in which they are written but allow them to stand as markers that set out a recent history of feminism and contemporary art. Chapter 1 expresses the pleasure and tensions found in the returns to feminism's histories in the mid- to late 2000s, a moment in which political art practice and the possibility of protest was being debated within the art world. Chapters 2 and 3 chart the late 2000s and early 2010s and the growing visibility of activist feminist communities, both outside and within the art world, alongside the staging of a huge range of feminism's histories in contemporary art as forms of learning from history. Chapter 4 frames a range of group practices that span from the gallery to the classroom to the street, charting shifts among feminist groups speaking together, and speaking to one another, from the late 2000s to the mid-2010s, imagined as versions of a "feminist chorus." Chapter 5 takes up the ways in which two influential artists—Lubaina Himid and Mary Kelly—have articulated their own histories through an emphasis on conversations and communities that are formed across time. I narrate their parallel feminist constellations, which refuse a neat historical mapping of the artists and cultural practitioners found in this book, looping through the 1970s and '80s in Britain and New York, linking with their present communities in the art world and universities across North America and the United Kingdom: a transnational feminist community. The chapter, like the book as a whole, emphasizes that there is not one historical narrative to be told about feminism's histories in contemporary art but, instead, a constellation that should be constantly rearticulated so it can be learned from in each particular moment. The book ends with a conclusion that moves away from the discussion of artworks and instead provides a way to think about the forms of writing that have been necessary to write about the critical and creative engagements with history found within them. One crucial aspect of a time of one's own—having time to be creative—is explored from the perspective of the time it has taken to write this book and how Virginia Woolf's text *A Room of One's Own* has been used by generations of feminists as a model to resist, remake, and reimagine the possibilities that creativity, writing, and learning mean within feminism. This leads into a discussion of Woolf's provocative notion of a "new, poor college" in *Three Guineas* in relation to Stefano Harney and Fred Moten's concept of the undercommons.

The period starting in the early 2000s and leading up to the end of the 2010s is one in which artists have found a huge array of feminist predecessors, experienced as a community and continuum of possibility by some and as authority figures in need of reconfiguring by others. Across the book, this is explored through different models, starting with fandom, then looking to other modes of communal learning. I argue that many contemporary artworks try to imagine feminist communities that are "at once discovered, invented and constructed" (to borrow Teresa de Lauretis's phrase).[22] Not restricted to those who identify as women, while often (but not always) insisting on the importance of attending to the experience of those who identity as women and/or lesbian and/or queer and/or trans to understand the structures of heteronormativity, contemporary artists are finding new ways to connect with these histories. I hold the awkwardness of this listing as a way to underline the complexities of contemporary artists' relationships to feminism. Various identity formations across moments in time are a topic in many works and are explored in more detail later in this introduction through a multiscreen video by the American artist Sharon Hayes.

This imagined community of feminists holds divisions and conflict as well as intimacy and kinship. The discussion of racial politics and the position of women of color within feminism has been an urgent one as I have researched this book.[23] As a white art historian, I explore how artists and curators of color are addressing the need to return to histories of Black feminism, foregrounding conversations between women of color while also allowing space for a white viewer. Through the idea of a "feminist chorus" and the concept of the constellation, explored later in the introduction, I look at different communities of feminists and the sometimes antagonistic relationships among women artists along lines of race, particularly in regard to visibility and art-world success. While writing, I returned to conversations between the poets and writers Adrienne Rich and Audre Lorde as they navigated their friendship, shared passions and the need to find common ground between Black and white women, and expressed moments of tension as well as kinship.[24] These conversations are also found within their writing. For example, Rich begins the essay "To Invent What We Desire" by asking, "What does a poet need to know?"[25] One of her answers to this question comes in the form of a quotation from Lorde, the title of her famous essay, "Poetry Is Not a Luxury." In it, Lorde argues that poetry is the space of imagining where new possibilities come forward; that it is "a revelatory distillation of experience."[26] She presents poetry as one way into the unspoken, unrepresented realities of women's oppression and contends that seeing such activity as a luxury means that "we give up the future of our worlds."[27] Poetry as a space of imagining new possibilities can also be seen as a way of thinking about the artistic practices tracked in this book and how they imaginatively bring together different moments in time to learn from history and remake it for the present.

With her emphasis on what poetry can do, Lorde pays close attention to feelings and their political implications in regard to gender, sexuality, and race, anticipating recent interest in affect in queer theory. Many writers have used Lorde's writing as a map to imagine a new politics and an archive of feelings in the present, with her words being central to Sara Ahmed's *Living a Feminist Life* and the theorization of intersectional feminist politics.[28] Echoing Lorde, Ahmed writes that, for her, "feminism is poetry," a way of taking up words, histories, and objects.[29] Lorde initially wrote "Poetry Is Not a Luxury" while serving as poetry editor at the feminist journal *Chrysalis*, employing the pages of the journal to reach a community and to create one. However, this potential community was short-lived, as Alexis Pauline Gumbs has explored. Lorde and her fellow poet June Jordan resigned from *Chrysalis* in protest over the marginalization of women of color.[30] These tensions have not disappeared in the decades since and have become part of the conversation about how to create intersectional feminist communities; these tensions are reflected in a number of the artworks I explore, including the London-based, artist-run Women of Colour Index Reading Group, discussed as an example of a feminist chorus in chapter 4.

LEARNING FROM HISTORY

From the figure of the fan, this book moves through the possibilities of learning from history, starting with an expanded definition of *reenactment*. To extend the group work and collective learning that takes place in fannish communities, I focus on the pedagogical relationships that occur in many art practices and relate them to Bertolt Brecht's considerations of how to turn the theater into a space of group learning. Drawing on his speculative outlines for the learning-play (his translation of *Lehrstück*), I propose that feminist histories become scripts that are starting points for discussion and embodied revisions, a rehearsal of possibilities that also creates a feminist community in the present. This return to Brecht is also a feminist repetition, as his writings were influential in the 1970s in thinking about the politics of representation, with key ideas taken up by many feminist artists and writers.[31] However, his concept of the learning-play was not taken up with the enthusiasm given to others, such as *Verfremdungseffekt* (defamiliarization or alienation effect). Here I treat his model as historical material that is only now coming into a Benjaminian constellation with the present.[32] As set out later in this introduction, Walter Benjamin's enigmatic theories of history have been crucial for the development of queer temporalities as well as for discussions of re-performance and reenactment. I take Benjamin's concept of the constellation as a way to think about our relationship with the contemporary moment and its potential for illuminating moments in the past (with Brecht's learning-play as a method for enacting this). I put these discussions of disrupted temporalities alongside feminist approaches to history writing and consciousness-raising to show how they hold potential for analyzing the performance of anachronistic relationships to time. I propose that the artworks explored in this book rework Benjaminian ideas by creating a sense of community across time and space, rather than by foregrounding an individual's relationship to moments in time, in which the anachronizing of history is felt as a visceral connection to others in the present moment and through crucial moments of the past.

I have used a reworking of Woolf's famous phrase "a room of one's own" to bring together these ideas. I take her explorations of the necessity for a space to be creative and a sense of a location within a history (or, at the very least, a fantasy of one) and reimagine them as "a time of one's own." A time of one's own is a way to think about bringing together different moments in time and how this can facilitate creativity, a sense of identity, and the possibility of a community. By focusing on the time rather than the room in Woolf's arguments, I join her historical text with contemporary concerns about time-poverty, as some of us now have a room but no time to use it. Many feminists have taken up *A Room of One's Own* and reimagined it. There is a continued possibility contained within the book's title, its argument, and the method of its presentation through personal experience, fantasy, and research. A quotation from the Italian feminist group Milan Women's Bookstore Collective is just one reworking: "The room of one's own must be understood differently, then, as a symbolic placement, a space-time furnished with female gendered references, where one goes for meaningful preparation before work, and confirmation after."[33] This version of a room of one's own as a "space-time" that enables feminist work is threaded through the artworks and ideas explored in this book. This space-time is also a way to think about the layers of time that come together in acts of anachronizing, allowing for them to be seen anew as they are put together in different combinations in our contemporary moment. The "female-gendered references" have expanded over recent decades to encompass complex feminist communities and histories that are reworked by artists, writers, and curators.

A multiscreen video work by the artist Sharon Hayes exemplifies engagement with the potential of the radical past and the communities found within and through it. Hayes is one of the artists who has risen to prominence across the time mapped in this book. Her presence is found in a number of chapters, but only tangentially—her early work *In the Near Future* (2005–2009) appears as an opening illustration of what it might mean to be a fan of feminism, and her connections to the group LTTR thread through to the discussion of a collaborative work with Andrea Geyer. Hayes reappears in chapter 5 as she takes part in conversations published by Mary Kelly, by whom she was taught, and her genealogical description is included in the exhibition catalog *Trigger: Gender as a Weapon and a Tool* (2017). Hayes continues (and most likely informs) Kelly's practice of using memories of political movements to see how they might be reanimated in the contemporary moment.[34] From this one artist, a network among other projects starts to emerge. These networks also include the historical material on which Hayes draws.

"Dear Reader: . . ." This is how Hayes's five-channel video work, *In My Little Corner of the World, Anyone Would Love You* (2016), begins, but it is not necessarily how viewers will experience it. Projected on a loop, the video begins when the viewer enters the gallery; for me, this was with the reading of "The Black Lesbian," written by Elandria V. Henderson in 1971 for *Lavender Woman*, a "Lesbian Newspaper" published in Chicago (although when I heard it, I didn't know where it had come from). In "The Black Lesbian," written in the collective-voice *we*, Henderson outlines the triple oppression of Black gay women, refusing to separate out her identity to fit neatly within movements for women's liberation, gay liberation, and Black liberation. After outlining her experience of racism, sexism, and homophobia within mainstream society and within liberation movements, she states: "We will continue to demand our right to exist as productive, free, equal, black, gay beautiful women. We are not for a second to forget that we are against racism, sexism and heterosexual bias." She signs off: "Get-it-together, because we are. Elandria." In this powerful short address, Henderson asserts a position of intersectional Black feminism addressed to a lesbian community from which she demands support and awareness. The young African American woman filmed reading her text speaks the words as if they still have resonance for her today, and, in the context of the growing Black Lives Matter movement—and the queer women who founded it—there seems to be a strong historical link with the present (figure 1.3).

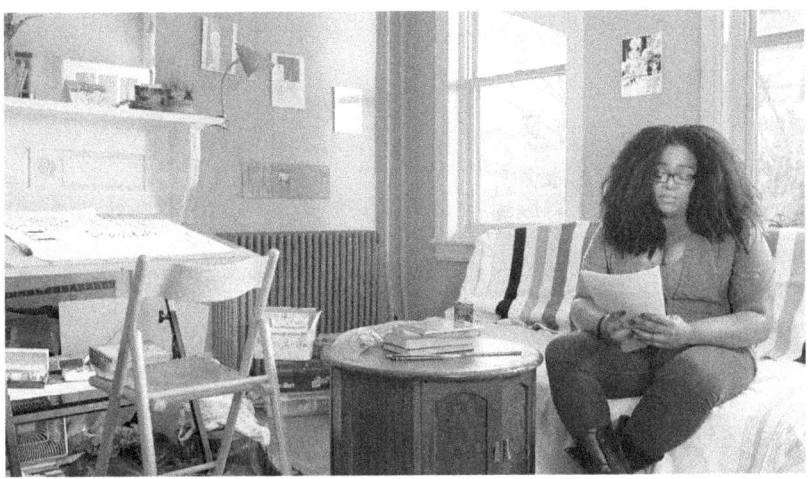

FIGURE I.3. Sharon Hayes, *In My Little Corner of the World, Anyone Would Love You*, 2016, film still. Pictured: Mahogany Rose. Five-channel H D video, color, sound; risographs, plywood. Dimensions variable, 36:40 minutes. Courtesy of the artist and Tanya Leighton, Berlin.

For the project, Hayes (with help from researchers) undertook archival research in the United Kingdom and the United States, exploring "material from lesbian, feminist and proto trans and queer newsletters and small-run magazines in the United States and the United Kingdom from 1955 to 1977."[35] A script drawn from these archival sources is read by a group of performers from "the contemporary queer and feminist community of Philadelphia," where Hayes lives (figure I.4).[36] Across the other texts read aloud, varying emotions are expressed toward members of feminist and queer communities. Nearly all the texts begin with an opening address such as "Dear Readers," "Dear Amazons," "Dear Womyn," "Dear New Friends," "Dear Sisters," and "Dear Editor." Many assert problems with the contours and assumptions of particular identities, ranging from butch readers protesting being characterized as "exhibitionists" or objects of pity to angry descriptions of heterosexist feminists, and call for connections and actions across diverse communities (e.g., lesbians in prison) and for ideas on tackling Ku Klux Klan bookstores and newspapers. This push and pull among desires, bodies, and politics traces a variety of passionate voices that were seldom captured in the collections of more famous feminist and queer writing from across this period.[37] By focusing on the letters and editorials in these publications, the texts demonstrate the historical presence of debates around race

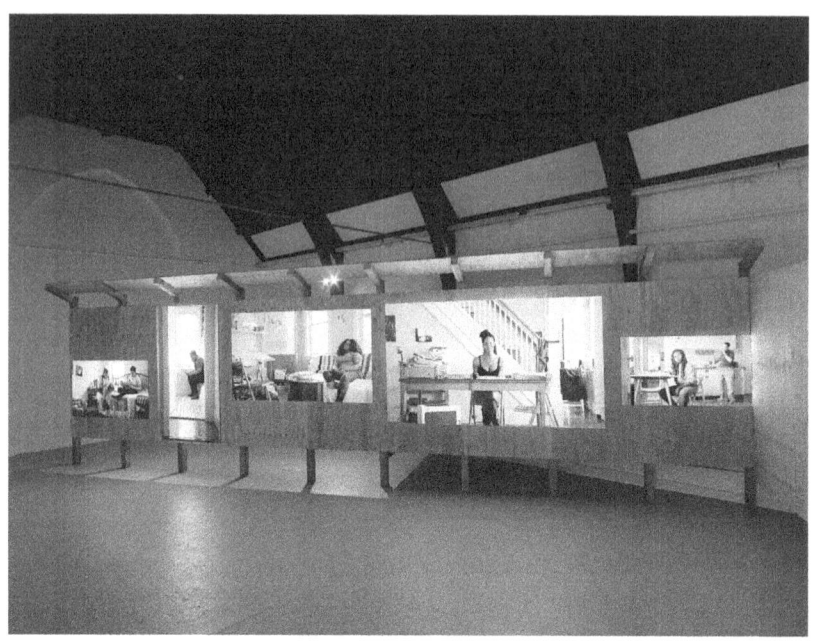

FIGURE I.4. Installation view of Sharon Hayes, *In My Little Corner of the World, Anyone Would Love You*, 2016, Studio Voltaire, London, April 15–June 5, 2016. Photograph by Andy Keate. Courtesy of the artist and Tanya Leighton, Berlin.

and trans politics within gay, lesbian, and feminist communities that resonate with contemporary discussions. While historical anachronisms within the texts are not glossed over, the form of the published letter tracks the creation and transmission of politics through a community connected by writing, conjuring a sense of aliveness within the moments in which they are being written and shared. The texts are presented in domestic living spaces—a bedroom, kitchen, bathroom, lounge, and dining room—and the speakers perform on their own or to one or two others. Many of the rooms feature folding chairs and a table and thus are available for work, writing, or study. As performers of varying ages, genders, and ethnicities read, the five channels sketch out a house that constitutes a community. Evoking the movable, changeable spaces of a house share, the performers variously knit, prepare snacks, send text messages, draw posters, type, and collate texts. The action of typing (done on an antiquated word processor), and what appears to be the collation of the sheaf of extracts that have been read, joins this contemporary group with the writers who have been picked out of the archive and the viewers who come to the gallery to sit, watch, and listen. The historical texts are made to resonate with the present through both their synchronicity and anachronism. The need for community is underlined in many of the letters, from an editor who requests more submissions in the face of an empty mailbox to stories of isolation and prejudice that a contemporary viewer hopes are a thing of the past. One woman writes: "On reading this news-letter, I feel that there is now hope for the future."

For Hayes, the use of archival material is animated by a number of strategies, which she has outlined as respeaking, anachronism, and citation.[38] On the use of the term *respeaking*, rather than *reenactment*, she says: "Respeaking is not re-enactment. Respeaking is not about a seamless or authentic transmission; on the contrary, it is resistant to such tidiness. The transmission of the text is halted, fragmented, and distorted, making it impossible to access the past moment as any kind of projected wholeness."[39] Her description is closely allied to what I ex-plore as expanded forms of reenactment, with chapter 3 paying attention to the process of rehearsing and chapter 4, to respeaking. In Hayes's video, respeaking is presented as an act of learning rather than affectless citation, with the presence of the other readers providing a sense of reading to another as well as to oneself. Here the transmission of historical material that was intended to build commu-nities is used to think about what kind of queer and feminist communities are needed in the present.[40]

The idea of anachronism as method that Hayes puts forward is one way to understand what might be at stake in bringing historical material into the pres-ent through an expanded notion of reenactment. Hayes explains why the term is useful for her: "I'm invested in deploying anachronism as an active error, a willful mistake, a deliberate confusion of temporality that exists as or insinu-ates itself into/as experience."[41] In this use of anachronism as a form of making strange, Hayes points to its Brechtian potential, something I pick up through an engagement with Brecht's concept of the learning-play. Anachronism also points to the potential in reenactment of creating a sense of "syncopated time," as set out by the performance scholar Rebecca Schneider.[42] Anachronism indi-cates that something or someone is out of place—coming either from the past into the present or from the present into the past. The disjuncture between times is what creates anachronism, something that normally is seen as negative. To be experienced as anachronistic can be painful and is part of what Elizabeth Freeman has so deftly explored in her discussion of (lesbian) feminism's "tem-poral drag" on queer theory.[43]

"What does it feel like to be an anachronism?" asks Carolyn Dinshaw in rela-tion to the experiences of the fifteenth-century English mystic Margery Kempe.[44] Her answer is that Kempe is "a creature of another time altogether—with another time *in* her, as it were."[45] This sense of having another time *in* the body pinpoints the way in which reenactment is thought of in this book: as a form of embodied quotation that cannot be seen as simply repetition, but is instead altered through its processing, whether through speech, gesture, or writing. This sense of having a time *in* the body also points to how anachronism allows for the revelation that subjectivity is the result of experience rather than essence, and, as de Lauretis has termed it, that which feels subjective is "in fact social and, in a larger perspective, historical."[46] In the artworks explored here, to anachronize is perversely celebrated, a refusal to see feminism's pasts superseded.

WHAT IS THE CONTEMPORARY?

To anachronize is to bring out what is needed from the past while altering the historical material in its re-presentation. This is an approach that I see as underpinning the numerous returns to feminist histories in contemporary art and one that draws on a rich interdisciplinary legacy on what is meant by history and, consequently, *the contemporary*. In the wide range of scholarship on queer historiography and temporalities since the late 1990s, many writers draw on older traditions of disruptive and affective models of history writing, often referring to Benjamin's writing, including his enigmatic essay "On the Concept of History" (1940).[47] In *Getting Medieval*, Dinshaw approaches Benjamin via Homi K. Bhabha's critique of what she calls the "closed sentences of history, the closed narrative of nation."[48] Following Bhabha, she discusses Benjamin's image of the constellation between the historian's own era and an earlier era as a way to understand the potential of historical moments to affect the present, something that Freeman refers to as history's "undetonated energy."[49] As Dinshaw sets out: "Benjamin's brilliant image of the 'constellation' revises any positivistic relation of past events to each other and to the present: its starry lights are emitted at different times even as they are perceived at once, together."[50] I bring these ideas together with recent discussions of what it means to be contemporary and the impact of these discussions on definitions of contemporary art. There is often a separation among discussions that take place in relation to theorizing contemporary art, feminist history, and queer temporalities. The particularities of art practices that work through these questions requires the writing of a contemporary feminist art history that is also queer; an art history that takes place within a constellation of artworks, artists, and archives; an art history that pays close attention to feelings, places, and moments in time both in the gallery and in everyday life—in short, an art history that pays attention to the question "What is the contemporary?" from a feminist perspective.

In a reworking of Benjamin's "On the Concept of History," the Italian philosopher Giorgio Agamben takes up and reimagines a range of images, metaphors, and examples in "What Is the Contemporary?" (2008).[51] His engagement with Benjamin's thought is both scholarly and creatively critical, with the essay's quotations and reenactments of key Benjaminian ideas and images reflecting the combination of research and reimagining that dominates the art practices in this book.[52] As I have argued in relation to anachronizing, to be contemporary, for Agamben, one has to be slightly out of step with the time in which we find ourselves. He writes: "Those who are truly contemporary, who truly belong to their time, are those who neither perfectly coincide with it nor adjust themselves to its demands.... [P]recisely through this disconnection and this anachronism, they are more capable than others of perceiving and grasping their own time."[53] Agamben layers this notion of the contemporary with a sense of it as a threshold, a limit point between the past and the future as a "too soon" and a "too late," "an 'already' that is also a 'not yet.'"[54] This sense of the contemporary has an urgency, as Agamben puts it: "It is something that, working within chronological time, urges, presses, and transforms it."[55] As with Benjamin's assertion that the politicized historian "grasps the constellation which his own era has formed with a definite earlier one," Agamben ends his text by saying that someone who is contemporary "is the one who, dividing and interpolating time, is capable of transforming it and putting it in relation with other times. He is able to read history in unforeseen ways, to 'cite it' according to a necessity that does not arise in any way from his will, but from an exigency to which he cannot not respond."[56] In this book, a feminist perspective reframes this notion of the force of the contemporary coming from outside of the person and reads it instead as a coming together of what is needed by that person in relation to history and how it is experienced in the present.

Agamben's essay intersects with recent writing in art history that seeks to define what "the contemporary" of contemporary art might be and that thinks through what it means to be a contemporary art historian. In his book *What Was Contemporary Art?* Richard Meyer explores how the concept of contemporary art has a history. He explores how, as a periodization, it is flexible. Sometimes it means art from this year; sometimes, art from the last decade. Within art history, it often means art since 1989, 1960, or 1945.[57] Over the past decade, a number of books have theorized or questioned the boundaries of contemporary art. They include Terry Smith's numerous essays and books, including *What Is Contemporary Art?*; Peter Osborne's *Anywhere or Not at All*; Jane Blocker's *Becoming Past*; the e-flux reader that also asks *What Is Contemporary Art?*; and the *October* journal questionnaire on "The Contemporary."[58] The use of the question format in many titles, and the mentions of the paradoxes of defining both contemporary art and contemporary art history, reveal the volatility of the first decades of the twenty-first century in relation to framing art practices and epochs. Most of the writers in these volumes agree that *contemporary art* is a term that needs to be understood not simply as a historical time frame but also as a way to define art made during a period of increasing globalization and a rapidly changing digital landscape.[59] The term *contemporary art* is a way to designate the plurality of art markets and art worlds that no longer can be easily defined by nation or movement.[60] To understand the contemporary within art requires both understanding the specific histories and places from which it arises and marking a shift from the emphasis in art history on a series of art movements.[61] As Osborne puts it, there is a need to pay attention to "the distinctively conceptual grammar of con-temporaneity, a coming together not simply 'in' time, but *of* times."[62] This discussion of how to define *contemporary art* has taken place alongside a growing literature on reenactment and re-performance in art, with returns to previous artistic performances and historical events forming a key area of debate in performance studies and art history. However, much of the writing on reenactment has focused on it as a general trend rather than looking at the specific return to feminist histories.[63] In this book, I explore how artists are thinking about a coming together *of* times, exploring histories of Anglo-American feminism across a period in which the circulation of materials has moved from photocopies and VHS tapes shared by researchers to PDFs and videos freely available online. From the early 2000s to the late 2010s, there has been a huge shift in the availability of historical materials relating to feminism, with many digital collections and newly reprinted publications becoming available alongside a growing range of new writing that embraces feminist politics for the present. The artists and cultural practitioners explored in this book have been part of this shift to make archival material available through strategies of republishing, respeaking, rewriting, and reimagining, but they remain focused on the embodied experience of learning from these historical materials.

AN INCOMPLETE, CONTEMPORARY ART HISTORY

Alongside this drive to define contemporary art as a conceptual category, scholars are paying increasing attention to what contemporary art history might look like. Rather than treating the term as an oxymoron, which would have been the case a few decades ago, work on contemporary artists within art history has started to be theorized rather than simply accepted or vilified.[64] Within feminist approaches to art history there is a rich discussion of notions of temporality, generation, and lineage that offers much to the discussion of "the contemporary" of art and art history. The issues brought up around notions of feminist generations are discussed in chapters 1 and 3, with the figures of the fan and the scholar being proposed as alternatives to a maternal lineage. My argument draws on a number of feminist art historians who have looked to reframe notions of "generations and geographies," to use Griselda Pollock's phrase.[65] A wide range of thinking of what it means to include embodied modes of looking, making, and relating in feminist art history joins the work from performance studies on reenactment and re-performance that takes up similar issues from a slightly different perspective.[66] Julia Bryan-Wilson explores some of the ground that I cover here in her meditation on learning Yvonne Rainer's famous dance *Trio A* (which I discuss in chapter 3, as a young British artist, Faye Green, performs her own illicit learning of it). Bryan-Wilson ends her text with a reenactment of Rainer's "NO Manifesto," making her own "YES" version. Here she presents the issues that are urgent for feminist and queer contemporary art history, concluding, "Yes to looking to the past for a way to endure the present, yes to inventing mediums and yes to creating new muscle memories and yes to alternative models of transmitting knowledge and yes to potential humiliation and yes to possible failure and yes to passion and yes to aging and yes to the messiness of contemporary art history as an uncertain and vital and undefined platform and yes to queer temporalities and yes to desirous histories."[67]

The writer and curator Helen Molesworth has also explored the necessity of paying attention to disrupted temporalities and embodied histories. In her text, which explores "how to install art as a feminist," she asks: "Might we be able to give credence to the deferred and delayed temporality of the recognition of feminist art, to pay better attention to which artists become available and/or important to us, and at what point?"[68] Here, the way in which feminist art has had a belated or obscured relationship to the dominant narratives of art history, particularly within the museum, creates a sense of temporal disjuncture that is not adequately addressed by models of influence or familial relation but can be seen as enacting what Agamben explores in his essay on the contemporary. Molesworth also points to "how women artists have often forged connections over disjointed periods of space and time."[69] Drawing on the work of the feminist art historians Lisa Tickner and Mignon Nixon, who propose rhizomatic structures, elective mothers, and sibling relations as alternative models to conceptualize relationships between artists and moments of time, Molesworth asserts that by paying attention to these disjointed connections, we "could better understand the young woman who comes of age as an artist in the halls of [the Museum of Modern Art] but doesn't see her first [Joan] Snyder painting until it suddenly emerges at the (corrective) retrospective at The Jewish Museum."[70] This book is, in many ways, about the artworks made by that young artist (who, I would argue, doesn't have to be a woman) in Molesworth's text.

In her short essay, Molesworth asks us to imagine a young artist coming across the work of an older feminist artist within the museum and the particularity of that moment of convergence. This complicated need for predecessors and/as peers, the impact of their absence, and the ways in which they might be conjured, if not discovered, is a motif found across queer and feminist thinking. From an infected dance of "Salomania" to a range of art and activism linked to second-wave feminism, I focus on artworks that see feminism as a project that is needed in the present but approach it through the past. The quotations from past histories embrace cyclical and disruptive notions of time—from demands that have to be made and remade over and over again to forms of community building and world imagining that continue to have potential today.

Taking up elements from feminism's histories that might be seen as anachronistic, outmoded, or embarrassing, these histories are returned to for what can be reimagined, fantasized, and remade. The return to feminism's ideas, activism, and art in contemporary art does not see feminism as a political movement that has been superseded. Instead, as Clare Hemmings has argued, it sees feminism as a diverse resource that often has been diminished through its narration while also continuing in the present.[71] This book argues that feminist histories' queer temporalities underpin a varied range of artistic practice, with issues of reenactment, archival reading, and community building coming to the fore.[72] These practices all provide ways into thinking about feminism and art in a manner that is intergenerational, complicating ideas of familial lineage and influence. If there is a location to be had for these artistic practices, and for my own position as a writer, it is one of the in-between and alongside. I write as someone who has grown up alongside third-wave feminism, but without a community, finding feminism through books and artworks in a viscerally transformational manner while entering the contemporary art world of the 1990s and early 2000s, where feminism was seen as outmoded and superseded. The shift that this book charts, beginning in the early 2000s and continuing to the late 2010s, is of an intergenerational network of artists, writers, and curators returning to histories of feminism with a passionate attention that is also critical and not afraid to rewrite where necessary. Across the course of researching and writing this book, I have found connections and friendships with numerous writers, artists, and curators who span the generations, or waves, of feminism. These feminist constellations—actual and potential, real and imagined—are woven throughout this book.

1

Fans of Feminism

To be a fan of something often indicates an overattachment, an excessive engagement that goes beyond the intellectual. The idea of a "fan of feminism" will, for some, conjure up negative associations: of obsession, of embarrassing desire, of a loss of perspective. Why, then, try out this idea of being a fan of feminism?

Since the early 2000s, feminism has gradually crept back into view in the work of a number of contemporary artists, particularly as a historical moment or mode of collective production, focused on second-wave feminist art and activism. The 1970s as a fertile feminist moment has been highlighted by the huge wave of debate generated by the exhibition *WACK! Art and the Feminist Revolution*, which opened at the Los Angeles County Museum of Art in 2007 and then toured the United States. This coincided with the opening of the Elizabeth Sackler Feminist Art Center at the Brooklyn Museum, whose centerpiece is the permanent installation of Judy Chicago's *The Dinner Party* (1974–79). The art press in both the United States and the United Kingdom covered page after page on the subject of feminism in contemporary art and its relationship to a feminist history. Special issues and sections on feminism were produced in magazines from *Frieze* to *Art in America*, with articles ranging from those by influential writers such as Lucy Lippard and Carol Armstrong to opinion pieces by a younger generation of critics such as Polly Staple.[1] If second-wave feminism was now fashionable, what was it that drew such interest? Books and exhibitions on feminist art during the 1990s had not generated such discussion, and when projects such as Amelia Jones's *Sexual Politics: Judy Chicago's Dinner Party* (1996) were looked at, it was in the context of the problems and arguments that had been provoked rather than as an appraisal of feminist art history in a positive light.[2]

Somehow, the history of second-wave feminism was either far enough away from 2007 to be discussed or, perhaps, it felt closer to the current desire for an engagement with politics in art. After 9/11, and with the Iraq War having led to antiwar protests internationally, the necessity (and impotence) of protest culture became a topic within the art world, with both nostalgia for a political past as represented by the late 1960s and '70s and engagement with what politics might mean in art in the contemporary context. By using the figure of the fan to explore the contemporary interest in second-wave feminism, this chapter explores a reanimation of feminist politics that paradoxically highlights the difficulty of a political art practice. An opening example expresses this difficulty: Sharon Hayes's series *In the Near Future* (2005–2009), in which the artist stood in various cities holding placards that drew from various protest cultures (figures 1.1–1.3). In the series of nine actions in New York, in 2005, Hayes held placards proclaiming, "I AM A MAN," "WE ARE INNOCENT" and "Ratify E.R.A. NOW!"[3] Hayes has described the project as "a set of anachronistic and speculative actions in an ongoing investigation into the figure of the protester"; the photographs that document it show the melancholy and absurdity of a one-woman protest in the middle of busy streets.[4] Here, the dream of collective action is replayed through the single figure, an image of resistance that is ignored by passersby in the street. By considering such a performance as the act of a fan, one can, one hopes, articulate the relationship between different moments in history in ways that do not collapse into a golden political past and an apathetic present. Rather than an appropriation strategy that privileges irony and distance, the action of a fan focuses on attachment and desire. However, being a fan of feminism also maintains the difference between historical moments and what might be at stake in replaying historical modes of feminist activity and art. I want to consider the figure of the fan in terms of Henry Jenkins's idea of a "rogue reader," a rewriter of the text that has inspired the fan's desire in a way that radically reforms the fan object—in this case, the historical moment of second-wave feminism. As part of this consideration, my own position as a fan of feminism provides a frame for my discussion of a range of contemporary works, focusing primarily on the journals of the collective LTTR (2001–2006) and Mary Kelly's group of works *Love Songs* (2005–2007).[5]

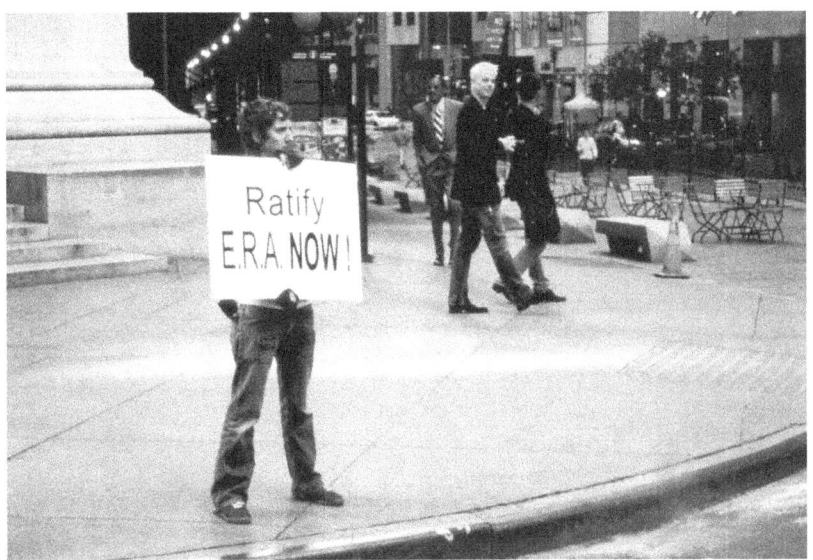

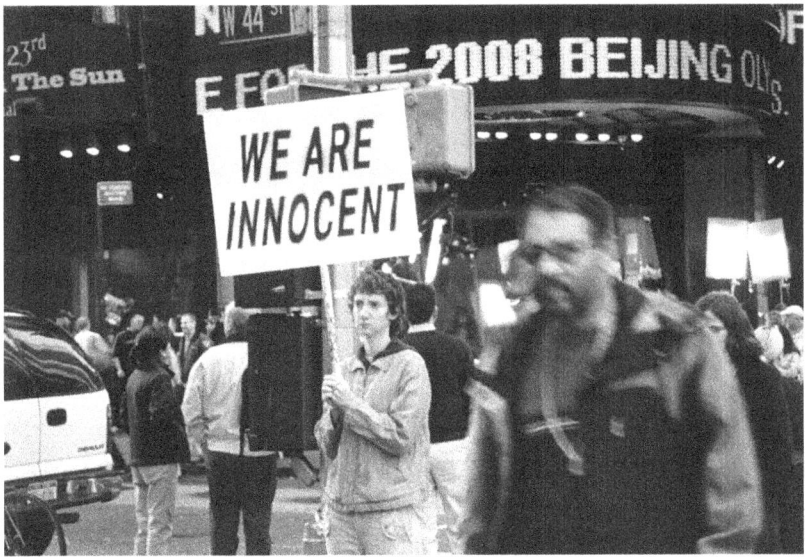

FIGURES 1.1–1.2. Sharon Hayes, *In the Near Future, New York*, 2005. Multiple slide projection installation, nine actions, nine projections; 223 original slides (729 in total), projection dimensions variable. Courtesy of the artist and Tanya Leighton, Berlin.

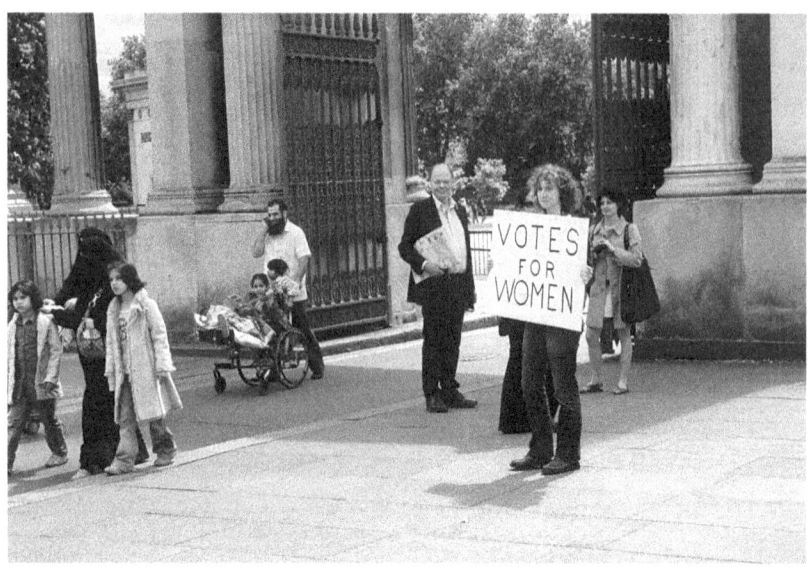

FIGURE 1.3. Sharon Hayes, *In the Near Future, London,* 2008. Multiple slide projection installation, three actions, three projections; 243 slides, projection dimensions variable. Courtesy of the artist and Tanya Leighton, Berlin.

DEFINING FANDOM

Within fan studies, fandom has been recuperated from the realms of obsessive loners and theorized instead as a creative, productive space of engagement with popular culture. As a model for rewriting histories, the differences between the fan and scholar seem to be blurred in many of the accounts of fandom, with a central debate being the self-definition of writers as being fans, academics, or "fan-scholars"—describing the in-between site of their work within an academic context or their participation in fan culture.[6] In this respect, my consideration of the artist as fan also incorporates the artist as art historian as well as the art historian as fan. Here the roles are blurred around a shared interest in a fan object—in this case, feminism. My position as a writer is equally colored by my own fandom, my emotional attachment to the history of feminism and feminist art. As an art historian influenced by the legacies of feminism, the figure of the fan provides a way to think through my relationship to a history of feminist art and writing. Having worked at the Women's Art Library in London from 1999 to 2002 and on the library's magazine, I experienced a gap between my own fascination with the archival material I found there and the lack of interest in, and sometimes distaste for, the idea of contemporary feminism among many artists and writers. At the time, I saw young artists and students coming to use the library and finding material that was inspiring and relevant to their writing and practice. This was in direct contrast to struggles that the library's magazine had in justifying its existence, with a funding cut in 2002 bringing to an end its almost twenty-year history.[7] It was during this moment of transition, when the Women's Art Library ended its active membership and magazine and became an archive, that I saw a video work by the London-based American artist Oriana Fox: *Our Bodies, Ourselves* (2003), the title a quotation from the famous women's health book first published in 1970 (figures 1.4–1.5). The short video shows Fox acting all four characters from the American TV series *Sex and the City*, lip-syncing to scenes from the series while dressed as '70s feminists.[8] As the character Carrie Bradshaw says, "Like every woman consumed with a relationship problem, I needed a project to keep my mind from obsessing and my hands from dialing his number," Fox is shown diligently sewing a Judy Chicago-esque vagina quilt. This humorous clash of historical moments and presentations of empowered sisterhood perfectly illustrated my own feelings of disjuncture between the powerful potential of activist feminism and the reworking of "empowerment" through the acquisition of shoes and boyfriends, as shown on *Sex and the City*. As Carrie might say: "Which got me thinking. . . . What does it mean to be a feminist in the twenty-first century?"

When I first saw Fox's video, I was not sure how to categorize it, but in the intervening years I have increasingly been struck by the number of artworks by women artists that involve a similar combination of humor, historical references, and hopeful reworkings of a previous political moment. Influenced by the activism of second-wave feminism, the do-it-yourself (DIY) spirit of riot grrrl communities, and digital platforms such as MySpace and YouTube, artworks were appearing that did not apologize for an interest in feminism but, instead, capitalized on a passionate attachment and often used video, performance, and self-publication as cheap and accessible modes of production that did not need institutional backing.

In his book *Textual Poachers*, Jenkins focuses on the subversive potential of fandom, describing the ways in which media fans interact with the TV show or group of shows that are the object of their interest. Jenkins describes these fans as "rogue readers," engaging with the shows with the attention normally deemed proper only toward high culture (e.g., art history).[9] Jenkins's definition corresponds to John Fiske's description of fans as "excessive readers," stating that "the fan is an 'excessive reader' who differs from the 'ordinary' in degree rather than kind."[10] Importantly, this intense mode of readership is also one that can generate

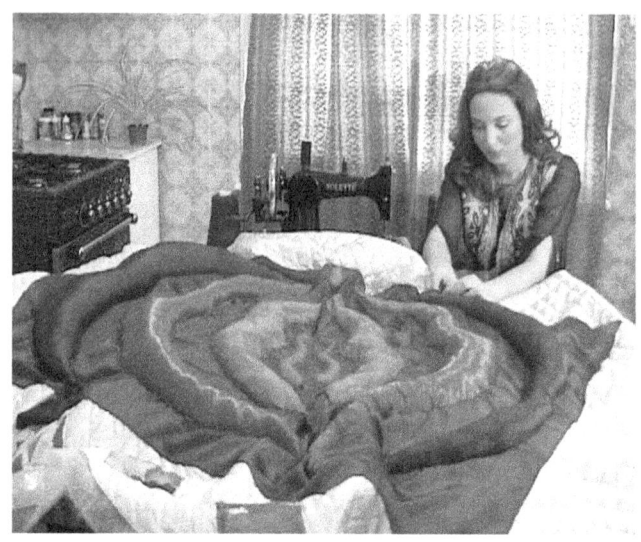

CARRIE (voiceover): Like every woman consumed with a relationship problem, I needed a project to keep my mind from obsessing and my hands from dialing his number.

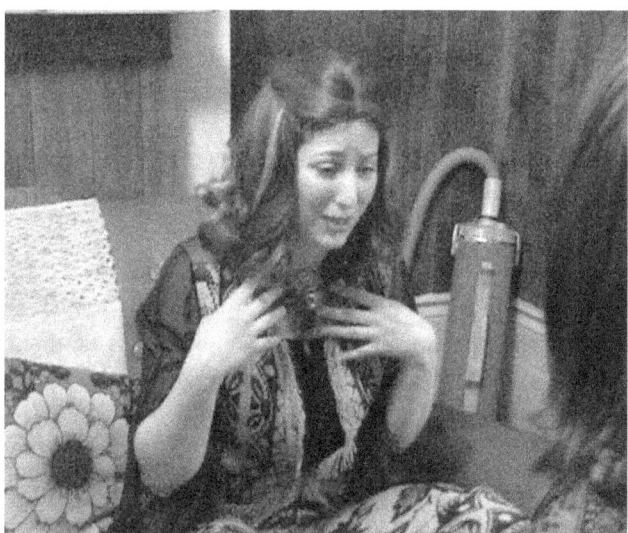

CARRIE (voiceover): You should see me around him. I'm not like me. I'm like "together" Carrie. I wear little outfits, sexy Carrie and casual Carrie. Sometimes I catch myself actually posing. It's just exhausting!

FIGURES 1.4–1.5. Oriana Fox, *Our Bodies, Ourselves*, 2003, video stills. Courtesy of the artist.

new texts as well as inform the fan's identity. Here the shift from scholar to fan allows for the desire of the reader to be incorporated into the study of the object of interest rather than remaining separate from it. For Jenkins, these rogue readers are also active producers of meaning, constructing the version of the TV show that they want rather than accepting what is given. As examples of this, Jenkins looks at various forms of fan writing, which can take marginal characters and create new plots for them or combine various members of the show and create narratives that take the show's storylines only as starting points rather than as boundaries to which to adhere.

The figure of the fan, then, combines the reader with the writer and sees the fan object as a key component in the formation of the fan's own identity. The passionate attachment to the object of interest is not passive but, instead, alters the object to suit the fan's needs; it takes a fascination for something as a starting point, which can then also start a process of negotiation and transformation of the object. "The fan's response typically involves not simply fascination or adoration but also frustration and antagonism," Jenkins writes, "and it is the combination of the two responses which motivates their active engagement."[11] This may be a productive model through which to think about the tensions between different generations of feminist artists and historians and how to relate to a feminist history in a way that moves beyond rejection or straightforward celebration. By approaching this work through the model of fandom, the engagement with feminism as a historical project also allows for a consideration of how feminism can continue in the present. Being a fan of feminism does not replace being a feminist, but it does articulate a particular relationship to histories of feminism.

In Jenkins's model of fandom, an active and resistant engagement with the object of interest is privileged.[12] This model tends to leave out the negative connotations of fandom. The term *fan* was coined in the late nineteenth century in relation to spectators of professional sports. *Fan* is a shortened version of *fanatic*, and in popular culture the fan is often associated with obsession—from the psychopathic stalker to the ridiculed "Trekkie."[13] By the late 1920s, fandom was primarily associated with teenage girls and young women who went to the cinema to see their matinee idols.[14] As Joli Jensen points out in "Fandom as Pathology": "The literature on fandom is haunted by images of deviance. The fan is consistently characterized (referencing the term's origins) as a potential fanatic. This means that fandom is seen as excessive, bordering on deranged, behavior."[15] This haunting "by images of deviance" is something that allows for the subjectivity of fandom to come into view, the violence that can be enacted on the fan object, even when that violence is committed in the name of desire. This alteration of, and intense engagement with, the object of interest allows for a more active model of contemporary art's use of previous political moments that focuses on what is *done* to the concept of second-wave feminism by this contemporary appropriation. Rather than a straightforward reenactment or scholarly research into a historical moment, the figure of the fan brings up the irrational, passionate, and violent aspects of the desire to embrace feminism.

LTTR

The journals of the art collective LTTR, based in New York, explicitly used a format borrowed from fandom: the zine (figure 1.6). A changing acronym, LTTR initially stood for "Lesbians to the Rescue"; it has also stood for "Listen Translate Translate Record" and "Lesbians Tend to Read." The collective was set up in 2001, and the first issue of its journal appeared in 2002; the founding members were K8 Hardy, Ginger Brooks Takahashi, and Every Ocean Hughes (then known as Emily Roysdon), with Ulrike Müller joining in 2005 and Lanka Tattersall working on issue 4. There are five issues of *LTTR*, which were accompanied by numerous performances and events.[16] On its website (www.lttr.org /about-lttr), LTTR is described as "a feminist genderqueer artist collective with a flexible project oriented practice. . . . LTTR is dedicated to highlighting the work of radical communities whose goals are sustainable change, queer pleasure, and critical feminist productivity." The manifesto quality of this description is borne out in the range of material that is presented in the *LTTR* journals, which showcase a range of writing and artwork, from personal stories to political essays, photography, music, and posters. The founding artists, who were in their late twenties when the journal started, borrowed from music and zines that came out of riot grrrl communities in the early 1990s in the selection and presentation of material.[17] The focus on creating a space for a community and the irreverent reworking of artworks, images, and texts ally the content with zine culture, although the issues' production values are nearer to an artist's book than a zine put together on a photocopier.[18]

Before considering some of the works in issues of *LTTR*, I want to mention a comment made Takahashi, a member of the LTTR collective. After I explained my project, she challenged my interpretation, saying: "I don't necessarily consider myself a fan. I see a lot of the work that people were doing in the '70s, not only feminists, but mostly feminists, as more existing on a continuum, and not necessarily trying to see it as history, as something in the past, and more as a spirit that lives through time and the work that a lot of people are doing now is really interrelated with that and carries that same kind of energy."[19] For Taka-

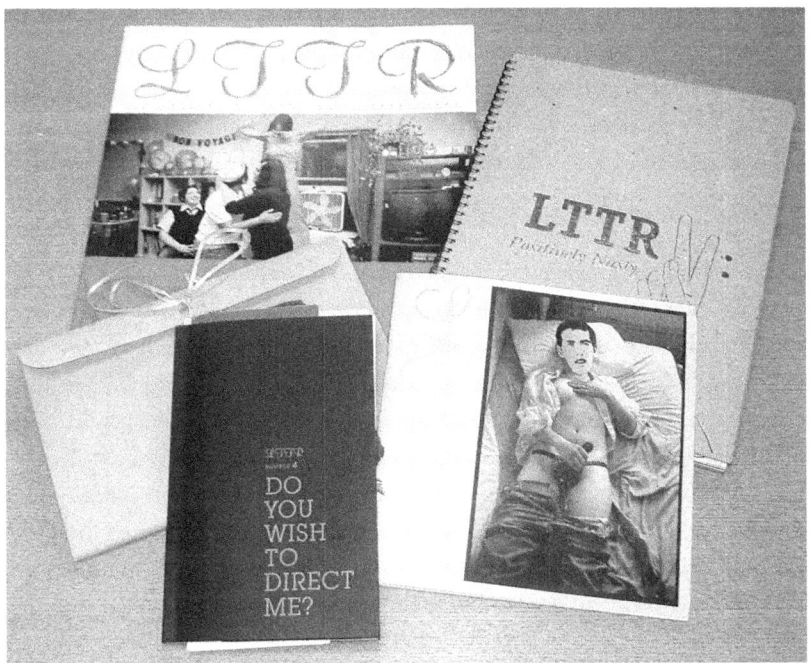

Figure 1.6. *LTTR*, nos. 1–5, 2002–2006. Photograph by Catherine Grant. Courtesy of the artists.

hashi, the figure of the fan remains separate from the object of interest and does not conceptualize the dynamic she sees taking place between her work and its relationship to earlier forms of feminism and gay rights movements. For me, the figure of the fan allows for an interrogation of the psychic dimension of the current interest in second-wave feminism and protest culture, as the fan both reenacts and mourns the desired moment of feminist revolution.

The figure of the fan also complicates the mother-daughter relationship that is often used to describe feminist generations. Already in 1986, B. Ruby Rich had commented: "Feminism has become a mother figure, and what we are seeing is a daughter's revolt."[20] While the mother-daughter metaphor does have some efficacy, conceptualizing younger generations as continually having to play rebellious daughters has obvious limitations. Another LTTR member, Ulrike Müller, takes up the problem of the generational model in a roundtable titled "Feminist Time," published in the journal *Grey Room*. Like Takahashi, Müller emphasizes her desire to see a continuum of feminist practice. In the discussion, the limitations and necessity of recognizing different historical moments are explored, with Rosalyn Deutsche proposing to "put 'generation' in quotation marks, problematizing rather than erasing it."[21] In my use of the term *fan*, I want to not only pay attention to the distance between the fan and the object of fascination but also look away from familial models. Particularly within the queer communities in which LTTR situates itself, the familial relationship evoked by a generational model obscures other desiring relationships between women. Elizabeth Freeman's notion of "temporal drag" explores the revisions needed when thinking about generational models of relationships. She writes, "'Generational,' a word for both biological and technological forms of replication, cannot be tossed out with the bathwater of reproductive thinking. Instead, it may be crucial to complicate the idea of horizontal political generations succeeding one another, with a notion of 'temporal drag,' thought less in the psychic time of the individual than in the movement time of collective political life."[22] Freeman's term combines the notion of performativity as described by Judith Butler in their use of the word *drag* with the act of dragging or suspending time that the replaying of historical moments enacts on both the present *and* the past. Freeman uses *temporal drag* to discuss Elisabeth Subrin's film *Shulie* (1996), a re-performance of an unreleased documentary about the second-wave feminist Shulamith Firestone, who would go on to write *The Dialectics of Sex* in 1970. For Subrin, what was at stake in re-performing the film were the points of identification with the documentary about a young woman at art school in 1968, focusing on issues of sexism and the construction of the self as a woman artist within the art institution. However, the potential for radical action is merged with the fear that this re-performance collapses politics into style. This notion of temporal drag may help to understand what kind of relationship is being played out between the contemporary artwork and the historical material with which it converses.

Across the five issues of *LTTR* are examples of reworkings of feminist artworks, texts, and communities in ways that bring into focus the different context of the contemporary artists while maintaining the importance of this feminist history. In issue 1, Rhani Lee Remedes presents "The SCUB Manifesto"—with SCUB standing for "Society for Cutting Up Boxes" (figure 1.7). Obviously riffing on the infamous SCUM Manifesto (1968), Valerie Solanas's far-out rantings on everything from war to the prevention of friendship, the "SCUB Manifesto" is a one-page, ironic call to arms that includes a request for "more beer on the streets." Defining boxes, Remedes writes: "Boxes: the thing in which restricts our thoughts and actions based on the square, cardboard and rigid stru[c]ture that groups and sub-groups use to suffocate [*sic*] and close in persons identities and/or non-identities."[23] The manifesto proclaims that SCUB is for improving

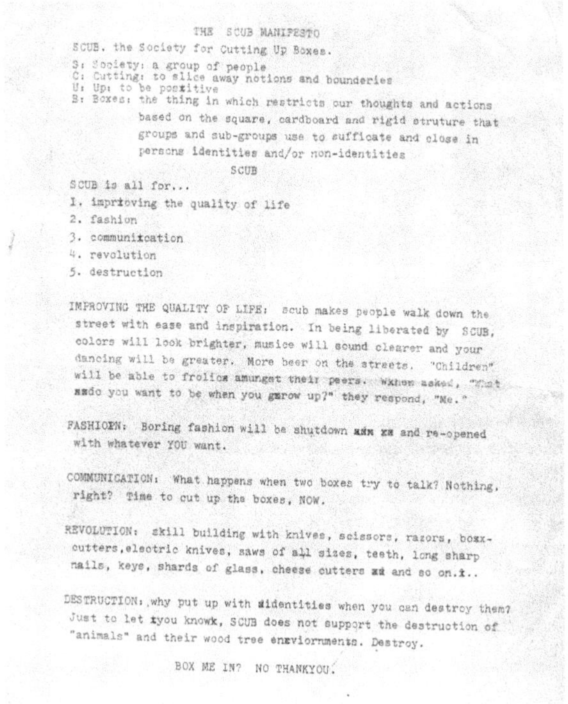

FIGURE 1.7. Rhani Lee Remedes, "The SCUB Manifesto," *LTTR*, no. 1, 2002. Courtesy of the artist.

the quality of life, fashion, communication, revolution, and destruction—a strange mixture of elements that characterizes how *LTTR* (following the structure of zines in general) incorporates the trivial with the political, the playful with the deadly serious.[24]

This investment in feminist politics while at the same time resisting rigid identity categories is a theme that runs throughout *LTTR* and can be seen in the combination of feminist with queer histories on the cover of issue 1, which, as discussed in the introduction, shows a photograph from Every Ocean Hughes's series *Untitled (David Wojnarowicz Project)* (2001–2008). This series reworks *Rimbaud in New York* (1978–79), in which David Wojnarowicz pictured himself and his friends as a modern-day Rimbaud, wearing a mask of the decadent poet while in New York hanging out, cruising, drinking coffee, shooting up. In Hughes's image, a woman is posed wearing a mask of Wojnarowicz's face and a strap-on dildo, re-creating Wojnarowicz's photograph of his modern-day Rimbaud masturbating. Here a queer female identity is constructed through a masculine gay history, with Wojnarowicz describing his series as already "playing with ideas of compression of 'historical time and activity.'"[25] Early publication of his photographs in a special issue of the literary zine *Little Caesar* dedicated

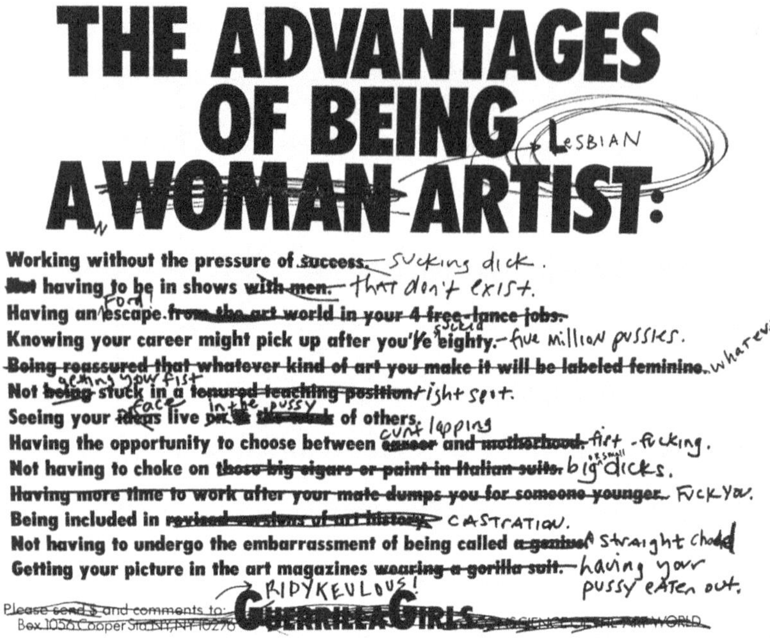

THE ADVANTAGES OF BEING ~~LESBIAN~~ A ~~WOMAN~~ ARTIST:

Working without the pressure of ~~success.~~ sucking dick.
~~Not~~ having ~~Ford!~~ to be in shows with ~~men.~~ that don't exist.
Having an ~~escape.~~ escape ~~from the art world~~ in your 4 ~~free~~ lance jobs.
Knowing your career might pick up after you're ~~eighty.~~ fucked eighty.—five million pussies. whatever
~~Being reassured that whatever kind of art you make it will be labeled feminine.~~ eating your fist.
Not ~~being~~ stuck in a ~~tenured teaching position~~ face in the pussy tight spot.
Seeing your ~~ideas~~ live ~~on in the work~~ of others. lapping
Having the opportunity to choose between ~~career and motherhood.~~ cunt flirt. fucking.
Not having to choke on ~~those big cigars or paint in Italian suits.~~ big small dicks.
~~Having more time to work after your mate dumps you for someone younger.~~ Fuck You.
Being included in ~~revised versions of art history.~~ CASTRATION.
Not having to undergo the embarrassment of being called ~~a genius.~~ straight chode
Getting your picture in the art magazines ~~wearing a gorilla suit.~~ having your pussy eaten out.
→ RIDYKEULOUS!
~~Please send $ and comments to: GUERRILLA GIRLS~~
~~Box 1056 Cooper Sta, NY, NY 10276~~

FIGURE 1.8. Ridykeulous (A. L. Steiner and Nicole Eisenman), "The Advantages of Being a Lesbian Woman Artist," *LTTR*, no. 5, 2006. Courtesy of the artists.

to Rimbaud also highlights Wojnarowicz's fandom.[26] These quotations bring to the fore a refusal of gender binaries and the construction of a queer feminism that reworks masculinity rather than rejecting it. Here the fraught histories of mainstream feminism, lesbian feminism, and gay liberation are rewritten on the body of a young woman who is articulating a queer sexuality that refuses to read these histories as boundaries.[27]

The queering of feminist histories is shown in "The Advantages of Being a Lesbian Woman Artist," by Ridykeulous (A. L. Steiner and Nicole Eisenman), in issue 5, a violently sexual reworking of the Guerrilla Girls' classic poster "The Advantages of Being a Woman Artist" (1989) (figure 1.8). As Freeman explores in her discussion of temporal drag, the act of queering history is a response to, and a transformation of, historical moments that allows for an emotive and political resonance in the present. At once both acknowledging the influence of the Guerrilla Girls' poster and challenging its politics with a campily aggressive lesbian sexuality, the fan here rewrites the fan object to create the stories that are missing.

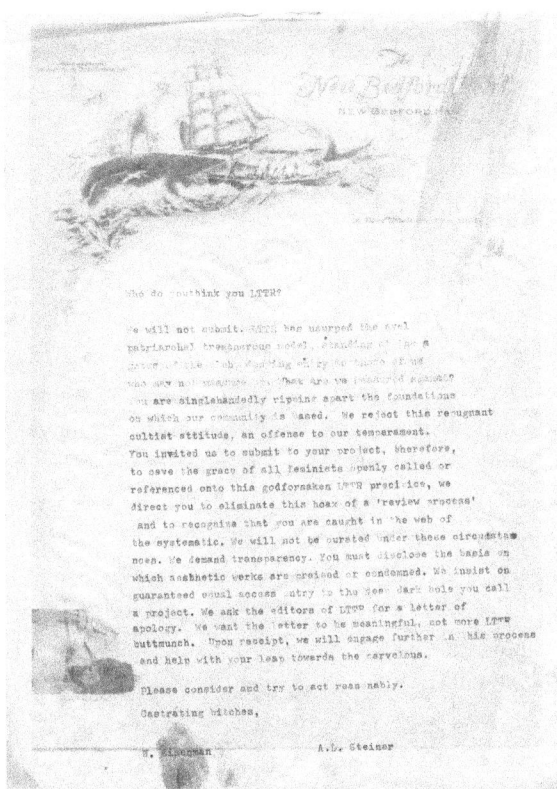

FIGURE 1.9.
Ridykeulous (A. L.
Steiner and Nicole
Eisenman), "Who
Do You Think You
LTTR?," *LTTR*, no. 4,
2005. Courtesy of the
artists.

Beyond these obvious quotations, the structure of *LTTR* itself borrows from the idea of feminist communities questioning hierarchies. A call for submissions that refers to a "reviews procedure" for issue 4 brings into focus the conflict between the ideal of a communal project and the tensions inherent in any such endeavor. At the beginning of this issue are two responses for submissions. The first is a letter from Ridykeulous (Eisenman and Steiner), who, as we just saw, contributed to *LTTR*. (Steiner has photographs in the same issue as the letter.) "Who do you think you LTTR?" (figure 1.9), the pair of artists ask in a letter, signed with bloody fingerprints, questioning the use of a "reviews procedure" rather than an open submissions policy. "We will not submit. Lttr has usurped the evel [*sic*] patriarchal treacherous model, standing at the gates of the club, denying entry to those of us who may not measure up."[28] Their indignation is echoed by an email from A. K. Burns, which asks, "Are you a marketing team? your venture stinks of shopping mall."[29] After protesting the system of selection, Burns ends by saying, "Thank you for creating something that makes me feel so much./consider this my submission."[30] As for the fan who both loves and hates the object of fandom, for Burns *LTTR* becomes the space of feminist possibility that is both adored and never enough.

By including these two protests, which are already ambiguously marked between "actual" letters of dissent and ironic artworks, *LTTR* performs the tensions within a feminist community, particularly around issues of control and hierarchy. Politics is blended with posture so that it is difficult, if not impossible, to untangle them. This ambiguity and camp approach to the dynamics of feminist communities is offset by the editors' essay in the same issue, which presents a desire for politics in a more straightforward, melancholic mode: "Halfway through the process of reviewing and discussing, we, as editors, faced each other feeling an absence. 'Where were the political demands of our queer community?' we asked. We felt hungry for some direct analysis of current state politics, government war tactics and homophobic strategies and their effects on our rights and daily life. We are all being directed through several wars by a government whose 'US' does not include me."[31] This need to engage with politics in an unironic mode is represented across the issues of *LTTR*, from Dean Spade's article on transgender politics in issue 1 to the reprinting of Eqbal Ahmad's 1965 essay on guerrilla warfare in relation to Vietnam in issue 5. Temporal drag is pictured both playfully and literally, as texts, ideas, and artworks from the past are re-presented to have an active impact on the present. As the issues progress, there is increasing awareness that having a successful platform for discussion within the art world can provide a place to disseminate information that goes beyond playful reworkings. The feminist project is used as a starting point for a consideration of inequality and politics in a much broader context, in which the act of being a fan leads into an interrogation of how to be an activist. There is pleasure in being a fan reader of *LTTR*, in recognizing the structures being replayed and the references to previous artworks and models. But alongside this, there is frustration at the limitations of the art context, as Müller comments in issue 5: "In a recent discussion the skeptical question about art's potential to change the world came up. I said that I am sure it can, because it has changed my world in many ways. I remember feeling polemical as I said that, and I also remember hearing conviction in my voice. I'd like to hear that again. So I want to know what we can do for each other now."[32] Müller's question is answered differently across the issues of *LTTR* and in the different approaches that circulate around the feminist maxim "the personal is the political." Being a fan of feminism in the context of *LTTR* is both pleasurable and a project that provokes uncertainty.

I now want to consider a contemporary project by an artist who became famous through work she made in the 1970s: Mary Kelly. Her project *Love Songs* (2005–2007) explores the relationship between feminist generations and her own history of activism. The fans of feminism depicted by Kelly both celebrate and obliterate the feminist past that is pictured as just out of reach while always being present through the attraction it presents for this new generation. As Kelly says about the relationship of *Love Songs* to activism, "People often talk about my work in terms of activism, but, ultimately, I think it's really a reflection on what that means."[33]

First shown at Postmasters Gallery in New York, and then in an expanded version at documenta XII in Kassel in 2007, *Love Songs* considers the relationship between Kelly and her students.[34] While *Love Songs* is very different in tone from the often confrontational works in *LTTR*, the project also engages with an emotional attachment to a political history, this time from the perspective of someone who was instrumental in second-wave feminism. The centerpiece of the documenta XII version of *Love Songs* was *Multi-Story House*, a small house permeated with text and light (figure 1.10).[35] Viewers could enter the house and read texts by second-wave feminists recounting their experience of the 1970s or stand outside and read comments about 1970s feminism by a younger generation of women. Above the door is the statement: "Everything was so clear then." This yearning for a political past is reflected and complicated by the different cultural and historical responses to feminism. One of the younger women states, "Second wave, third wave, missed everything. I went through puberty in Saudi Arabia. There wasn't even a first wave yet," while another says, "I grew up dodging bullets in Angola. So the term 'feminist' didn't mean much." Others recount a more romantic attachment to an imagined feminist history: "I love my birthday—May '68. But I wish my parents had been part of something like the German student movement. Now, in my way, I'm trying to be more revolutionary" (figures 1.11–1.12).

Kelly has provided a theoretical framework for *Love Songs* that focuses on identification and fantasy, which she explores in relation to a generational model. Before I consider *Love Songs* in relation to the concept of fandom, I sketch out Kelly's model and the ways in which it might intersect with the idea of "fans of feminism." In an interview with Ian White, Kelly describes the genesis of the *Love Songs* project:

> The impetus for *Love Songs* came from my students. I noticed that they were preoccupied with that pivotal moment we refer to as "the events of

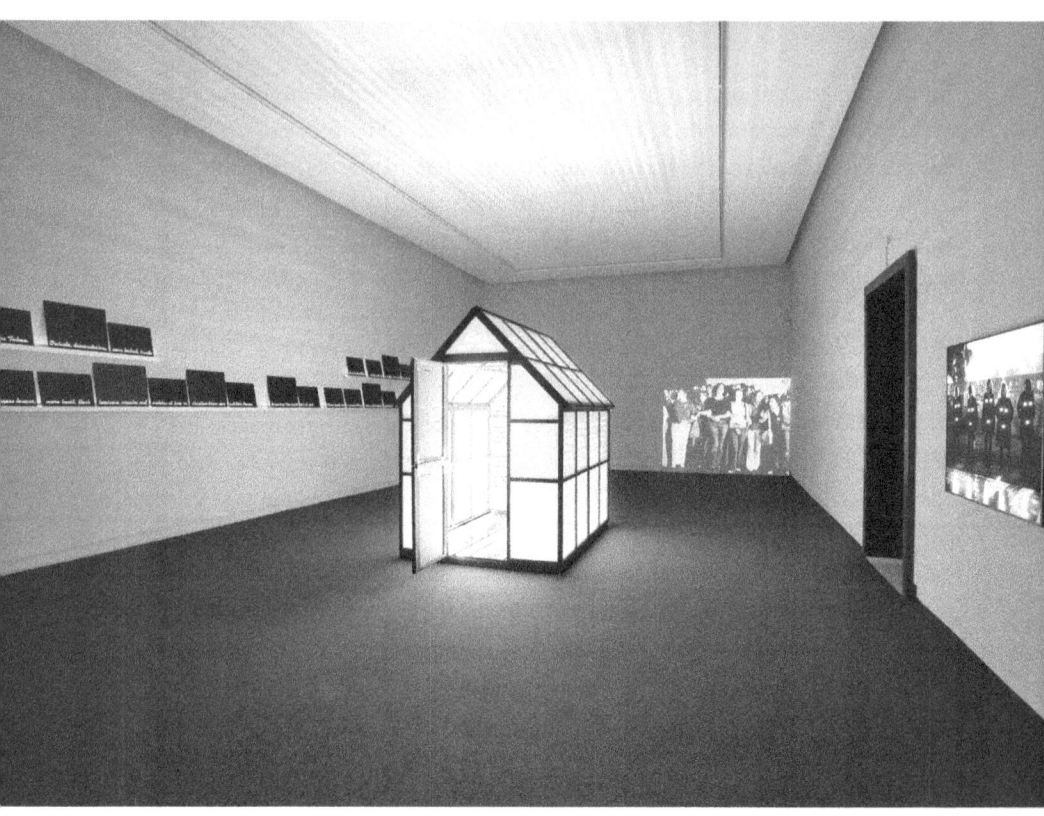

FIGURE 1.10. Mary Kelly, *Love Songs*, 2005–2007, at documenta XII, installation view, 2007. *Multi-Story House* is at the center. Courtesy of the artists.

68." Then I realized they were born around that time, so their fascination was partly to do with figuring out where they came from: what I like to call the "political primal scene." On one level, *Love Songs* is about the appearance of the past in the present, this generation imagining what they missed or what we were trying to achieve: on another, it's about my identification with them.[36]

The notion of a "political primal scene" is key for Kelly: a moment with which a generation identifies. Just as the personal search for origins is always characterized by absence (as presented by Sigmund Freud), Kelly emphasizes the fantasy that is evoked in this re-creation of a moment, linking the urgency of the inquiry with a generational concern.[37] Kelly also recounts how her students in 2003–2004 were the same age as her son (who was born in 1973), bringing an-

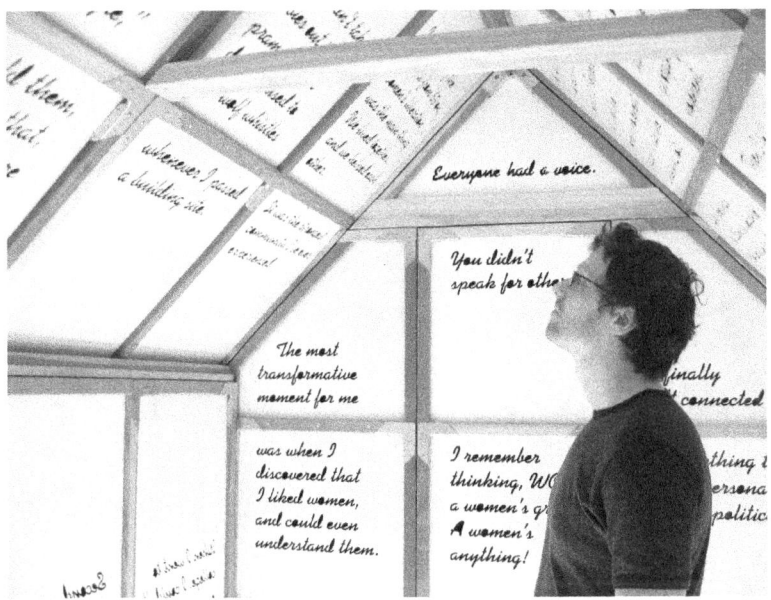

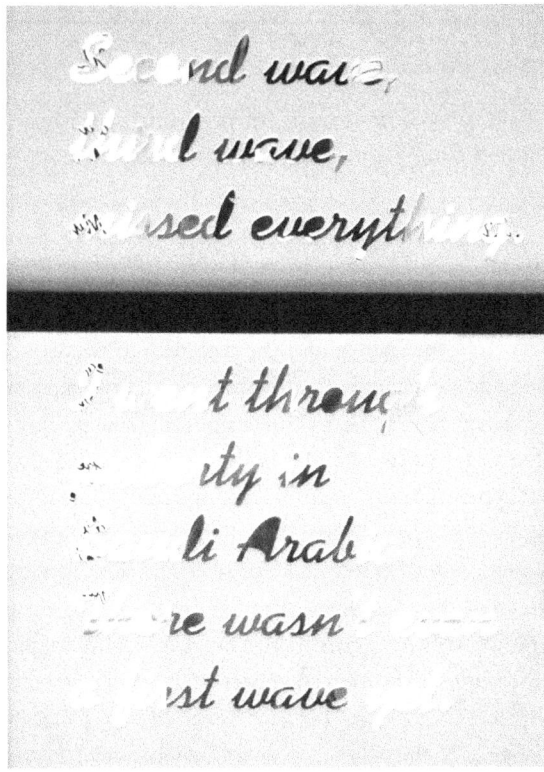

FIGURES 1.11–1.12.
Mary Kelly and Ray
Barrie, details of *Multi-
Story House*, 2005.
Collection, Whitworth
Art Gallery, Manchester.
Courtesy of the artists.

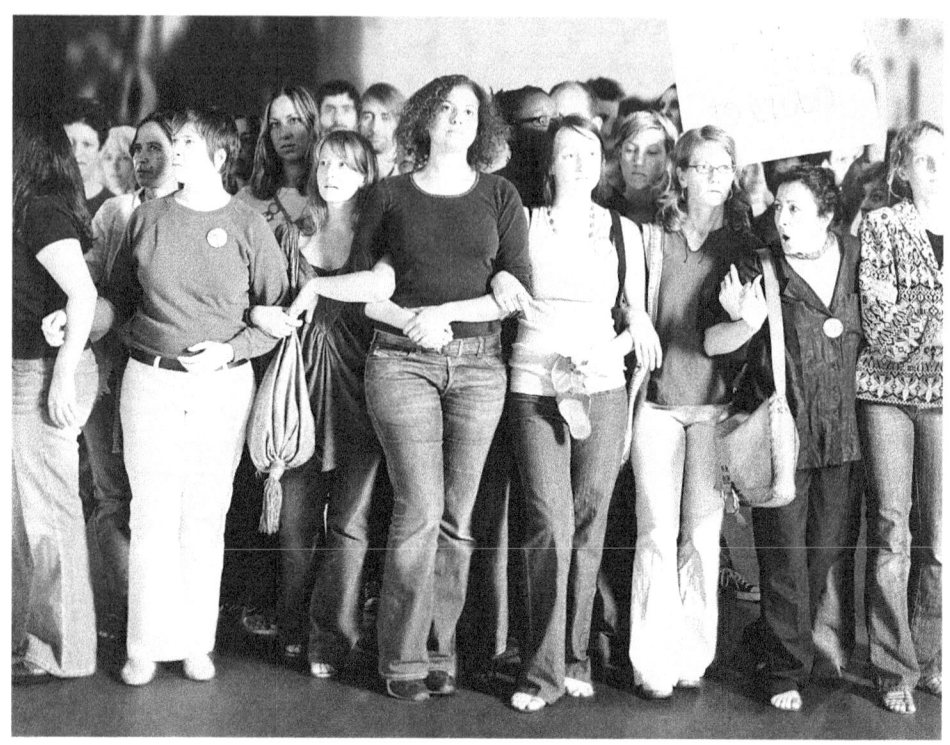

FIGURES 1.13–1.14. Mary Kelly, *WLM Demo Remix*, 2005, stills, 1.30 minute film loop. Collection Centre for Contemporary Art, Warsaw. Courtesy of the artist and Pippy Houldsworth Gallery.

other layer of generational correspondence.[38] When talking to me about *Love Songs*, Kelly repeatedly used the word *euphoria* to describe the tone of the work, remarking on the importance of "the humor and the pleasure" in the work, which sets it apart from the focus on trauma that unites her work on war from the 1990s.[39] The narcissistic identification that Kelly describes as taking place on both sides of the work mirrors the positivity found in the zines and collaborations of LTTR and defines much of the current embracing of feminism.

To think through the figure of the fan in relation to Kelly's project requires some work. Who is the fan here? Is it Kelly herself? Her students? The viewer? Or is it somehow the excitement that Kelly feels through her students? How does her position as an iconic artist of the 1970s change my relationship to this work? Kelly's position is rather different from the positions of the young women featured in a number of the pieces (figures 1.13–1.14). (Incidentally, Every Ocean Hughes, wearing a LTTR badge, is in the video loop *WLM Demo Remix*.) How-

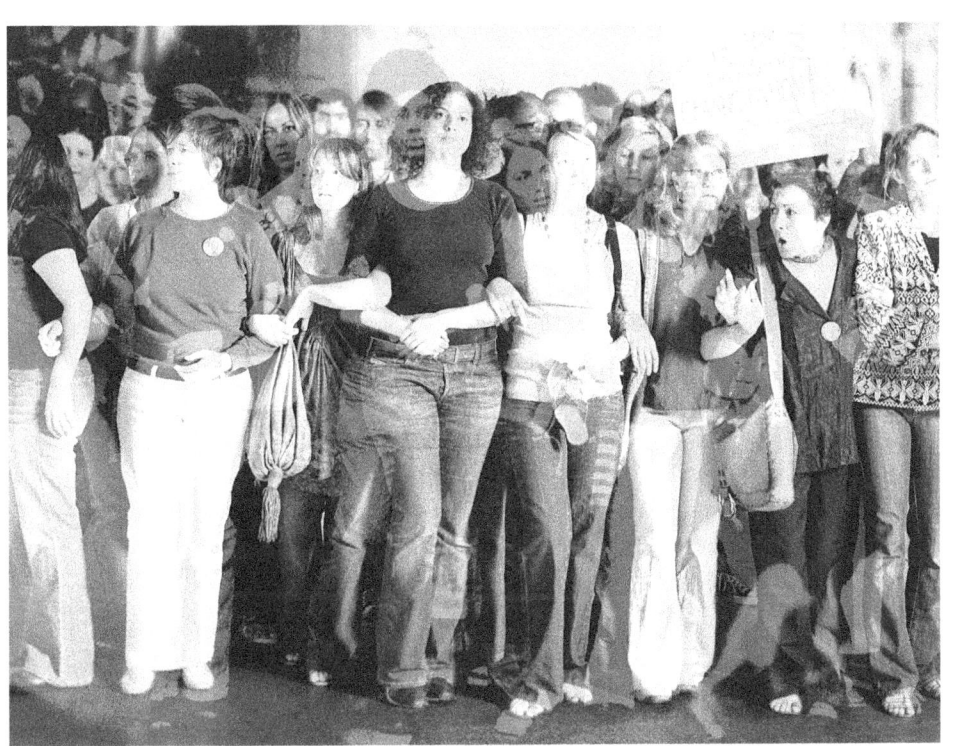

ever, her relationship to feminism has shifted in this work, a shift that can be described as taking up the position of a fan. The seeds of *Love Songs* can be found in the "Historia" section of Kelly's *Interim* (1989), but rather than the "euphoria" expressed in relation to the latter work, a sense of needing to claim the ground won by second-wave feminism is at the fore. In "Historia," Kelly presents four first-person narratives, distinguished by the age of each speaker in 1968: twenty-seven, twenty, fourteen, and three. Unlike *Love Songs*, "Historia" is dominated by a sense of loss and a relationship to the past that is inflected with doubt for the future. This sentiment is explored in the essay by Kelly that accompanies the artwork; in it, she discusses the notion of identification within feminist communities, focusing on the importance of sameness to provide political cohesion. In the face of this fantasy of a collective identity, the fear of difference causes fundamental problems, especially as awareness of the diversity of the feminist community is brought into focus through its lengthening history. Discussing the present moment (in 1990), Kelly comments: "The unity of feminism is not threatened by men but by a different generation of women who 'don't understand'— postfeminists and others. Our enjoyment as a movement is stolen, displaced by the new social, racial, ethnic, and sexual politics of the present. The mythology of feminism, *our* history, comes into being at the moment it is left behind."[40] While this statement seems to offer no way forward, Kelly also points to how second-wave feminism is being used in the present: as "the mythology of feminism," which "comes into being at the moment it is left behind."

This concept is presented visually in the video loop *WLM Demo Remix*, from *Love Songs*, in which an archival photograph of a women's liberation demonstration is merged with a reenactment staged by Kelly's students. As the two images merge in and out of focus, the archival image is always overlaid with the contemporary reenactment, a reminder that the past is always refigured by the present. In the archival image, a placard is held that reads "Unite for Women's Emancipation." In the re-performance, Kelly has replaced the text with "From stone to cloud," a quote from Sylvia Plath's poem "Love Letter."[41] This change of text resituates the scene and points to the framing of this piece by Kelly. The poem is said to address Plath's newborn child, describing the shift that has taken place with the baby's birth. Plath describes coming to life, with the solidity of stone replaced by the diffuse image of a cloud, mobile and airborne. In the closing lines of the poem, Plath describes the event as "a gift." Kelly comments: "Plath probably wrote it about one of her children, but for me it also captured something that you could think about in terms of collective love."[42] The change of title—from Plath's "Love Letter" to Kelly's *Love Songs*—also points, probably unintentionally, to the rise of rock-and-roll in the 1960s and a different kind of collective love. Here the fandom of the teenage girl haunts Kelly's project, a moment of collective desire that allows for an excessive embracing of the fan object, as with the Beatlemania of the early 1960s that has been described as, "in its own unformulated, dizzy way, revolutionary" through the demonstration of an active sexuality disallowed at that time to "nice girls" in Europe and America—a precursor to the liberation of women's sexuality in the late 1960s and 1970s.[43]

The quotation from Plath's poem also points to a shift in focus from the demand of the 1970s placard: "Unite for Women's Emancipation." The demonstration that is photographed was itself a reenactment, as it was staged to celebrate the fiftieth anniversary of the passage of the Nineteenth Amendment, which gave American women the vote.[44] The placard quotes from the women's suffrage movement of the early twentieth century, so the second-wave feminists are in conversation with their suffragette forebears. This conversation continues in Kelly's reenactment, but with an important difference—one that pervades the current interest in feminism in art. Rather than holding a demonstration in the street, Kelly's students re-perform the 1970 event as an artwork, with the call to arms replaced by a meditation on the relationship among generations of women. It is here that the figure of the fan may help to understand the shift that has taken place in relation to feminist politics in artworks from the early 2000s. Rather than taking place in the street, the work is placed within the gallery, a place where the fantasy and loss implied by the reenactment, rather than its political impact, comes to the fore.[45] To Kelly, the women in her reenactment represent "a gift"—if we follow the lines of Plath's poem—but how do these women perceive themselves in relation to the fantasy of a feminist past that they perform? In discussion with Ian White, Kelly states: "What you see in that image is not just a reenactment of the moment, but an unconscious identification."[46] This identification that takes place does not claim to speak for all women, as in the exhortation "Unite for Women's Emancipation." Rather, it re-performs a moment of collectivity that is based on a shared fantasy of the past, as a group of fans replay their favorite moments from a film or TV show. It is the changes that are enacted on the object of fandom by the fan that point to the desires for and engagement with feminism that are taking place in contemporary art, which go beyond a familial relationship.

In the context of fandom, the failure of the fan object to fulfill the fan's desire is often the cause for production, for the construction of an alternative narrative. As Jenkins discusses in relation to zine culture, a TV show is just the beginning for complete alternative universes written and circulated among fans, creating the stories that they need.[47] This movement between a fantasized identification and a lived history is reflected in the contrast between the texts on the outside of Kelly's *Multi-Story House* and the more personal moments of revelation that are scripted in the house's interior. Kelly describes the importance of the interior and exterior texts not being read at the same time: "I wanted them not to be seen from the same place, because you could never be *in* the same place."[48] From the diversity of comments seen from the outside, the interior, which is also the work's source of light, radiates a sense of common experience and purpose, perhaps the lost center that the younger generation is trying to re-create.

In speaking to Kelly about *Love Songs*, my position as a "fan of feminism" and of being a different generation from Kelly came into focus. In contrast with LTTR, made by artists who are my peers, Kelly has a standing within the histories of feminist art that made me uncertain about how to frame her within an idea of fandom. Perhaps Kelly could be seen as an actor from a TV series appearing at a fan convention, a character who is there to be adored without dictating the discourse of the fan. However, Kelly positions herself as a fan of a history that she lived through, a moment that is reanimated for her through her students' interest. It is here that the figure of the fan reveals itself as more flexible than a generational model, as the different fandoms of Kelly and the artists in LTTR cannot simply be split into those of mother and daughter. However, the different positions of Kelly and her students leave questions about *Love Songs* that I have only touched on—particularly how the voices and bodies of these younger women are situated in relation to the maternal authority of Kelly.[49] In subsequent chapters, I explore these dynamics by focusing on the back-and-forth of the pedagogical relationship. But also, in relation to my position as an art historian, how does the figure of the art historian intersect with the figure of the fan? In many cases, the actions of interpretation are similar, but with a distancing of emotional affect. The evolving presentation of feminist art history and theory still requires analysis of the art historian's subjectivity, especially as feminism's history within the institution lengthens.

ENDING AT THE BEGINNING

When I was first thinking about being a "fan of feminism" I went to what I thought was going to be a talk between Laura Mulvey and the artist and filmmaker Emma Hedditch about Mulvey's classic essay "Visual Pleasure and Narrative Cinema" (1975).[50] Instead of a talk, Hedditch presented a film in which Mulvey read sections of her text to a camera, interspersed with clips from the Hollywood movies that had inspired her analysis and fragments of her original text. The film, made as a collaboration between Mulvey and Hedditch, brought the essay to life in a way that corresponded to my thoughts on the creative potential for fandom and the reworking of the fan object. The filming of fragments of text allows phrases to stand out in both the visual representation and Mulvey's reading of selected excerpts. Words and phrases are solidified in a manner that underlines the increasingly iconic status of Mulvey's essay, which has come to distance it from the complexity and detail of her original argument (figures 1.15–1.17). Watching clips of synchronized swimmers performing perfectly; Marilyn Monroe as a glittering showgirl; and Greta Garbo in seductive close-up gave a specificity to Mulvey's argument that often has been elided in the paraphrasing of her discussion of the male-identified gaze of Hollywood cinema. Mulvey has described her essay as being an act of both cinephilia and iconoclasm, with her love for the films discussed coming to the fore in her compilation of clips.[51] Hedditch describes her collaboration not in terms of fandom but as a way to learn about Mulvey and her essay, stating that she did not know the text well before they began.[52]

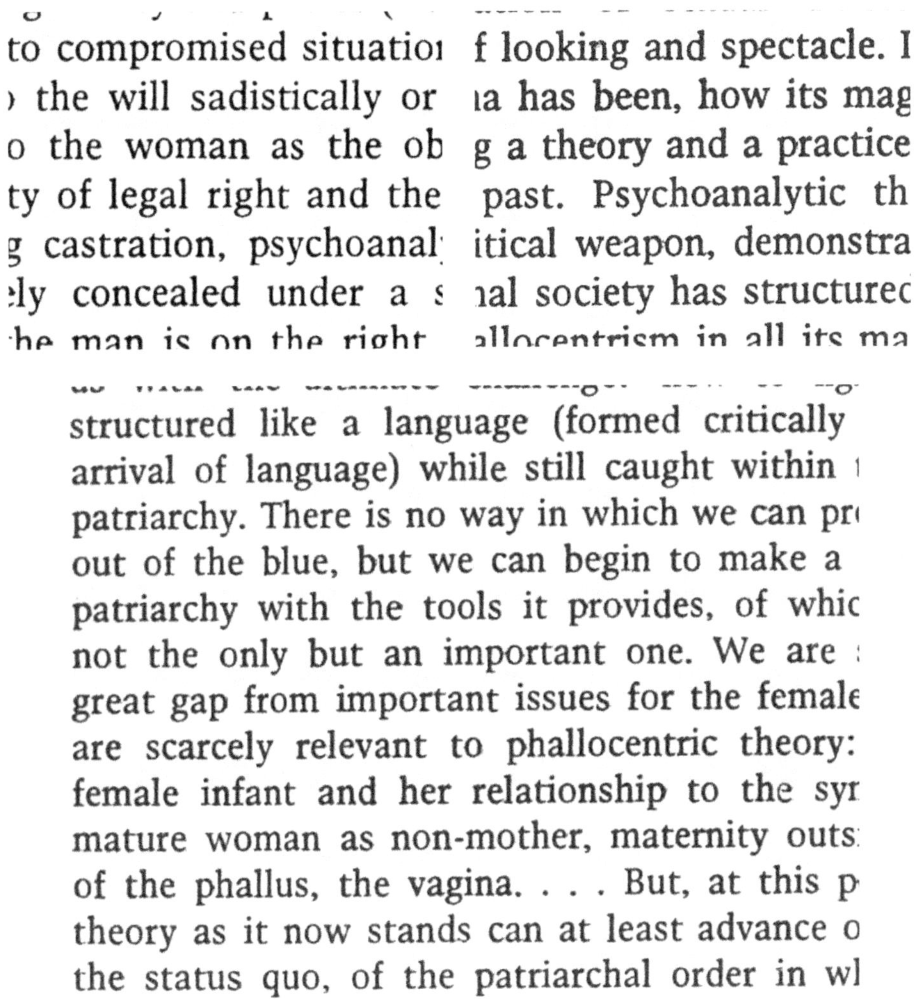

to compromised situatio f looking and spectacle. I
) the will sadistically or la has been, how its mag
o the woman as the ob g a theory and a practice
ty of legal right and the past. Psychoanalytic th
g castration, psychoanal itical weapon, demonstra
ly concealed under a s lal society has structurec
he man is on the right allocentrism in all its ma

structured like a language (formed critically
arrival of language) while still caught within
patriarchy. There is no way in which we can pr
out of the blue, but we can begin to make a
patriarchy with the tools it provides, of whic
not the only but an important one. We are
great gap from important issues for the female
are scarcely relevant to phallocentric theory:
female infant and her relationship to the syr
mature woman as non-mother, maternity outs
of the phallus, the vagina. . . . But, at this p
theory as it now stands can at least advance o
the status quo, of the patriarchal order in wl

FIGURES 1.15-1.17. Laura Mulvey with Emma Hedditch, *Visual Pleasure and
Narrative Cinema*, 2007, video stills. Courtesy of the artists.

Here my reading of this work as a fan production paid more attention to my
own fandom and the DIY, improvisatory approach that Hedditch and Mulvey
adopted in their filming. When Hedditch introduced the film, she discussed
how Mulvey wrote the essay not within academia but while working in a book-
shop, inspired by her involvement with the Women's Liberation Movement.
This context cast the canonical text back to its original intention as polemic, a
conversation across historical moments that brought back the urgency of Mul-

vey's original. Accidentally, perhaps, the film also echoes Mulvey and Peter Wol-len's film *Riddles of the Sphinx* (1977), in which Mulvey is shown reading to the camera, the action interspersed with fragments of text, linking Mulvey in her midthirties to a similarly aged Hedditch in the present and invoking the absent body of the younger filmmaker (figures 1.18–1.19).[53]

These conversations across historical moments that bring into focus the importance of feminist histories and the fantasies that they hold seem to be increasing in number. Not only in contemporary art but also in feminist institutions, reflections on feminist legacies are widespread and manifest in smaller, more marginal spaces as well as in large-scale exhibitions such as *WACK!*[54] While researching second-wave lesbian art collectives at the Lesbian Herstory Archives in Brooklyn at the beginning of this project, I was struck by the similarities to the work of LTTR in the graphic style, emphatic text, and DIY presentation of many leaflets, calls for submissions, and magazines. Coincidentally, there was an exhibition at the archives of material related to lesbian activism spanning from 1970 to 2005, with a range of material that would not be out of place in many contemporary exhibitions; the photographs, posters, T-shirts, and badges showed a shared interest in communal action and queer feminist visibility that artists such as those of LTTR and Hedditch are continuing.[55] Takahashi explained how important archival research is to her practice: "I do a lot of research. I regularly go to archives, especially when I'm traveling. . . . I go to lots of archives, like queer archives, like women's archives, and I just look at whatever I'm interested in at the time."[56] In this way, the temporal drag of the present reexamines aspects of these feminist pasts that have been neglected or relegated to embarrassing footnotes within mainstream feminism. As I sat among the numerous files at the Lesbian Herstory Archives, sifting through leaflets, memoranda for obscure collectives, calls for submissions, and meeting agendas, I realized that the contemporary artists had managed what I had not.[57] By engaging with these histories of second-wave feminism in their art projects, they had creatively reworked these historical moments in ways that were not possible for an art historian. For example, Hedditch's collaborations with a number of LTTR members includes a reading with Müller based on the inventory list of the Lesbian Herstory Archives' T-shirt collection.[58] Every Ocean Hughes's projects after LTTR include the exhibition *Ecstatic Resistance*, in which protest is presented in an explicitly phantasmatic space.[59] Material that I had collected, pored over, and been fascinated by, but had not been able to write about, was now activated within the public realm, whether by revitalizing Mulvey's thoroughly quoted essay or bringing to light forgotten elements of collective activism. Within the model of fandom that privileges fantasy in reenactment

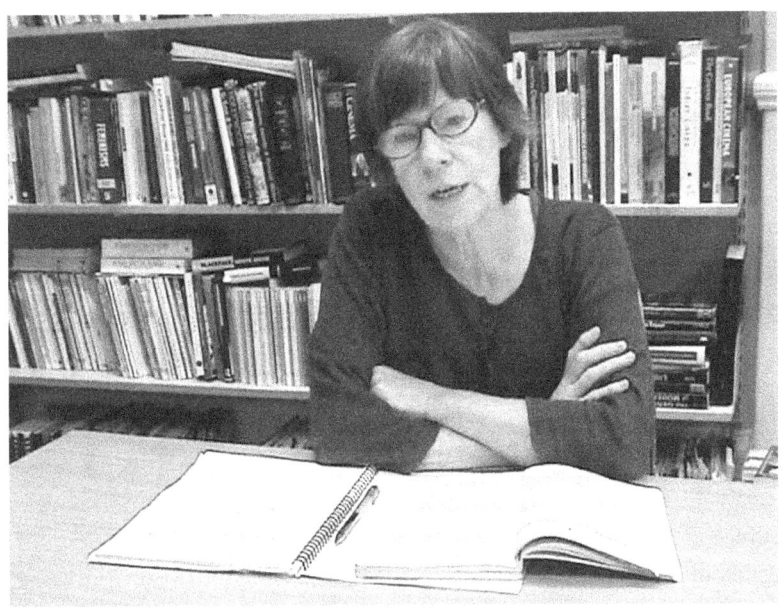

FIGURE 1.18. Laura Mulvey with Emma Hedditch, *Visual Pleasure and Narrative Cinema*, 2007, video still. Courtesy of the artists.

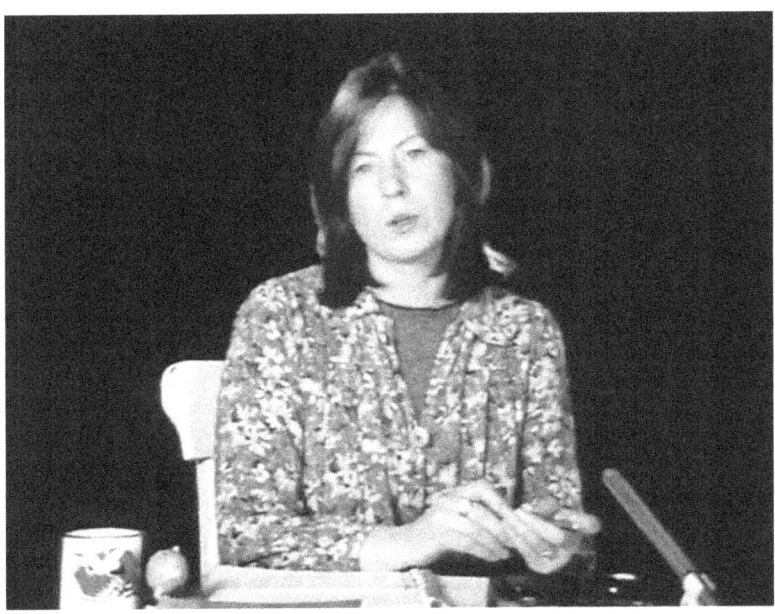

FIGURE 1.19. Laura Mulvey and Peter Wollen, *Riddles of the Sphinx*, 1977, film still. Courtesy of Laura Mulvey.

and reworking of the fan object, a canonical text can be treasured as much as a T-shirt slogan. With the fortieth anniversary of the first Women's Liberation Movement conference in the United Kingdom taking place in 2010, the revival and discussion of second-wave feminism's relationship to the present continued with exhibitions, talks, and screenings, the most provocative of which engage with this subjective reimaging of the past within the present.[60]

The figure of the fan, then, is not a way to belittle the current reworkings of second-wave feminism in contemporary art, but a model through which to explore the psychic and political pull of the past on the present. In an interview about *Love Songs*, Kelly says: "Emotions are also a form of knowledge."[61] This is echoed in an exhibition title by Hedditch: *A Political Feeling, I Hope So*.[62] Just as Hedditch and Mulvey collaborate to revisit a moment in second-wave feminism in a very practical way that crosses generations, the artists I have discussed here are in a wide range of conversations with the archival residues, iconic images, and cultural fantasies of feminist art and activism. As artists and writers such as Mulvey and Kelly were involved together in the Women's Liberation Movement in London in the 1970s, new connections are being made among contemporary feminist artists, particularly within queer artistic and activist communities, with projects such as LTTR documenting and instigating these conversations. It is here that the communal aspect of fan cultures, particularly around the creation of new writing, imagery, and film, can provide a flexible and psychically invested model for these generational crossings.

To conclude, I return to the final article in *LTTR*'s issue 1. It documents a series of interviews with women from various cities repeating a set of questions, including, "How is feminism articulated in the present moment?" and "What does feminism mean to you?"[63] For the authors, the interest is in the diversity of answers, and their cultural specificity, reflecting the range of voices and sense of freedom that *LTTR* fosters. For these fans of feminism, feminism is still in process, a place of negotiation, from the rewriting of classic texts and images to the creation of new communities and the expression of art practices that take feminism seriously enough to rewrite its stories. This approach allows for interaction with feminist histories that does not simply revere or reject, combining the past and the present in an active dialogue, or seek to simply reinstate the past. It allows us to rework feminist histories differently, passionately, and perhaps even politically in the present.

2

Killjoy's Kastle
in London

I went to see Allyson Mitchell and Deirdre Logue's *Killjoy's Kastle: A Lesbian Feminist Haunted House* in March 2014, when film documentation was installed as part of the Flare season (previously the London Lesbian and Gay Film Festival) at the British Film Institute (BFI). Mitchell and Logue's interactive work draws on American evangelical hell houses, with the horrors depicted coming from lesbian feminist literature, icons, stereotypes, and myths. In the original version of *Killjoy's Kastle*, participants were guided around by a "demented" women's studies professor, who instructed them on the queer dimensions of women's studies and dramatically introduced a lively cast of riot grrrl ghouls, ballbusters, and polyamorous vampiric grannies, ending with a Processing Room where visitors could talk about their experience of the installation with real-life feminist killjoys.[1] These reworked histories of lesbian identities, histories, and politics pick up on many fannish elements explored in chapter 1. In this chapter, this large-scale installation, first displayed in Toronto and then in Los Angeles, is the focus of thinking around an expanded concept of reenactment in returning to histories of feminism.[2] Following from the brief discussion of reenactment in Mary Kelly's *Multi-Story House*, this crucial aspect of fannish returns to feminist histories is explored over the next two chapters. Alongside the literature on reenactment from performance studies, a Benjaminian model of history underpins my use of Bertolt Brecht's outline for the "learning-play"

(*Lehrstück*) as a politically motivated form of reenactment that privileges rehearsal, discussion, and reimagining. I introduce Brecht's concept of the learning-play as a political and experimental format for reenactment and reimagining that continues the possibilities found in Elizabeth Freeman's model of temporal drag and the fan as rogue reader, as set out in chapter 1. The learning-play is a model to connect the collaborative elements of Mitchell and Logue's installation with a series of encounters with British feminist, lesbian, and Black organizations, archivists, and activists, activated through the work of Nazmia Jamal, curator of the installation in London, and her friend, the activist archivist and artist Ego Ahaiwe Sowinski.[3]

The installation of *Killjoy's Kastle* demonstrates how reenactment's historical returns do not have to be factually accurate but can play with our mythologizing and fantasizing about feminist pasts. Alongside film footage of the haunted house in Toronto in October 2013, the installation at the BFI re-created some of the cheesy, faux-creepy imagery from the original, including a series of gravestones that marked the passing of various feminist and lesbian organizations and institutions (figures 2.1–2.2). Alongside SCUM, dated "1968–infinity," there were a range of markers specific to the United Kingdom and London—including Silver Moon, Circles, and the Lambeth Women's Project—that made the installation a space of campy mourning and reflection. Individual memories of various organizations were invoked by the presence of these gravestones, a wake for feminist and queer pasts that doesn't always make the history books. By tracing this web of defunct groups and gatherings, Jamal, curator of the London version of *Killjoy's Kastle*, continued the haunting that had begun with Mitchell and Logue's charting of lesbian feminism's herstories in Toronto.[4] In this chapter, I propose that the gravestones operate as a form of script to be inhabited by the installation's participants, a script that is activated through our memories and fantasies about the lesbian-feminist herstories being staged. Through my research into *Killjoy's Kastle* and conversations with Jamal, I was set on a path to explore some of the Black British feminist groups included in the London version of *Killjoy's Kastle* and their continuing impact in feminist and queer communities. The difficulty of archiving and commemorating Black British feminist and lesbian organizing is a key narrative within the stories memorialized by the gravestones, and it provides an important UK perspective on the growing literature on queer people of color activism, archiving, and history writing. Borrowing from Brecht, I argue that the form of participation that *Killjoy's Kastle* invites is a kind of learning-play, Brecht's term for a play that is undertaken by a group, with the focus on the analysis and rehearsal of its content rather than a finished performance for an audience.

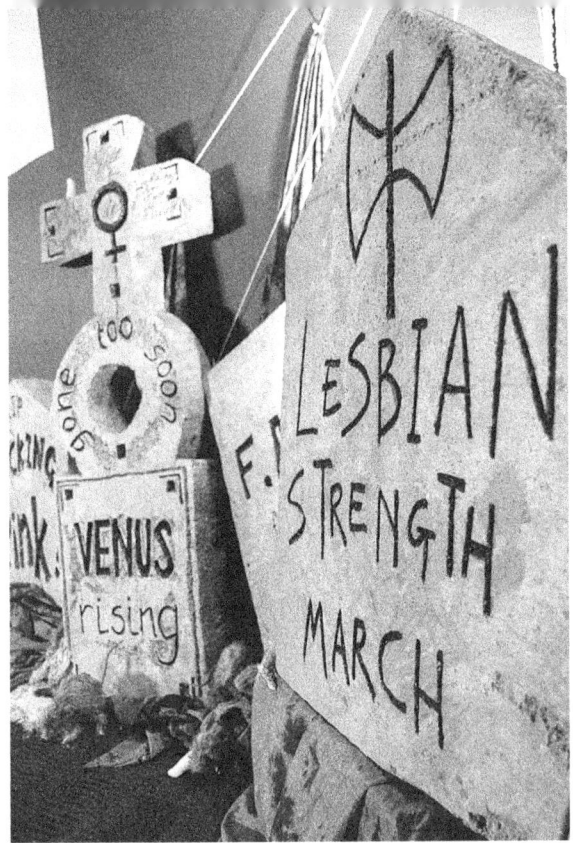

FIGURES 2.1–2.2.
Installation of Allyson Mitchell and Deirdre Logue's *Killjoy's Kastle: A Lesbian Feminist Haunted House* at the British Film Institute, London, 2014. London grave makers: Nazmia Jamal, Blake Baron Ray, Ros Murray, Ochi Reyes, Arvind Thandi, Sita Balani. Photograph by Nika Zbašnik. © www.nikazbasnik.com. Courtesy of the artists.

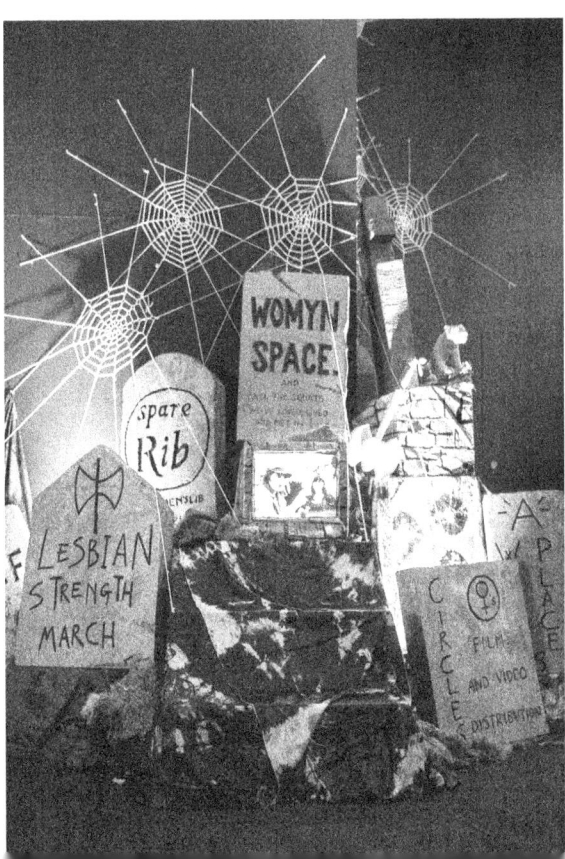

I went to see *Killjoy's Kastle* on a quiet afternoon. It was the last day of the installation, and the films played to a mostly empty room. Surrounded by polystyrene gravestones and crocheted cobwebs, I watched film documentation and photos from the installation's initial incarnation in Toronto. The ghoulish Gender Studies Professor and Riot Ghoul dance party; the butch Ball Bustas; the signs warning of "Two Adult Womyn in LOVE": this campy and humorous parade of lesbian feminist herstory and mythology was immersive and compelling. However, my experience of *Killjoy's Kastle* was very different from that of those who visited the installation in its full-blown glory, complete with a cast of performers to guide the hapless souls who enter. Plunged into the darkness of the *Killjoy's Kastle* installation on a sunny afternoon, I found my attention held by the gravestones. The list of organizations inscribed on their painted polystyrene surfaces included many that I recognized, sparking memories and giving me a feeling of unease. The gravestones documented lesbian and feminist organizations that were deceased, tracing a map of a community mainly based in the United Kingdom that included women's centers, film distributors, and club nights.[5] Many of these organizations and events had begun in the late 1970s or 1980s and petered out in the late 1990s and 2000s because of lack of funding, rent rises, or organizers' burnout. Although I didn't realize it as I sat there, my memories of these organizations formed a nodal point of collective experience. I had come to London in the mid-1990s, and my own history was wrapped up with these gravestones. Reading the names led to a recognition of how many places, organizations, and groups had been lost over the past twenty years.

A Script / A Poem / An Invocation

Black Widows / Zamimass / A Women's Place / Peckham Black
Women's Centre / The Gateways Club / Quim / Spare Rib / Out
Write / Lesbian Strength March / Venus Rising—gone too soon /
RIP: Shocking Pink / F.A.F. Feminist Activist Forum / Lesbian
Avengers / First Out / Black Fist / Lambeth Women's Project / Glass
Bar / Chain Reaction / OWAAD / SCUM 1968–∞ / London Lesbian
and Gay Centre / Cinema of Women / Silver Moon / Circles
Women's Film and Video Distribution / Womyn Space and all the
squats we've loved, lived and met in / Sheba Feminist Publishers

Reading the list of gravestones forms a kind of poem. I write their names on the page to try to continue the invocation of the places, spaces, and groups that the gravestones activate. As a wake for a queer past that is still desired and remembered by many of the visitors to BFI Flare, the gravestones were both poignant and pathetic as they called out to the visitors who found themselves among them. One of the London-based collaborators who had worked on the gravestones described the collective activity of making them as a chance to find out about the organizations being inscribed into the slabs of polystyrene.[6]

Intrigued by this process of creating the gravestones, I arranged to interview Jamal.[7] She explained how working on the gravestones had been partly collaborative but also a rather solitary activity, as she made them in her front room (figures 2.3–2.4). The group of grave makers had worked with her on some of the gravestones, but the time it took to make them far exceeded what could be done together, and Jamal ended up making many of them on her own. She described the act of carving the polystyrene as melancholic, a working through of her own relationships to the organizations that she had elected to commemorate. The list of organizations included in the graveyard was drawn up from her experience of London's feminist and lesbian groups and institutions, as well through asking friends such as Helen DeWitt at the BFI (who had worked at Circles, a feminist film distributor included in the gravestones) and Louise Carolyn at *Diva* magazine to contribute.[8] Also included in the list are names of organizations Jamal hadn't heard of but was intrigued by, names taken from the backs of books such as *Lesbians Talk: Making Black Waves*.[9] She drew on the now mostly defunct "Resources" section featured in many feminist publications before the internet. The gravestones provide a mainly London-specific account filtered through Jamal's contact with lesbian, feminist, and Black organizations. Here "Black" is understood in the political sense, prevalent in the United Kingdom since the 1980s, as a term that includes all people of color. This is not uncontested, and these discussions have led to combinations of terms being used, although the term *Black British Feminism* continues to be understood as including multiple perspectives by women of color. I use the term in this chapter because it is historically resonant with many of the organizations in the gravestones.[10]

As the "grave makers," Jamal and her collaborators produced a space of reflection and analysis on the organizations commemorated, both for the producers and, in the subsequent installation, for the viewers to discuss and bring to mind. Jamal's formation of the list of gravestones as a curator and activist rather than an artist, and their creation by Jamal and a small group of friends, is a version of the learning-play generated collaboratively through research, personal memory, and calls for information. When I sent Jamal a draft of this chapter, she emailed back listing gravestones I had missed and commented, "They are all carved into my brain. Playing is learning."[11] For Jamal, the installation at the BFI produced a space similar to the final Processing Room in Mitchell and Logue's original version, a space of discussion and conversation that used the material on show

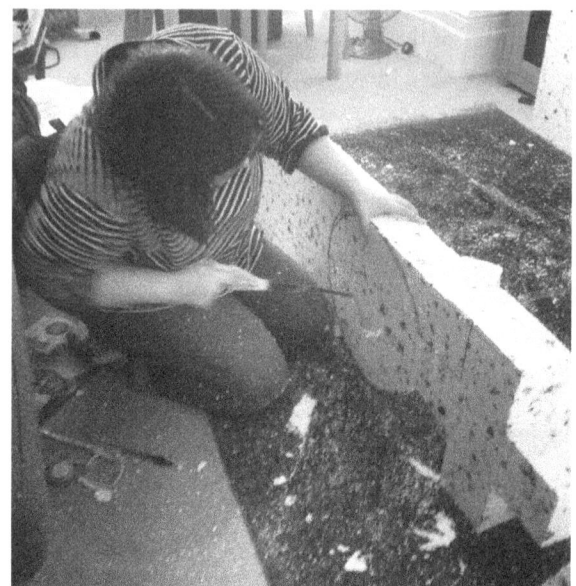

FIGURE 2.3. Nazmia Jamal carving a gravestone in her front room, London, 2014. Photograph by Blake Baron Ray. Courtesy of Blake Baron Ray and Nazmia Jamal.

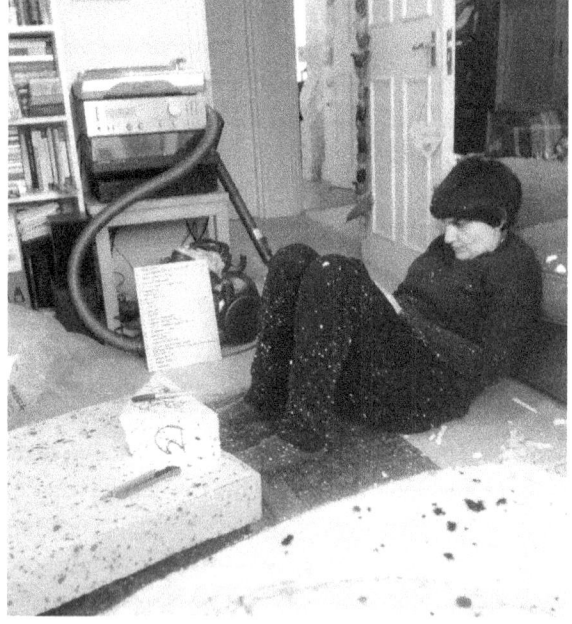

FIGURE 2.4. Ochi Reyes, one of the London grave makers, in Nazmia Jamal's front room, London, 2014. Photograph by Nazmia Jamal. Courtesy of Nazmia Jamal.

as a starting point for viewers to reflect on their own relationship to a network of lesbian and feminist communities that had faded into obscurity.

Jamal's involvement with *Killjoy's Kastle* points to the evolution of the installation as initially conceived by Mitchell and Logue, and it produced an iteration of the artwork that continued its participatory logic. Drawing up the list and making the gravestones was not simply a practical piece of outsourcing by Mitchell and Logue. Instead, it was another part of the intense process of collaboration that marked all versions of *Killjoy's Kastle*, which involved populations of performers working on the immersive installations.[12] Jamal's friendship with Mitchell led to the installation's occurring at the BFI, and rather than holding a straightforward screening, they worked together with Logue to create a new environment that took over the building's foyer.

THEATER FOR LEARNING

The process of collaboration is also central to Brecht's concept of the *Lehrstück* (learning-play).[13] He gives this concise summary of the learning-play's aims: "The learning-play is essentially dynamic; its task is to show the world as it changes (and also how it may be changed)."[14] To do this, Brecht imagined a form of play that foregrounds the process of rehearsal and all of its attendant discussion, repetition, and improvisation.[15] In a description that fits closely with the group of collaborators on whom Mitchell and Logue drew for *Killjoy's Kastle*, Brecht explains: "We organized small collectives of specialists in various fields to 'make' the plays; among these specialists were historians and sociologists as well as playwrights, actors and other people of the theatre."[16] He proposes that, with the learning-play, "the theatre becomes a place for philosophers, and for such philosophers as not only wish to explain the world but wish to change it."[17] In my repurposing of his concept, we could change "theatre" to "gallery" and "philosophers" to "feminists."

The development of *Killjoy's Kastle* also had a profound collaborative element, which led to a change of authorship from sole to coauthored project. Since the BFI installation in 2014, Mitchell's partner, Logue, has been credited as cocreator rather than producer, which had been her initial credit on the project. When I asked Mitchell about this, she wrote to me:

> At the end of the Toronto installation [in 2013] we realized that this project was much more of a collaboration between the two of us than we had ever imagined. We are a couple and live in close proximity in every way so this melding was inevitable but also needed. KJK [*Killjoy's Kastle*] took

over our whole lives, our home, our bank accounts, our time, our psychic space. The labor, conceptualization and execution of KJK is well beyond the ability of one person and it was weird and misleading to continue calling it only my project.[18]

Here, the normal practice of glossing over help from significant others is turned on its head. Rather than remaining as art-world gossip (as in, "Of course, his girlfriend did all the work"), Mitchell and Logue's collaboration moves into focus.[19] The shift that Mitchell describes is an indication of the intertwining of domestic and professional lives that is a reality for many artists and the queer communities that *Killjoy's Kastle* honors as well as interrogates. The feminist slogan "The personal is the political" could be extended to read "The personal is the artistic is the professional is the political." This is something Mitchell and Logue went on to explore in their film *Her's Is Still a Dank Cave* (2016) as well as in the gallery they run, the Feminist Art Gallery (FAG). *Killjoy's Kastle* is a product of these intense modes of doing and being. Mitchell has also proposed the concept of "Deep Lez" to frame her artistic practice, outlining an affectionate, but critical, update to lesbian feminist politics. She explains: "Deep Lez was coined to acknowledge the urgent need to develop inclusive liberatory feminisms while examining the strategic benefits of maintaining some components of a radical lesbian theory and practice in dreaming big queer worlds."[20] Mitchell presents Deep Lez as a proposal to be developed, a "a macraméed conceptual tangle" that "is not meant to become its own dogma."[21] In this respect, Mitchell's concept has many similarities with the historical model of the learning-play set out by Brecht, a model that, I propose, provides a flexible and political framework for an expanded notion of reenactment. To explore the learning that took place as part of the London installation of *Killjoy's Kastle*, I turn to one of the organizations inscribed in the gravestones: the Lambeth Women's Project.

ARCHIVAL THERAPY: LAMBETH WOMEN'S PROJECT

The Lambeth Women's Project (LWP) was an organization initially known as the Lambeth Girl's Project. It began in 1979, was housed in Stockwell, London, and closed in 2012. Stockwell Primary School evicted the LWP after an extensive refurbishment that had seemed to represent a new beginning but turned into a fast, ignoble end.[22] As with so many of the organizations charted in the gravestones, the LWP ended not because the need for its resources had expired but because funding was pulled.

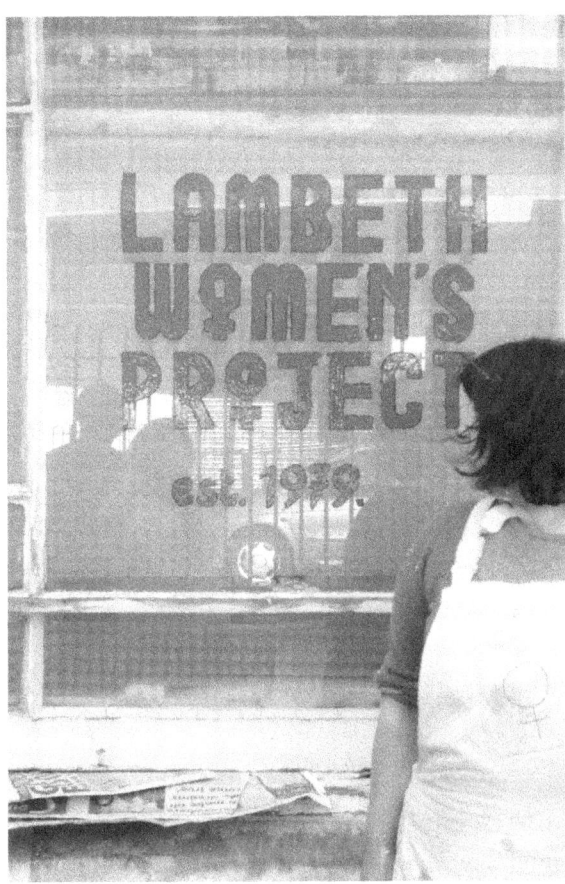

FIGURE 2.5.
Nazmia Jamal at
Lambeth Women's
Project during its
refurbishment, 2010.
Photograph by Ego
Ahaiwe Sowinski.
Courtesy of Ego
Ahaiwe Sowinski.

Jamal had been involved with the LWP, including the campaign to stop its closure in 2012, as were other grave makers (figure 2.5). Their very recent activism joined a longer history of resistance to closure due to funding cuts and austerity measures biting into key community services. One of the key members of the LWP, Ego Ahaiwe Sowinski, described how the project was "a lifeline for women in Lambeth," providing a physical place for various community groups to meet as well as services for women that included counseling, sexual-health advice, crafts, yoga, art, and music.[23] In a talk about her involvement in the LWP, Ahaiwe Sowinski asserted that, even after its demise, the organization had continued to exist in the memories and legacies of those who were part of it (figure 2.6). In an essay by Yula Burin and Ahaiwe Sowinski titled "Sister to Sister," the demise of the LWP is the starting point for thinking about the importance of archiving Black British feminist history and the process of what Ahaiwe Sow-

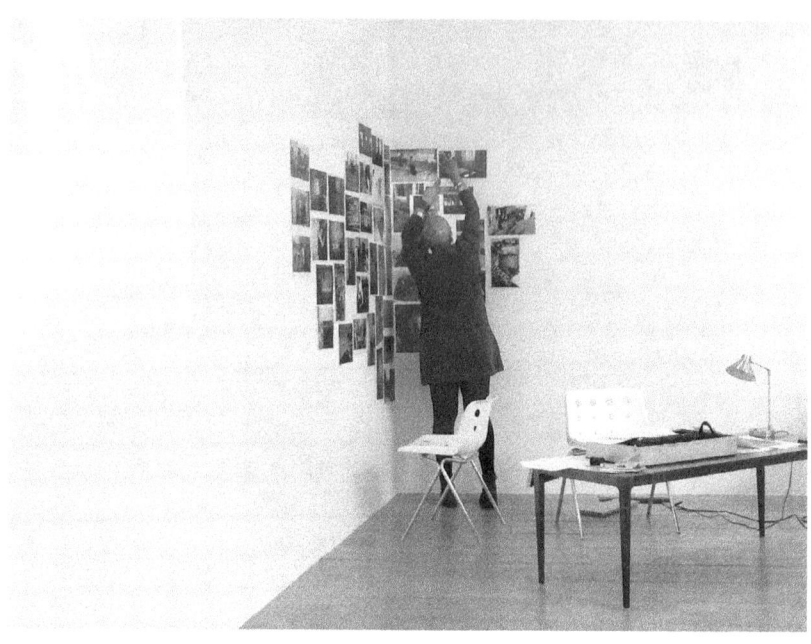

FIGURE 2.6. Ego Ahaiwe Sowkinski installing her photographs of the Lambeth Women's Project for her talk at Raven Row, London, 2017. Photograph by Nazmia Jamal. Courtesy of Nazmia Jamal.

inski calls archival therapy.[24] This process was inspired by Jo Spence and Rosy Martin's practice of phototherapy. They describe how the LWP was "a crucible for black feminist transformations. And now it has gone."[25] They recount their anger about the closure of the LWP and their involvement in feminist organizing in London and state that "there is a need to connect the dots, to find and create our UK black feminist narrative through archives, and to consciously preserve our history."[26]

Ahaiwe Sowinski has spent a lot of time archiving the collection of the LWP, which is now in the Lambeth Archives in London (figure 2.7). She has described this activity as a labor of love that is hampered not by any lack of material but by a lack of resources to process the archive.[27] For example, there is extensive video documentation of the activities of the project but no funds to edit and present it. Despite the lack of institutional support, Ahaiwe Sowinski has found ways to open up the archive through films, presentations, and activities by X Marks the Spot, a group that describes itself as an "art and archive research collective."[28] At a symposium charting a number of radical-feminist spaces in London, Ahaiwe Sowinski described her work on the Brixton-based activist Olive Morris and her work as an oral historian, including an ongoing collaboration with the artist Rita Keegan, who set up the Women of Colour Index at the Women's Art Library, recording her memories and work with her archive. For Ahaiwe Sowinski, being an archivist also means being an activist and being an artist. All these roles are woven into collaborative ventures, including publications such as *Human Endeavour: A Creative Finding Aid for the Women of Colour Index*, published through the Women's Art Library in London and produced as part of X Marks the Spot. After sending me the picture of the LWP sign in the Lambeth Archives, Ahaiwe Sowinski emailed to say that she had had to fight to have it included in the archive because it wasn't deemed archival material, but she imagined it being needed for a future exhibition (figure 2.8).[29] Like Jamal, Ahaiwe Sowinski uses the space of art to extend her activist archival practice, which prioritizes the history of Black British feminism. As she put it when describing her archival work: "Our history is still out there, under beds, in cupboards. We've got to think about how to collect it."[30]

For me, the gravestones that Jamal made, and the histories of which they speak, demand that the audience take part in this process of archiving and remembering and reflecting on how history is shaped. This means that we are being asked to take responsibility as historians of our feminist communities, something that Jamal and Ahaiwe Sowinski have put at the heart of their activist archival activities. Elin Diamond frames the role of the historicization from a Brechtian perspective, which can help us see what the installation of the gravestones is doing as part of *Killjoy's Kastle*: "When Brecht says that spectators should become historians, he refers both to the spectator's detachment, her 'critical' position, *and* to the fact that she is writing her own history even as she absorbs messages from the stage. Historicization is, then, *a way of seeing*, and the enemy of recuperation and appropriation."[31] The organizations inscribed on the gravestones present the audience with *a way of seeing*, refusing to allow these histories—particularly of Black, British, lesbian feminist organizing—to become invisible or remain as whispers in the margins of mainstream feminist history.[32]

Burin and Ahaiwe Sowinski's discussion of the LWP archives reminds us of the unfinished business represented by the organizations named on the gravestones and how their existence needs to be continued. As they put it, work on the archive can also be a form of therapy, to understand that what has gone has not been lost: "The experience with LWP left us feeling quite simply robbed, but the process of archiving has helped to support our road to recovery, serving as a kind of 'archival therapy.' Archives have offered us an opportunity to find ways to heal and be empowered through being exposed to a variety of narratives by black women who have paved the way."[33] I would like to put this concept of

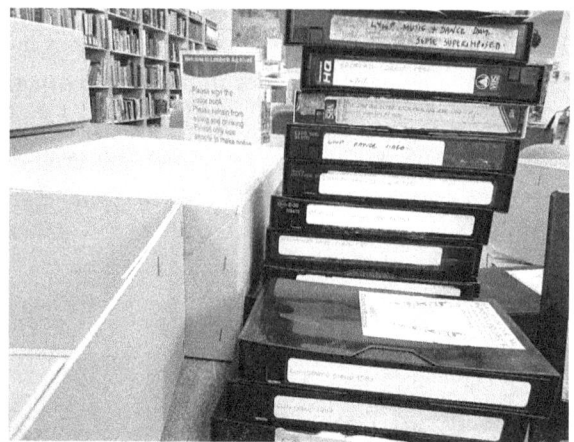

FIGURE 2.7. Videos from Lambeth Women's Project at the Lambeth Archives, 2010. Photograph by Ego Ahaiwe Sowinski. Courtesy of Ego Ahaiwe Sowinski.

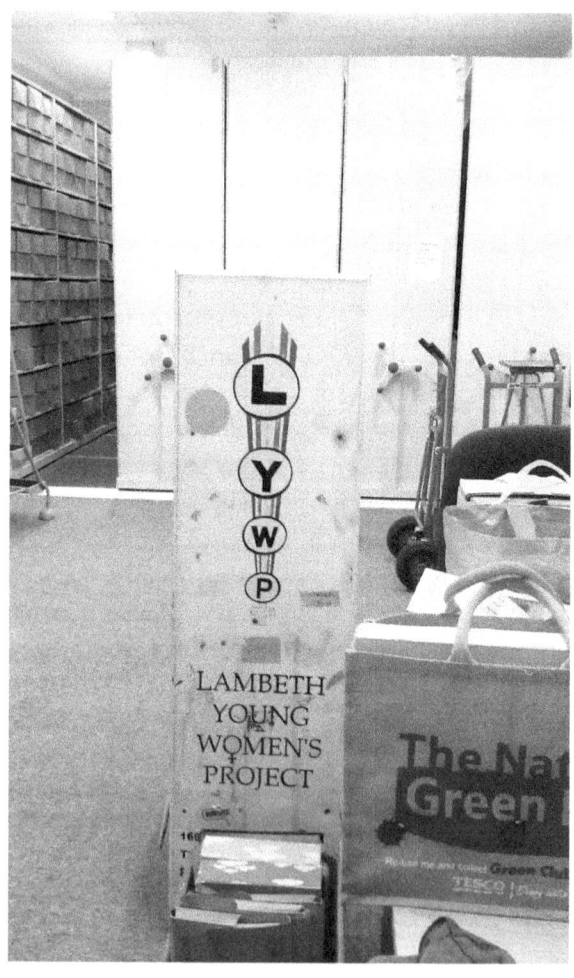

FIGURE 2.8. Picture of Lambeth Young Women's Project sign in Lambeth Archives, 2010. Photograph by Ego Ahaiwe Sowinski. Courtesy of Ego Ahaiwe Sowinski.

archival therapy alongside the activation that Brecht's learning-play demands.[34] For me, Jamal's work in choosing the names for the gravestones creates a scene that is ongoing, a script that can be taken up. Similarly, it is not by accident that Burin and Ahaiwe Sowinski's essay was published as part of a special issue celebrating the thirtieth anniversary of "Many Voices, One Chant: Black Feminist Perspectives" (1984), *Feminist Review*'s special issue on Black British feminism. Within this commemorative issue, writers such as Heidi Safia Mirza and Yasmin Gunaratnam reflect on the contemporary revival of Black feminism by a new generation of activists and scholars, exploring "a genealogy of black feminism as 'lifelines.'"[35]

AN INTERESTING BOOK

This process of returning to histories is also central to Brecht's idea of the learning-play. He compares the process of taking part in a learning-play to reading: "In studying an interesting book we must 'look back,' we reread passages in order to grasp them entirely, and so too in theatre. Revisiting a play is like rereading a page of a book. Once we know the contents of it, we can judge more closely of its meaning, or its acting, and so on."[36] This embodied rereading is playfully literalized in *Killjoy's Kastle* at the Gender Studies Dance Party, as riot grrrl ghouls are pictured dancing with huge covers of queer feminist books (figure 2.9). Hand-painted papier-mâché versions of Jack Halberstam's *In a Queer Time and Place* are brandished alongside Margaret Cruikshank's *Lesbian Studies: Present and Future*; Judith Butler's *Gender Trouble*; and Angela Davis's *Women, Race and Class*. In the background, drawings of the books housed at the Lesbian Herstory Archives in Brooklyn paper the walls.[37] Books and learning come to life, not to be read carefully, but as symbols of a politics that can be both enticing and dangerous.

These large-scale hand-painted covers of feminist classics highlight their power in shaping our worlds. For many people, encountering books such as these is literally life-changing, a moment of self-recognition or consciousness-raising.[38] (The importance of reading, and sharing books within feminist communities, is explored further in chapter 3.) Seeing the photographs and film of this part of *Killjoy's Kastle* also brought to mind the "Book Blocs" at protests against cuts to university education during the early 2010s, which started in Italy.[39] As the UK group Arts Against Cuts describes it: "Books are our tools—we teach with them, we learn with them, we play with them, we create with them, we make love with them and, sometimes, we must fight with them."[40] In an interview published as part of the exhibition *Disobedient Objects*, one of the orga-

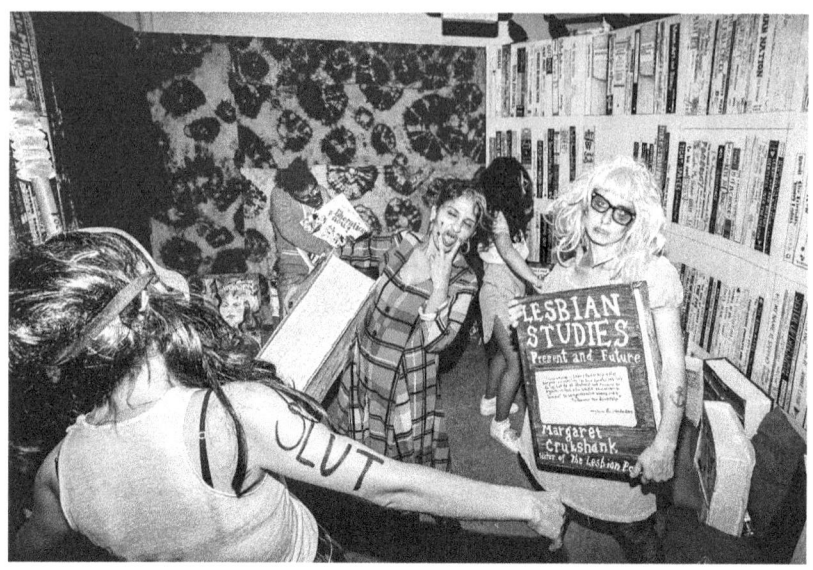

FIGURE 2.9. Documentation of Deirdre Logue and Allyson Mitchell's *Killjoy's Kastle: A Lesbian Feminist Haunted House*, Toronto, October 2013. Gender Studies Dance Party including riot grrrl ghouls. Photograph by Lisa Kannako. Courtesy of the artists.

nizers of the London Book Bloc said, "Whoever made their book chose what book it was. It was great because it was something collectively made but also individually expressive, with different modifications."[41] The large cardboard covers of significant tomes generated images of the protests that visualized the fight to keep education freely available. As instructions published as part of *Disobedient Objects* described it, by making a book cover as a shield "you are turning the media's 'story of the battle' into a battle over the story."[42]

In the essay "Theatre for Learning," Brecht explains how, in epic theater, events do not appear simply to "take place" but are the outcome of various social and political forces. His description summarizes the layering of information found when books become dance partners or protest shields: "The stage began to narrate. . . . Not only did the background make its own comment on stage happenings through large screens which evoked other events occurring at the same time in other places, documenting or contradicting statements by characters through quotations projected onto a screen."[43] When Brecht explained his new vision for theater, he employed a list that defined the differences between epic theater and what he termed Aristotelian theater. For my discussion here, what is important are the aspects of epic theater that encourage argument, investigation, and, importantly, the focus on "the world as it is becoming."[44] The use of the archival material (such as book covers or the gravestones) as a script to be embodied sets into play a particular engagement with material that can be thought through Brecht's idea of a learning-play. In *Killjoy's Kastle*, the process of performing history creates new possible futures.

FEMINIST ACTIVIST FORUM

At the end of the BFI installation, Jamal arranged for the gravestones to have a literal afterlife, auctioning them off to raise money for the Lesbian Immigration Support Group (LISG). As I tried to choose from the list of gravestones that I wanted to own, I decided on an organization that I had never heard of: Feminist Activist Forum (FAF). In the United Kingdom, "to faff about" is slang for procrastination, taking too much time to do something or, as a dictionary definition puts it, "spend time on ineffectual activity."[45] The humorous acronym seemed appropriate for my sense of time as disrupted, stretched, filled with family care and teaching, or the tedium of administration at work. I put the gravestone in my office as a hopeful reminder to try to use some of my time for research and writing, to create a space in which the residue of my research is visually present, and as a talking point for visitors and students (figure 2.10). Later, I found out that Jamal had included FAF because its name had become a self-fulfilling prophecy: an organization that began life as the UK Feminist Forum but disbanded before agreement could be made on what action it should take across issues of race, gender, sexuality, and class. Jamal recounted: "I don't think it lasted a year and I included it in the graves as a bit of a joke for those people who remembered how faffy it was. . . . It is an excellent lesson in why people should support existing organizations instead of immediately trying to set up their own!"[46] Jamal's comments point to the necessity of having a history that joins together feminist communities rather than having each new grouping inventing spaces and places that have already existed or still do exist. Jamal's involvement in FAF also pointed to the incorporation of her own activist history as well as research in compiling the list of organizations to commemorate.[47] This commemoration was also imagined as an activation, recalling Brecht's desire for the learning-play to teach new attitudes to a collective by embodying historical moments critically.[48]

To explore the names on the gravestones in more detail, I bought a second-hand copy of the book Jamal had mentioned: *Lesbians Talk: Making Black Waves*. This slim volume, published in 1993, charts the rise of Black lesbian organizing in the United Kingdom from the early 1980s onward. Starting with

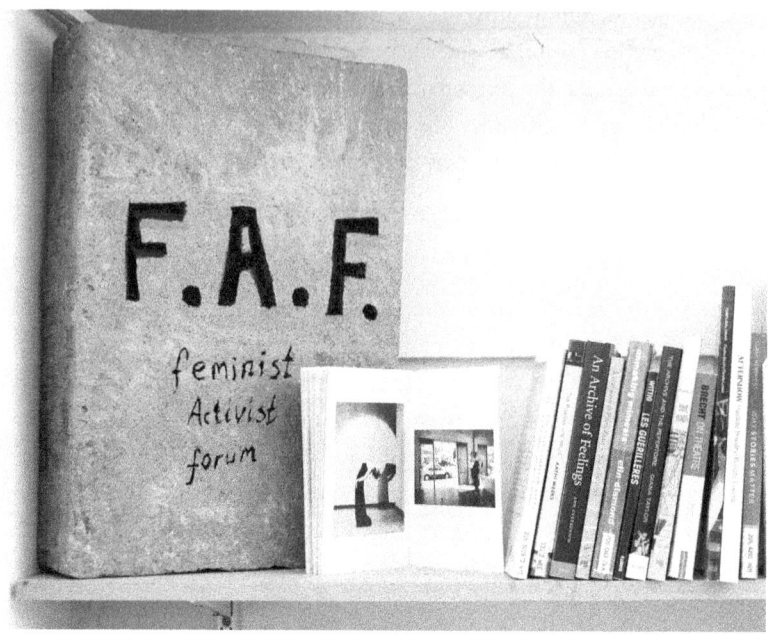

FIGURE 2.10. Bookshelf with gravestone from Allyson Mitchell's *Killjoy's Kastle*, 2014; spread from Pauline Boudry and Renate Lorenz, *Toxic: a play in two acts*, artist zine, 2013. Photograph by Lisa Castagner. Courtesy of the photographer.

a lesbian workshop at the 1981 Organization of Women of African and Asian Descent (OWAAD) conference, the book documents "an explosion of events organized by and for Black lesbians."[49] In reading this book, I was taken through a history of London and the United Kingdom that I had only scant knowledge of: an intense series of groups, organizations, and publishing ventures that had mostly disappeared by the time I moved to London. Funding from the Greater London Council meant that a number of Black feminist and lesbian organizations were able to have relative financial stability during the 1980s, and the book charts the range of activities that were made possible. Even so, its introduction demonstrates that the sense of precarity that I felt while sitting among the gravestones was not a new phenomenon: "Our lives have occasionally been documented in sections of anthologies, but many of the newsletters and articles we have produced or contributed to have disappeared. The few relevant archives and libraries—the Black Lesbian and Gay Centre, Lesbian Archives and Feminist Library face threats to their future. It is therefore essential that we chronicle our achievements, struggles and debates before they are forgotten and disappear."[50] From 1993, when the book was published, to 2014, when Jamal and her grave makers carved the gravestones using names from the book, the sense of urgency to keep hold of a history remained alive.[51] In one of the final sections of the book, "Now and Then: A Black Lesbian Chronology," the authors describe how the chronology is drawn from the three archives mentioned in the quote as well as from their own experiences and memories. Many of the groups, newsletters, and centers mentioned are then followed with the phrases "Folded due to loss of funding" or "Folded due to burn-out" or simply "Folded" and the date. Many of them are not part of the dominant narratives about queer and feminist organizations in the United Kingdom.

Jamal said that she chose some organizations, such as Zamimass, because they sounded intriguing. Listed in the resources section of *Making Black Waves* as a working-class lesbian group, "Zamimass (London)[,] set up initially to organize an alternative Xmas celebration, continued as a monthly group."[52] Coming out of discussions at Zami I, the first Black lesbian conference in the United Kingdom, Zamimass began as an alternative Christmas celebration, offering a glimpse into the kinship networks and political organization happening within the Black lesbian community in the 1980s in the United Kingdom.[53] Following the brief history of Zami I, the authors mention that a series of interviews on "the experience of lesbians from immigrant communities" led to the setting up of the Lesbian and Gay Immigration Group, which survived for five years, from 1985 to 1990.[54] About thirty years later, Jamal auctioned off the gravestones to support the Manchester-based LISG, set up in 2007. As I read about this earlier organization, I realized how the two groups, separated in time, had been brought together by Jamal's actions in the present and by her activation of a Black lesbian feminist past. As in the reading across the issues of *Feminist Review* on Black British feminism, the thirty years that separate these two immigration support groups are not felt as part of a linear progression. Instead, there are moments of intense recognition as well as of difference—powerful ways to learn across and through history, as Brecht aspired to with his model for the learning-play.

THE FEMINIST LIBRARY, LONDON

My final destination to trace the gravestones' afterlife was the Feminist Library, London. I asked the librarian (Gail Chester, one of the founders) if I could see the gravestones from *Killjoy's Kastle*. She looked at me blankly. Then I mentioned Jamal's name and that she had donated a selection of the gravestones following the installation at the BFI. Chester exclaimed, "Oh, the haunted house!"

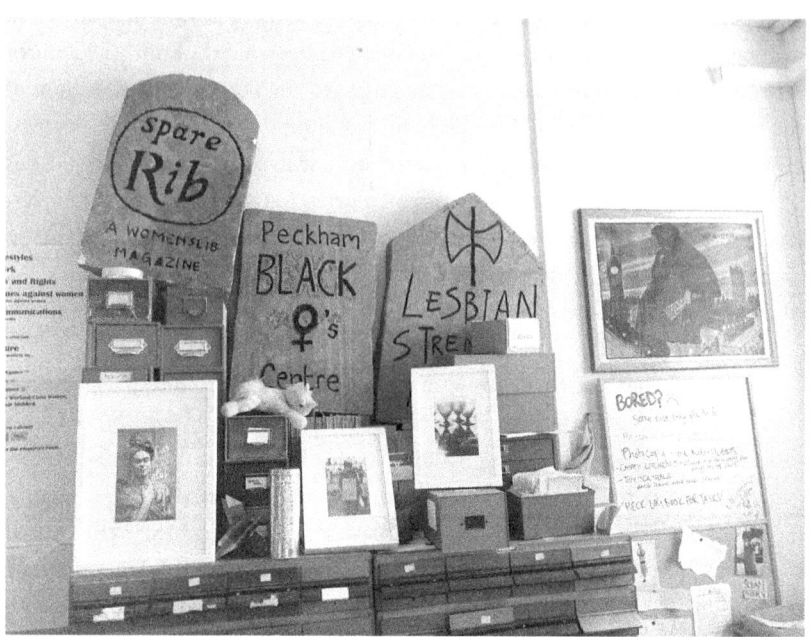

FIGURE 2.11. Gravestones in the Feminist Library, London, 2017, with "The Haunted House" suffragette poster on right. Photograph by Catherine Grant.

and pointed to three gravestones propped up over a series of pictures and files (figure 2.11). She said they were put there because of a 1907 suffrage poster titled "The Haunted House."[55] The title refers to the Houses of Parliament, and the poster features the outline of a woman looming over them, a specter calling for women's emancipation. Here, the histories of lesbian feminism activated by *Killjoy's Kastle* meet with a previous moment of feminist haunting and activism.

As the gravestones sit patiently in the Feminist Library, an organization that has been on the brink of extinction itself for a number of years, they are waiting to be activated again, part of the library's idiosyncratic archival flow. Like Ahaiwe Sowinski's insistence on the sign from LWP being held in the Lambeth Archives, the gravestones are objects that are hard to place in a folder and forget about. They act as visual reminders of what needs to be reclaimed from history, and activist archivists and curators such as Ahaiwe Sowinski and Jamal are continually trying to find new ways to allow these histories to be active in and for the present.

When I visited, the Feminist Library was housed in a crumbling, damp local government building that has been home to a range of community resources for decades but was in the process of being emptied. The library had fought against eviction for a number of years in the face of large rent increases, and although it had secured new premises, there was, and is, a need for huge amounts of help, funding, and resources. During my visit, Chester told me there are other gravestones in the library, but she couldn't access them at that time. She led me into a room that was full of books, boxes, and posters. The gravestones were nowhere in sight, presumably hidden beneath the piles of boxes waiting to be moved. Like many of the histories captured in the names on the gravestones, there was a sense that the gravestones are lying dormant, not quite lost but barely remembered. As with Ahaiwe Sowinski's careful archiving of the LWP, the gravestones are being kept for their potential in the future, although questions about the security of the places that house them loom large. As for many of the organizations described in *Making Black Waves*, their histories are still in need of reclamation. As I searched through books on Black British feminism, I found that their names are mostly absent.[56] Like Brecht's learning-play, these gravestones are reminders of archival material waiting to be reactivated, to become part of our conversations again.

SCRIPT, ONGOING

This chapter is my reply to the invitation to listen to the histories contained within the gravestones as well as to *Killjoy's Kastle* as a whole. In the process of tracing the names from the gravestones, I learned about many places and groups and that the tracking of Black British lesbian organizing was one of Jamal's most vital choices. The gravestones activate these histories and underline Jamal's presence and activism as a British South Asian woman who has been deeply involved in Black, feminist, and queer communities. As a curator, educator, and archivist, she champions and orients her work toward people of color, although she often finds herself presenting to majority-white audiences, including me.[57] Sitting among the gravestones in 2014, and continuing now as I write this, I can feel the fierce desire not to lose the histories of all the communities represented by the gravestones, to make sure their archives stay active and present for us today. What is written here is a small gesture toward keeping these histories alive and taking strength from the gravestones' gathering of powerful feminist communities and their refusal to be silent, invisible, buried. In the chapters that follow, the possibilities of reimagining feminist histories as forms of learning-plays are continued, foregrounding the provisionality of rehearsal and the ways in which feminist ideas and histories are communicated through books, artworks, and gestures.

3

A Time of
One's Own

I'm in the library. There is a low shelf, near the exit, by the librarian's desk. I can't remember what it was labeled, probably something like "Women's Studies" or "Women's Psychology." I've been working my way through the titles that appeal to me. I think this is where I first pick up Germaine Greer's *The Female Eunuch*, drawn to its title and vaguely disturbing cover that shows a female torso hung up like a jacket. I definitely read Sheila Jeffries, Andrea Dworkin, maybe Sheila Rowbotham, alongside numerous Virago Classics, chosen from their own dedicated cardboard display case on the other side of the librarians' desk, their dark green spines brought together in a feminist chorus.[1]

A few years later, probably 1997. I'm finishing my undergraduate studies, and a feminist conference is being hosted by the History of Art Department. I see Amelia Jones give a paper on cunt art; she has one or maybe two children in tow, looked after by her husband. As I remember it, Griselda Pollock is the keynote speaker. My overriding impression is of her charismatic presence. This is the first time I've seen either Jones or Pollock in the flesh, and this experience of feminist art history taking the stage stays with me.

2004. Emma Hedditch curates an exhibition at Cubitt in London titled *A Political Feeling, I Hope So*. In the space hangs a "separatist curtain," made in collaboration with Henriette Heise, which the artists describe as "a homemade fantasy of fake differentiation" (figure 3.1).[2] Due to regulations around discrimi-

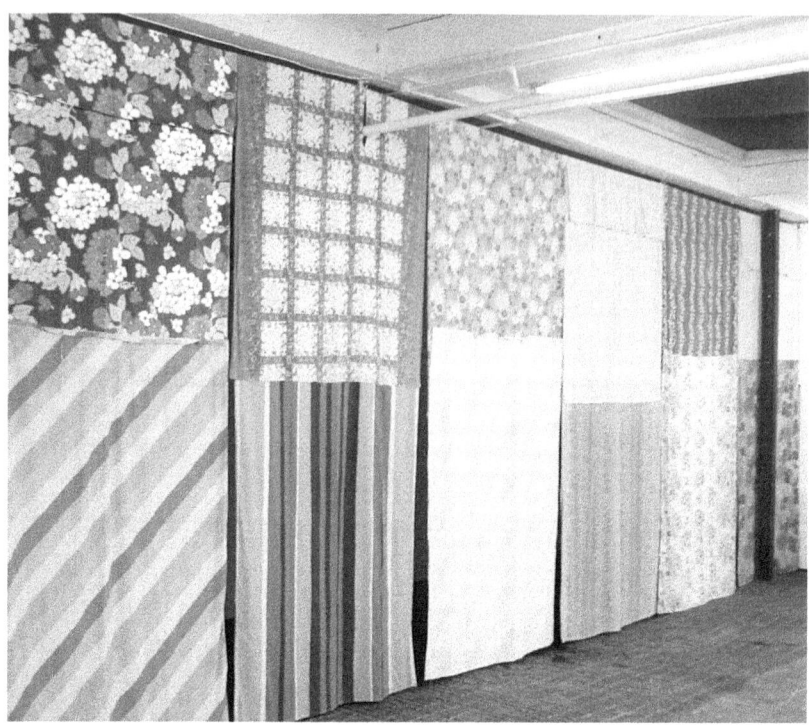

FIGURE 3.1. Emma Hedditch and Henriette Heise, *Separatist Curtain*, made for the exhibition *A Political Feeling, I Hope So*, Cubitt, London, 2004. Courtesy of the artists.

nation, the gallery cannot be made into a woman-only space, but the curtain reminds participants of this idea. The exhibition consists of film screenings, reading groups, meetings, and a journal that includes contributors' reflections on their feminist pasts and desires. The text introducing the project reads: "For three days Cubitt gallery will become a feminist autonomous place (that is, we will commit to that idea)."[3]

These three scenes are from my feminist past. They are slight but intellectually and pedagogically important. I start with these recollections to explain, in part, this chapter's title. "A Time of One's Own" obviously plays on Virginia Woolf's famous book *A Room of One's Own*. In this chapter, I want to look at reenactment as creating a time of one's own made up of disparate historical moments that, when brought together, become alive and vital for the present and the future. Picking up on the emotional attachments explored in chapter 1 through the figure of the fan, and the ways in which viewers can collaborate in reenactments that are a form of learning in chapter 2, the focus here will be on creating space and time for histories to come to life and to be remade. As I explore later, a time of one's own also points to the necessity of having time: time to spend in that room of your own, time that is not instrumentalized toward paid work or domestic labor.[4] For Woolf, "a room of one's own" is a way to visualize the freedom to be creative—imagined by having enough money and space to obtain creative autonomy. Today, we might have a room but often no time to use it. This sense of time poverty—both of being in an increasingly full present and having only a dim awareness of the past in the face of the new—is something that underpins my argument here.

Artists engaging with the histories and fantasies of feminism are creating a time of their own by bringing together a cast of both historical moments and characters for us to use in the present. They are also providing a durational space for us to engage with this material. This chapter discusses a series of artworks—primarily the film *Salomania* (2009), by Pauline Boudry and Renate Lorenz, as well as Kajsa Dahlberg's *A Room of One's Own/A Thousand Libraries* (2006) and Faye Green's *NOT TO DISCOU[RAGE] YOU* (2013)—all of which use reenactment as scenes of learning. To think about this, the process of rehearsal will be foregrounded: whether rehearsing an argument in text or in conversation or rehearsing gestures alone or in a group. Rehearsal is a pedagogical tool that helps to conceptualize what is happening when historical material is reenacted. Rehearsing an idea through the body is one way to imagine Rebecca Schneider's description of reenactment as an "embodied inquiry."[5]

Rehearsing material also necessitates a critical relationship to it, a willingness to rework and return, a repetition that is not traumatic but generative. Bertolt Brecht's theorization of the learning-play (*Lehrstück*), as set out in chapter 2, understands this exchange between script and players as including rehearsing alone or in a group, exchanges between teacher and student, between friends, and as an audience watches a play or hears a script. In the examples explored, this rehearsal is also motivated by an affective charge, a desire to know while accepting and celebrating that this knowledge will always be partial. This desire is key to my relationship to histories of feminism, staged here as a continuing rehearsal, where feminist ideas are inhabited to see what their possibilities might be now.

My past and present are woven with the writings, ideas, and art from second-wave feminism. I've read feminist history, poetry, politics, philosophy, and fiction in a fairly random manner from my late teens. I hold the experience of reading and imagining these histories as a dear and important activity. As a teenager and young woman I wasn't involved in a political group and often felt anachronistic in my feminist politics. They were closely linked to my personal feelings of not fitting in with a heteronormative model of feminine identity or sexuality and thus were part of a self-discovery through the creation of an alternative history and community. I wasn't directly involved in the so-called third wave and experienced riot grrrl from a historical remove similar to that from the second-wave ideas I read in my local library as a teenager. In an important sense, I experienced the second wave as immediate in that I related to and reimagined narratives of becoming feminist as messy, confusing, and exhilarating in my own present moment. Rather than becoming feminist in the historical moment of the Women's Liberation Movement, I became a feminist in feminisms' histories, helped by friends, teachers, and books.

While working on the reimagining of feminist histories in contemporary art, I've been drawn back to my autodidactic process of learning and how pedagogical scenes—whether featuring teachers, academics, peers, or students— continue to form my ideas of feminist histories and temporalities. This is why I don't relate to familial metaphors around generations but, instead, proposed to start thinking about histories of feminism in art as a form of fandom. As Rosalyn Deutsche suggests, generations should be understood as relations rather than as entities so "we can move away from casual linearity toward multidirectional models of history."[6] This concept of generations as relations rather than time-specific identities is also found in Julia Kristeva's essay "Women's Time," which has been inspirational for many feminist writers on this topic.[7] For Kristeva, the concept of generation implies a "*signifying space*," which she describes as "both a corporeal and desiring mental space."[8] This chimes with work on queer temporalities, beginning with Carolyn Dinshaw's influential discussion of connecting "affectively with the past" to create "communities across time."[9] Elizabeth Freeman's book *Time Binds* argues for the necessity of disruptive models of temporality to explore what has not yet been realized within feminist and queer histories. Freeman, along with many other writers, draws on Walter Benjamin's enigmatic theorization of history and its relationship to the present, with his essay "On the Concept of History" (1940) also being an important reference for much art-historical discussion of reenactment, which I return to later in this chapter.

Brecht's notion of the learning-play suggests a prosaic model to grapple with a Benjaminian notion of history, particularly in being able to historicize the present through an engagement with the past.[10] The learning-play focuses on the community formed in the rehearsal, discussion, and performance of a script. This creation of a community through an engagement with the past links the artworks discussed here and is one way to understand what is meant by "a time of one's own." Despite not belonging to an easily identifiable feminist group, I have witnessed a rise in the number of academics, artists, and writers who want to think about feminism's histories in a multitude of ways, with communities formed around reading groups, art events, and seminars. Indeed, this chapter is the product of an evolving conversation that owes a great debt to many friends, colleagues, and students. Increasingly, contemporary artists have worked in this space and time of feminisms' histories to figure out what we might get from them now.

Reenactment has been prevalent in contemporary art and performance since the early 2000s, so I will now sketch out my own use of this term. In exploring the ways in which artists engage with feminist and queer histories, I have looked at artworks that take a preexisting film, image, text, or idea and re-present it in some way. This can be a faithful replay or a fantastical reimagining. I am using an expanded idea of reenactment, so rather than literal re-presentation, I'm interested in the process of embodying and analyzing an event, text, or idea. There has been wide-ranging critical discussion of reenactment and re-performance, with Rebecca Schneider providing one of the most thorough and nuanced accounts of the disruptive temporalities and possibilities that reenactment can allow. She explores how "the experience of re-enactment . . . is an intense, embodied inquiry into temporal repetition, temporal recurrence."[11] She works through a wide range of philosophical models for thinking about how reenactment might "open-up" history while acknowledging that reenacting a past event can also spectacularize or stabilize it.[12] A key term for Schneider is "syncopated time," describing "the warp and draw of one time in another time—the *theatricality* of time—or what Gertrude Stein, thinking about *Hamlet*, referred to as the nervousness of 'syncopated time.'"[13] This syncopated time is also referenced by Elin Diamond's repurposing of Brechtian ideas for feminist theater, exploring how "syncopatedness, the visceral and cognitive sense of temporal otherness, becomes methodological, a praxis of seeing/knowing and performing/writing in which the object belongs not to me but to a historical force-field which is never fully knowable."[14] Diamond's words might also be used as an explanation of Freeman's often used term "temporal drag," discussed in chapter 1, which conceptualizes how anachronistic feminist and queer histories can pull on and resonate in the present.[15] Across the literature on reenactment there is this attention to temporal disruption as a space of possibility, and I see it as a space of learning.

LEARNING-PLAYS

By using a very specific version of a play—Brecht's concept of a learning-play—I want to foreground how the rehearsal and analysis as well as the presentation of a reenactment can offer a starting point for further investigation. This return to Brecht might be seen as another layer of reenactment in relation to second-wave feminist art and ideas.[16] Developed during the 1920s in Germany, a period of profound social change and possibility, the learning-play feeds into Brecht's broader ideas of epic theater.[17] With the learning-play, he focused on the act of rehearsing, watching, and discussing a play, as much as on the performance of it. As explored in chapter 2, he compared the process to reading: "In studying an interesting book we must 'look back,' we reread passages in order to grasp them entirely, and so too in theater. Revisiting a play is like rereading a page of a book. Once we know the contents of it, we can judge more closely of its meaning, or its acting, and so on."[18]

By translating the process of reading and rereading to that of embodying, discussing, and viewing a script, Brecht provides ways to think about gesture, collective learning, and discussion, which are often key to contemporary artworks that return to feminist and queer histories. He made a number of experiments, often written collectively, that included audience participation or dispensed with the audience entirely so that the process of rehearsal and reflection formed the key activities.[19] His model of the learning-play is suggestive rather than programmatic.[20] Roswitha Mueller also points out that "Brecht writes the central concern of the *Lehrstück* into the text itself—namely, the education of individuals to enable them to become members of a collective."[21] After Brecht returned to more realist modes of dramatic presentation in the late '30s, Devin Fore has argued, the emphasis on quotation and reenactment of gesture continued to create plays that are to be analyzed and interrogated through a process of "demonstration": "Instead of eliminating representation entirely, Brecht compounded it by reproducing the reproduction, as it were, by quoting secondhand speech, by acting out the film. 'Show that you are showing!' Brecht enjoined his actors."[22]

SALOMANIA

In Pauline Boudry and Renate Lorenz's film *Salomania*, a collective is pictured across time as well as through the audience, bringing together iterations of Salome's dance of the seven veils as a form of infectious image (figure 3.2). Circulating around this dance as pictured in Alla Nazimova's experimental film *Salomé* (1923), the artists excavate the queer potential in various embodiments of Salome and her dance as it was performed through the late nineteenth and twentieth centuries. The artists say, "We liked the idea of a dance as 'infectious' in terms of denormalising practices."[23] In one of the statements published to accompany the film, they tell us how, "at the beginning of the twentieth century in

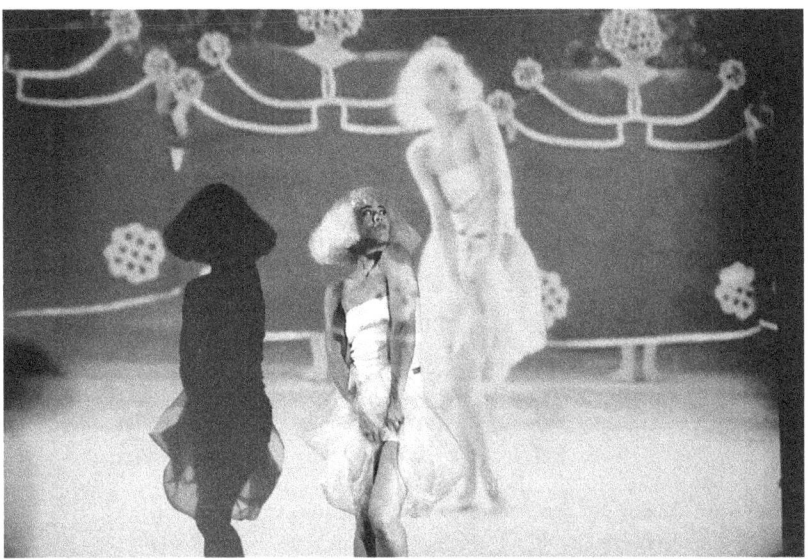

FIGURE 3.2. Pauline Boudry/Renate Lorenz, *Salomania*, 2009, film still. HD/ Super 8 film installation, 17 min. Performer: Wu Tsang. Courtesy of Marcelle Alix, Ellen de Bruijne, and the artists.

England, women met privately to perform the dance of the seven veils, a movement which, like a kind of viral infection, was called 'Salomania.' Shortly after the appearance of the Strauss opera 'Salome,' an article in the *New York Times* urged President Roosevelt to act to prevent the fad from spilling over into the USA."[24]

In the film, this Salomania is continued through a montage of fragmented scenes, which include Wu Tsang and Yvonne Rainer reenacting Salome's dance as it is performed in Nazimova's film as well as interacting as Rainer teaches Tsang her own Salome-inspired dance, "Valda's Solo," from her film *Lives of Performers* (1972 [figure 3.3]). Between these dances, the process of rehearsal and discussion are foregrounded, with Tsang questioning Rainer on her "NO Manifesto" and the campy eroticism in her interpretation of Salome's dance.[25]

As in other films by Boudry and Lorenz, many elements within and alongside *Salomania* indicate the process of its making and research. Clapboards are shown at the beginning (marked "Scene 1, Take 3"—although this scene is actually scene 2); a scene between Rainer and Tsang appears to be a rehearsal for one of the others, and they are shown getting ready for the performance of Nazimova's dance (figures 3.4–3.5). The artists explicitly reference Brechtian strate-

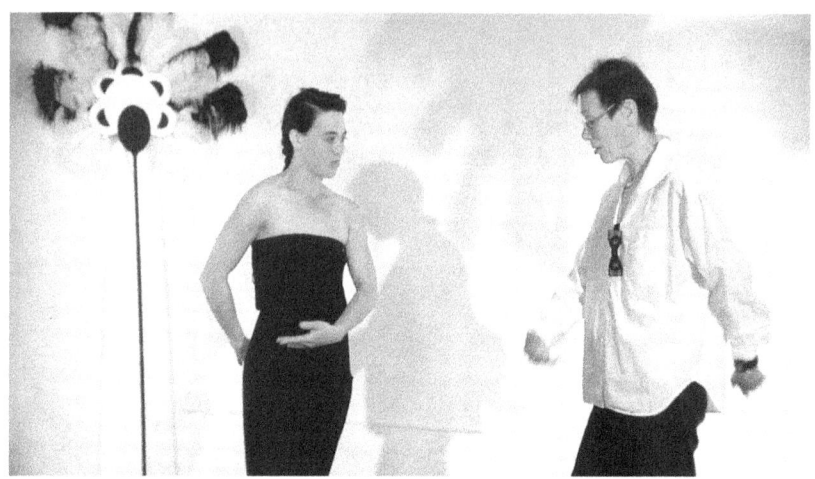

FIGURE 3.3. Pauline Boudry/Renate Lorenz, *Salomania*, 2009, film still. HD / Super 8 film installation, 17 min. Performers: Yvonne Rainer and Wu Tsang. Courtesy of Marcelle Alix, Ellen de Bruijne, and the artists.

gies of showing in commentaries on their work, although they emphasize that this act of showing is done without a sense of explaining what is being shown.[26] In Boudry and Lorenz's work, the *bodies* of performers, as well as the reenactment of speech, transform the scripts. Here the concept of "embodied inquiry" is thought through the dancing figure of Salome; the communities that historically have formed around the dance; and the differently gendered, raced, and aged bodies that have taken up Salome. By working with the trans performer Tsang, who plays Salome, Nazimova, and the student of Rainer, the history of Salome as an exoticized, perversely sexualized character is animated. Boudry and Lorenz have discussed how the figure of Salome was taken up by Nazimova as a way to perform her Jewish identity as well as to take charge of her typecasting as "exotic." By the late nineteenth century, Salome was a figure used to embody racial and sexual degeneracy, a circular logic in which a fictional character became the justification for pseudoscientific debates that located excessive female sexuality within a nonwhite, non-Christian body.[27]

The artists work as fan scholars, researching and responding to the historical figures and events and objects that they weave into the film.[28] They also encourage the audience to take up the position, with the film being only one element in a range of material that invites the viewer to investigate further. When the film was shown at the South London Gallery, a zine was published alongside the exhibition that included material on historical embodiments and performances of

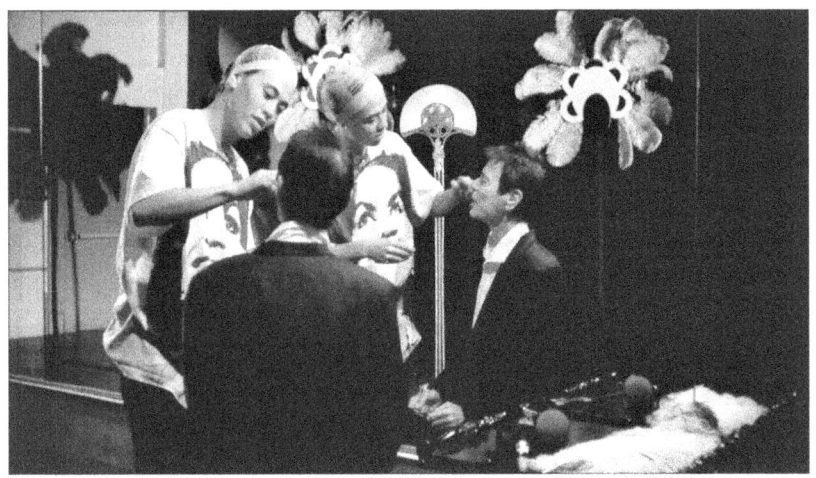

FIGURE 3.4. Pauline Boudry/Renate Lorenz, *Salomania*, 2009, film still. HD/ Super 8 film installation, 17 minutes. Performers: Yvonne Rainer and Wu Tsang. Courtesy of Marcelle Alix, Ellen de Bruijne, and the artists.

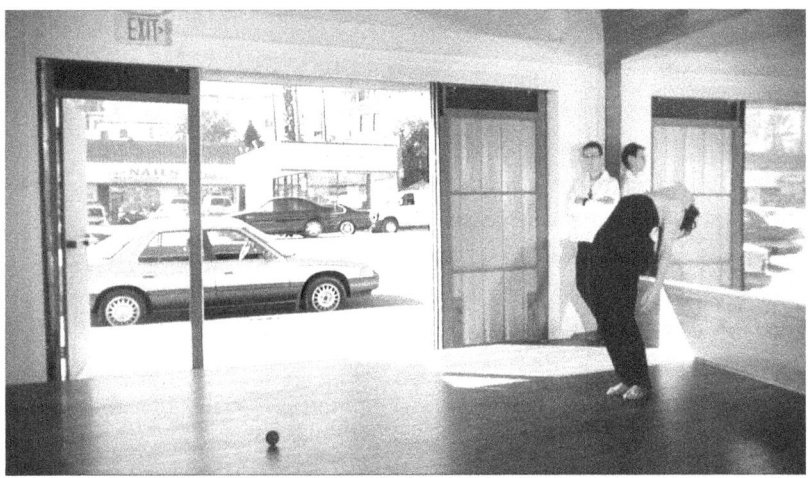

FIGURE 3.5. Pauline Boudry/Renate Lorenz, *Salomania*, 2009, film still. HD/ Super 8 film installation, 17 minutes. Performers: Yvonne Rainer and Wu Tsang. Courtesy of Marcelle Alix, Ellen de Bruijne, and the artists.

Salome, focusing on their queer feminist potential. When asked about the relationship of the research and associated materials with the film, Boudry and Lorenz stated: "The films should also work without any further information. But since our works are based on research on the one hand and they also might produce 'theory' or 'thinking' on the other hand, other dimensions might open up if you are able to look at documents or read a text that is related to the different elements of the film."[29] In interviews, the artists have explained why they are not interested in historically accurate reenactment, with Boudry saying, "The way that performers engage with the archive is not a mere reenactment; it very often involves anachronistic elements."[30] They discuss how the idea of temporal drag underpins their use of reenactment, describing it as "a connection of current performers (which include their embodiment of contemporary performance work) with materials from the past and the audience—connection understood as instigated by desire."[31] This desire relates to the discussion of fandom in chapter 1, and here reenactment is a form of fandom that prioritizes understanding, learning, getting inside a collection of historical moments and gestures to make them active for the present.

When we see Tsang dancing alongside film footage of Nazimova in the famous dance of the seven veils, Rainer performs the viewer; Herod, Salome's stepfather; and the man for whom the exchange of a dance for a promise leads to the execution of John the Baptist (figure 3.6). There is already a strange temporality to Nazimova's dance, as Tsang performs in a white wig and close-fitting dress that seems closer to punk than the actual moment of the performance in the 1920s. Rainer mimes the leering face of Herod watching Salome dance, a feminist mother transformed into a queer predatory stepfather, a parody of a familial relationship. In a later scene, we witness a conversation between Tsang and Rainer as Rainer teaches part of "Valda's Solo," her response to Nazimova's dance that is filmed for *Lives of Performers*, in which a ball is used to represent the head of John the Baptist. They talk about the relationship of "Valda's Solo" to Rainer's famous "NO Manifesto," with Rainer slightly exasperated. In contrast, when she is teaching Tsang gestures from the dance, she is much more precise. The act of learning and teaching is dramatized here, with Tsang's serious student contrasting with Rainer's casual, but nonetheless exacting, teacher (Rainer was Tsang's teacher at the California Institute of the Arts).[32] After Tsang asks Rainer about the relationship of eroticism and camp in "Valda's Solo" to the dictates of the "NO Manifesto," Rainer simply says, "That manifesto was never meant to be a Bible!" Her comment warns the good student not to be too studious and points to the impossibility of re-creating a historical moment or intention in the present, because in the moment of its making it was not completely

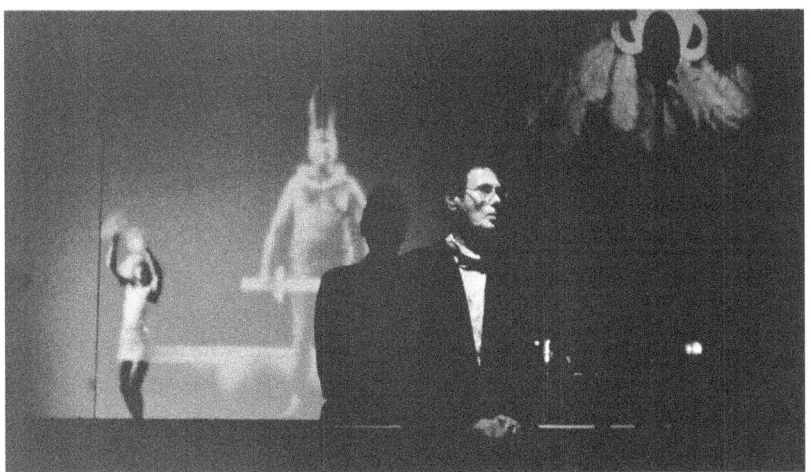

FIGURE 3.6. Pauline Boudry/Renate Lorenz, *Salomania*, 2009, film still. HD/ Super 8 film installation, 17 minutes. Performers: Yvonne Rainer and Wu Tsang. Courtesy of Marcelle Alix, Ellen de Bruijne, and the artists.

fixed. Instead, we are encouraged to join Rainer and Tsang in the seemingly formal act of learning a dance, which Tsang performs for Rainer in the subsequent, penultimate scene of the film.

In the opening speech (which could also be the closing speech), Tsang refers to Rainer as her "father-in-law."[33] If the two are performing the relationship between Salome and Herod, then this is a mistake, maybe of translation, as Rainer would be Tsang's stepfather. But if this is about a conceptualization of their relationship, then father-in-law might be apt. A father-in-law implies a relationship that is both familial and generational but bound by convention, not blood. The potential for this relationship to be an erotic one is therefore more possible, and the dynamic with an older generation is not straightforward between sons and fathers, just as these two characters are not men but are figured in a variety of masculine poses and positions. Tsang has refused to locate a trans identity as either male or female and, instead, remains resolutely queer.[34] Rainer has also located her identity outside binary notion of gender, instead describing herself an "a-woman."[35] As I watched the film, I had assumed that Tsang was a butch woman and what was being presented was a relationship between two queer women enacting different models of feminine seduction and female masculinity. Instead, like the artists' conception of Salome as an image that is not fixed but a combination of interpretations, gestures, and figures, the two performers are set up as a series of relationships to each other and to us, the audience. Rainer is the historical figure who has made canonical works such as *Lives of Performers* but also the wry teacher who watches her student critically but affectionately and camps for the figure of Herod, a fantasy of power that ultimately rests in the ring on his finger rather than anything about his own person. (In Nazimova's film, the ring on Herod's finger is taken by his wife and given to the executioner, who understands it as a command to execute John the Baptist.)

In *Salomania*, we are seeing the process of research and the process of performing. The montage of scenes is disruptive, stuttering, with different moments of performance, thinking, discussion, reflection. As in a Brechtian learning-play, the act of showing is foregrounded: showing us how the dance is performed, showing us how our viewing is positioned, showing us how the film is made. Returning to Brecht's "revisiting a play is like rereading a page of a book," I would like to propose that we are watching such an act of rereading—one that is passionately and creatively engaged with its potential for the present, using its historical sources as methods to teach us, to show us how we perform the act of viewing and to ask us to continue the act of researching. As we oscillate between the leering face of Rainer as Herod and the lithe body of Tsang as Nazimova as Salome, we are encouraged to take part in a Salomania that continues beyond the frame of the film: a fantasy in which the past is imagined in the present; a past that is as difficult and exciting to engage with as a person; a script that commands us to examine, perform, and discuss.

A TIME OF ONE'S OWN

While thinking about reenactment as bringing to life histories that have unfulfilled potential, I reread Woolf's *A Room of One's Own*. The emphasis on bodies in *Salomania* made me pay attention to the people and relationships found within the book. Woolf frames her argument by staging a lecture to a group of women students at a fictional Oxbridge college.[36] Repeatedly, she brings in her own embodied experiences and scenes of learning and thinking, from sitting on a riverbank to working in the British Library. She approaches her topic—"women and fiction"—through a combination of research, anecdote, imagined history, and fictionalized encounters. She invites the audience/reader to join her in the analysis of what appears to be an impossible topic to summarize. Like the artists considered here, Woolf combines fantasy with history, transforming what at first appear to be straightforward anecdotes into tools for analyzing the key problems around the production of creativity and the histories of women writers. As is well known, her precise, sardonic argument about "women and fiction" centers on the necessity of money and a room of one's own. As I work on artists engaging with feminist histories as forms of learning-plays, I think about Woolf's words and how we increasingly can reframe her call for a room of one's own as a time of one's own.

My use of this phrase "a time of one's own" is meant to suggest both the need for time in the present and an embracing of previous moments to create a context for our "now." Importantly, taking part in a learning-play requires time on the part of the participants and an insistence that close attention be paid to the historical material under analysis. For me, the time needed to be a creative or political person is brought to life in a number of sections of Woolf's text. The first occurs within a couple of pages of the book's beginning. She writes about sitting on a riverbank; while contemplating the scenery, a thought darts into her mind, which she vividly describes as catching a fish that flits in the water:

> Thought—to call it by a prouder name than it deserved—had let its line down into the stream. It swayed, minute after minute, hither and thither among the reflections and the weeds, letting the water lift it and sink it, until—you know the little tug—the sudden conglomeration of an idea at the end of one's line: and then the cautious hauling of it in, and the careful laying of it out?[37]

As we sit with her, Woolf tantalizes us with the statement that, although this thought is small, it can still be found within the pages of the book. However, as the scene continues, her moment of creative thinking is disrupted when she is apprehended by a Beadle, who tells her only fellows and scholars are allowed to walk on the grass. She must return to the gravel path. In this scene, as in many that follow, Woolf demonstrates the many, and often petty, ways in which creativity requires support: institutional, financial, and intellectual. While she appears to be alone in much of the book, she is in fact surrounded, first by the women students in the lecture hall to whom she first frames her fictional anecdotes, then, as we follow her through her research and musings, we meet the women from history, who either make it as writers or have to be imagined, as well as members of Oxbridge colleges enjoying (or not) their lunches and dinners. As readers, we take part in this collective, addressed by Woolf's intimate tone to join in the discussion.

The moment of creative thinking that Woolf describes is one that I have found in watching, reading, and participating in the artworks under discussion. Whether one is sitting in a gallery watching *Salomania* or sitting at home reading the zine that accompanied the film, the works provide a starting point, a way to enter into a process of research and reflection, with a view to creating new feminist possibilities and communities in the present. Reading *A Room of One's*

Own articulates the structures that often remain invisible behind the capturing of even a small thought, and how being creative so often requires being part of a collective, or community, in terms both of a history to identify with and as a peer group in the present. In the book's conclusion, Woolf exhorts the reader to work for the future of women writers, to make possible the realization of Judith Shakespeare, her fictional sister of William Shakespeare. Woolf's account of being a woman and a writer in the sixteenth century is a tale in which writing is impossible or destroyed, with Judith Shakespeare's suicide the tragicomic conclusion, buried underneath where omnibuses now pass through London's Elephant and Castle. In creating Judith Shakespeare, Woolf gives a figure of unfulfilled women's creativity, a figure to work for, as she tells us in the last line of the book: "I maintain that she would come if we worked for her, and that so to work, even in poverty and obscurity, is worthwhile."[38]

Woolf writes *A Room of One's Own* to a community of women—or, more precisely, a community of potential or actual feminists. These communities that are formed around reading are animated in a work by the artist Kajsa Dahlberg. In *A Room of One's Own/A Thousand Libraries* (2006), Dahlberg visited every public library in Sweden to collect the marginalia recorded in their copies of Woolf's book (figure 3.7).[39] Here, the invisible and cross-temporal communities of readers are brought to life through the residue of their interaction with Woolf's words. This recalls my own sense of autodidactic learning in relation to feminism's histories, which would imagine a community for me to try to actualize within my life. Here the act of reading might be equated with that most "second wave" of activities: consciousness-raising. A friend of mine pointed out that the learning-play might be a way to think about consciousness-raising, and the two forms share goals of reforming social structures and personal lives through sharing, researching, and analyzing.[40] Here consciousness-raising occurs not within an immediate space with a group of women but across time, sometimes in relation to actual bodies, and sometimes in relation to historical material. Dahlberg recounts that she wanted to give the book to a friend, and on finding that the Swedish edition was out of print, she photocopied and bound the pages of a library copy. This act of friendship, of communication through literature, is a version of consciousness-raising that takes place in the context of a rich tradition of feminist writing. Like the rereading of a book that Brecht recalls when he describes the process of learning, unlearning, and reimagining that happens in the learning-play, Woolf's words take place in a connected set of reenactments—fantastical and actual—from her restaging of her university lecture to the next reader who picks up her book and find inspiration in its pages.

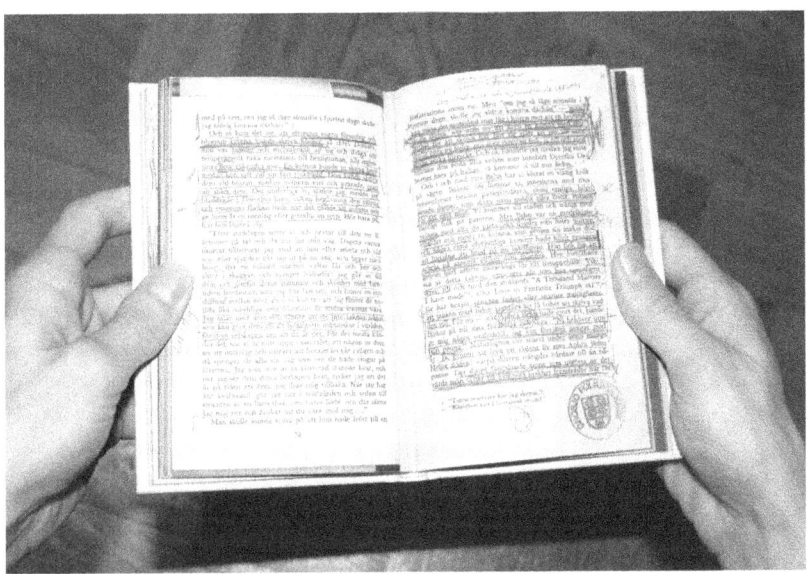

FIGURE 3.7. Kajsa Dahlberg, *A Room of One's Own/A Thousand Libraries (Ett eget rum/ Tusen bibliotek)*, 2006. Book in an edition of 1,000 copies. Courtesy of the artist.

As mentioned earlier, discussions of reenactment and notions of disrupted temporality often reference Benjamin's famous "On the Concept of History." Nicholas Ridout explores how theater can "undo" time when its syncopated time is mobilized through what would Benjamin would term a "constellation."[41] Both Brecht and Benjamin saw urgency in being able to keep hold of history in the present. As Benjamin put it: "The only historian capable of fanning the spark of hope in the past is the one who is firmly convinced that *even the dead* will not be safe from the enemy if he is victorious."[42] The artists who take hold of feminisms' histories echo this drive. Just as Dahlberg retrieves Woolf's famous book when it is out of print, a communication about different moments takes place—a communication that is an ongoing discussion, a rehearsal of a history fueled by an urgency for what it might teach us in the present.

A REHEARSAL

In a letter to Rainer, Boudry and Lorenz begin by asking her whether she agrees with the comment that certain scenes from *Lives of Performers* "are less a rehearsal of a performance than a performance of a rehearsal."[43] They continue: "Thinking through the question of rehearsal in this way, we learned a lot about

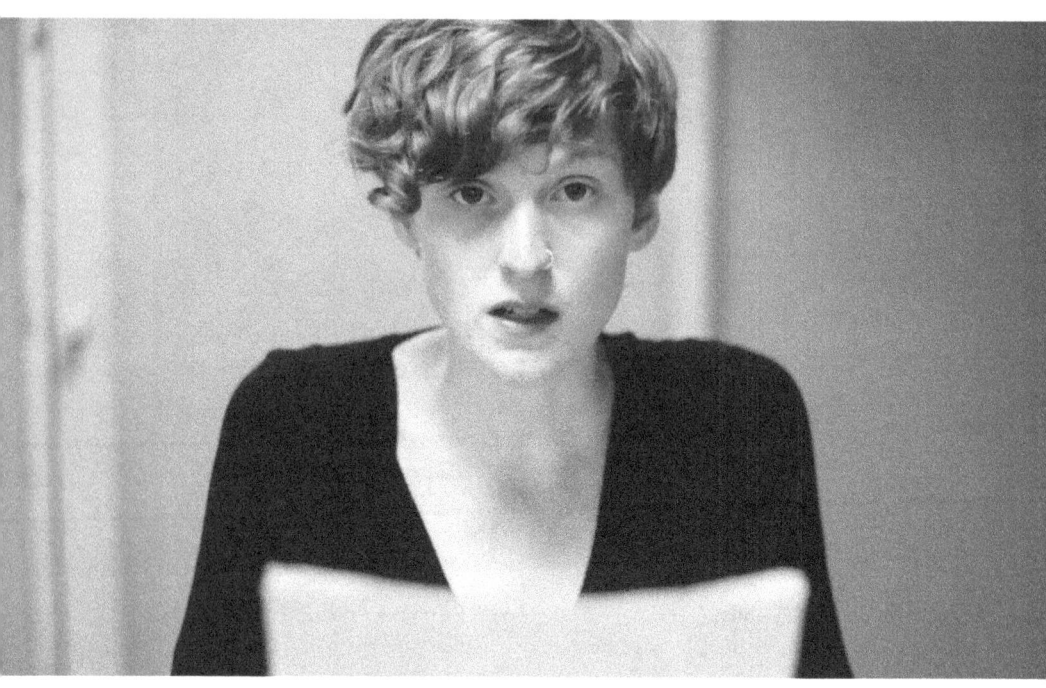

FIGURES 3.8–3.9. Faye Green, *NOT TO DISCOU[RAGE] YOU*, 2013 (made with Erin Buelow). Courtesy of the artist.

our interest in 'performing rehearsal.' . . . It seems to create bodies and sceneries [*sic*] of 'becoming' but never 'being.'"[44] Rehearsal as a process is key to the learning-play as a space in which the script is always under possible alteration. By working on a script as both text to be analyzed and gestures to be embodied, the collective engaged with a learning-play has to be aware of the specificity of their bodies and their temporality. Rehearsal also often requires a struggle, an embodiment of various possibilities without necessarily knowing which one to choose, a debate that takes place within and between bodies.

This sense of struggle is found in a performance by the British artist Faye Green: *NOT TO DISCOU[RAGE] YOU* (2013 [figures 3.8–3.9]).[45] In a filmed version, Green begins by reading to camera, closely framed. The stories she tells circulate around her passionate engagement with Rainer's famous dance *Trio A*. This is not a pedagogical exchange in person, as in *Salomania*, because Green cannot access the approved channels through which to learn *Trio A*. Instead, she pursues an unauthorized learning, an obsessive, incomplete taking hold of the dance through the available information: descriptions and film. Her passionate learning and embodying are accompanied by research, reading, feeling.

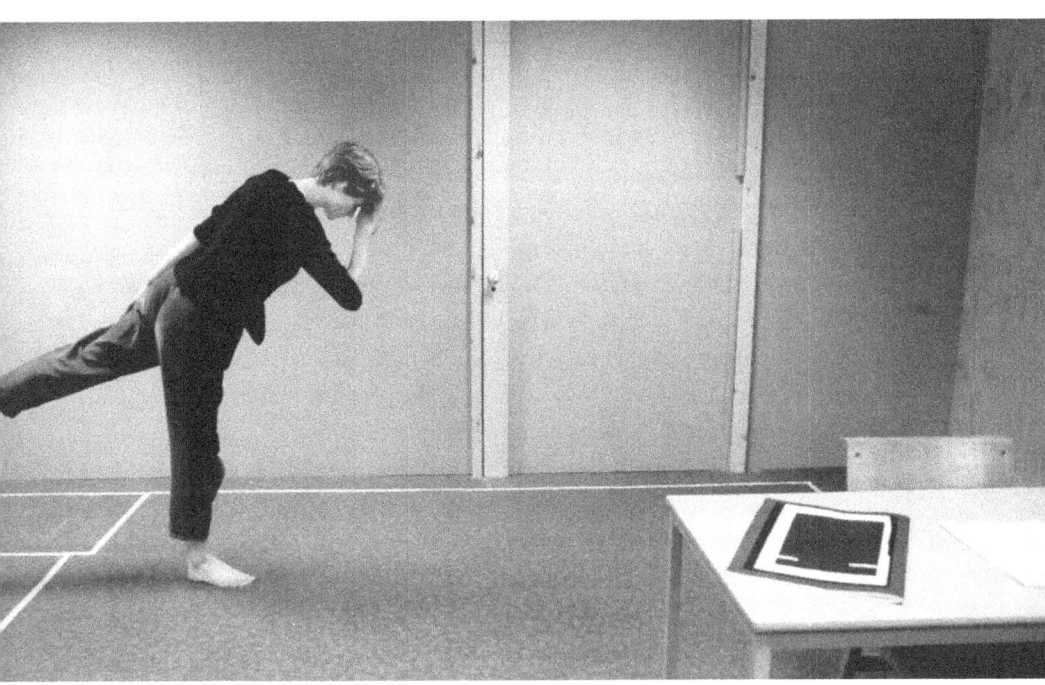

The moments of reading are alternated with Green dancing parts of *Trio A*, her body's movements confined by the small space in which the film is shot: a makeshift room that is made even more provisional through the masking-tape contours of the room in which Green learned the dance. A room of one's own is here constructed and performed within: Green tells us "she learns the room as she learns the dance."[46] Just as Woolf narrates scenes of embodiment to make viewers aware of their own, specific corporeality and temporality, Green insistently brings attention to her own body. Discussing the performance, Green says that what is being shown is not her final learned version of *Trio A* but, rather, "about learning my learning."[47] This learning is visceral, felt in the body in a manner akin to a hysterical symptom, not a good student but a ravenous one, one ready to steal what is needed. She talks about "the purgatory of an unread text, a bodiless dance." Taking up this dance is no simple exercise in technique for Green. Instead, it is a survival strategy of learning through reenactment, an infection in the form of a historical moment. Green's fragmented narrative tells how she stumbled upon Rainer's work while reading at a library, how she "read the dance before she ever saw it." The dance marks a return in her personal history, as she had stopped dancing when her body no longer fit what is deemed appropriate for a ballet dancer. She tells the viewer, "I am 23 remembering being 15 remembering being 8."

Green's performance and learning, undertaken alone and against the wishes of one of Rainer's transmitters, is a counterpoint to the performance of queer, intergenerational friendship in Boudry and Lorenz's film.[48] However, I propose that both films employ forms of learning from history that reveal some the tensions felt when taking up material from other feminists—in this case, the work of Rainer, who continues to be a practicing artist herself. Green is separated from the authorized learning of *Trio A* through her lack of finances (the transmitter will teach it to her only for a fee) and through a lack of network (unlike Tsang, Green is not personally connected to Rainer through art-school training). She describes isolated learning that takes place in the face of opposition, although she sees this as productive, and states that her performance is not "anti-Rainer."[49] There is something to be gained from resistance, and this is where the model of fandom rather than generations or waves becomes useful. A fan doesn't need to get authorization from an admired actor or writer or musician. Fans can still operate without needing a sense of filial connection, and I would argue that, for many feminists still, there is a sense of coming to feminist histories and legacies in an accidental manner, with relationships experienced as generational only after an initial connection with material that is often textual.

Green's performance begins with reading. She sits and reads from a text that explains her relationship to *Trio A*: her experience of reading about it, watching it performed online, emailing one of Rainer's transmitters to learn more, and illicit learning of it. It is a long time before she dances. Her text leads the viewer through her process of trying to access the dance and dramatizes her attempts to find a history without being located within a network that will assist her. The title of the piece comes from her circling the word "RAGE" inside the apologetic sentence of refusal sent to her from Rainer's transmitter: "*NOT TO DISCOU[RAGE] YOU.*" Rainer and Tsang's humorous exchange is replaced by a termination of contact, which Green then processes through her own experiences and that of Sigmund Freud and Josef Breuer's famous hysterics, stories of women acting out the past through their bodies when society cannot allow them to express themselves. Green takes the neutral pacing of Rainer's dance and reimagines it as the scene of repression, a holding in of desire in the face of patriarchal authority. A tapping foot is taken from Anna O's case study in which the patient hears music and wants to dance but cannot because she is at her father's bedside.[50] Green is the analyst and patient, dancer and choreographer, student and teacher: a Brechtian spectator and dramaturge who "is writing her own history even as she absorbs messages from the stage," promoting "unofficial histories and unofficial historians."[51] Here patriarchal authority is overlaid with the gate-keeping of artistic legacies, a complicated relationship that crosses time, bodies and disciplines.

In both *Salomania* and NOT TO DISCOU[RAGE] YOU, moments of exasperation, rage, eroticism, and dis-ease are found when historical material is experienced, rehearsed through the body. Tsang gets to converse with a queer stepfather, being gently chastised but ultimately still allowed to speak and dance her version, whereas Green celebrates her refusal to abide by the rules set out by Rainer's proxy, the transmitter.[52] These interactions thematize the problem of how older feminists relate to histories that they were part of, or that they remember, when they are engaged with by a younger generation. Many interactions have been fraught and bruising.[53] However, particularly within queer networks and pedagogical scenes, this has started to loosen, and a commonality and pleasure have started to be found for some, as explored with Kelly's relationship with her students in chapter 1. Through the foregrounding of the process of rehearsing in this chapter, the difficulties on both sides are framed by the possibilities found through conversation and dialogue, even if no agreement is reached.

In Green's hands, *Trio A* can only ever be in rehearsal, as she has no access to its finished version or authorization to perform it as "Trio A." Instead, the dance remains "dis-eased in her." This sense of embodiment, as a form of learning through discomfort or excess, is something that Julia Bryan-Wilson has explored in relation to her experience of learning Rainer's *Trio A*—this time from Rainer herself.[54] She writes about how learning gestures—as opposed to watching them or reading about them—creates an embodied intimacy with the historical material of the dance that has the potential to fold time in ways that have been theorized as queer by writers such as Freeman.[55] Like Bryan-Wilson, I want to propose that what happens in the reenactment of gesture is that the bodily experience of performing can be used as a vehicle for a creative quotation that remakes and reshapes the gesture that is being learned and replayed. In *Salomania*, the reenactments might be thought of as bringing an archive to life or embodying an archive. In that act of embodiment, the archival material is transformed, literally and figuratively acted on. In NOT TO DISCOU[RAGE] YOU, this reenactment is taken into the body and is reformed in its interactions with other experiences, other histories. Green performs on her own what Dahlberg collects through textual traces that betray passionate engagements with Woolf's own performances and arguments across the pages of *A Room of One's Own*. Both projects echo the urgency Kate Eichhorn describes in her discussion of feminist archival practices: "The archival turn under neoliberalism should not be primarily read as a desire to escape the present but rather as an attempt to regain agency in an era when the ability to collectively imagine and enact other ways of being in the world has become deeply eroded."[56] Eichhorn's words provide an overview to understand the attention to feminist histories in contemporary art, resonating once again with Brecht's and Benjamin's politicized returns to history.

My thoughts on a time of one's own should be read as a rehearsal, a proposition to be taken up. For Brecht, Benjamin, and Woolf, a critical, embodied engagement with history was a way to think beyond their "nows." I propose that reenactment thought through the learning-play can open up conversations among feminism's histories while also paying close attention to the specificity of our present, a form of consciousness-raising that can be performed in a group or with an imagined set of interlocutors. Brecht designed the learning-play to encourage the analysis of history and the acquiring of new attitudes in the mind and body. Here, a time of one's own imagines the learning-play as a cast with characters across history, using different media to bring them to life, rehearsing scenes across film, the pages of a book, or a gallery. These scenes are now handed over, with all their incompleteness, all their potential, to you, the reader. It is a call to claim time and rehearse whatever is necessary for your own sense of history, community, body; to refuse other people's definitions of what is over, or too much, or superseded; and to be open to reenactment's syncopated time and to use its embodied inquiries to engage with feminism's pasts in ways that make them alive for now.

4

A Feminist Chorus

Throughout this book there has been an interest in the formation of feminist communities. In this chapter, the notion of a feminist chorus explores how this community is staged. Focusing on collective acts of respeaking, a feminist chorus also includes conversations that take place in person and on the page. Various strategies for speaking to one another, as well as alongside one another, are key to feminist politics, beginning with the practice of consciousness-raising and the organizational structure of the small group, as touched on in chapter 3, and leading to the pedagogical and dialogic practices of artists working in or with groups. The feminist chorus brings together some of the ways in which re-enactment can be generative while also engaging with the problem of historical repetition. The chorus is a format that stretches back to Greek theater, but here I will also think about the chorus as a refrain in a song, or a chorus line. What does it mean to be part of a feminist chorus? Can this be a way to imagine a time of one's own—as a chorus that is picked up by different people at different moments in time? I explore how the feminist chorus stages the very feminist practice of presenting embodied experience as a form of learning, conceptualized as riffing on a well-known line, spoken by others as well as oneself, listening to the individual sound while aware of a community of others. The well-known line here is mostly archival material, which leads to conversations with others, both present and imagined.

By returning to texts, phrases, or moments and replaying or respeaking them together, we listen and speak to one another. Rather than a single figure, the group becomes the focus, although the experience of being within a group produces a very particular sense of self that is important to how we take part in a feminist community. Thought of as a feminist chorus, this group also returns to the theme of embodied reading as an entry point into rewriting: to pay attention to the scene of reading, which is imagined here as reading out loud, but also as taking place in writing that is circulated and added to, alongside conversation, discussion, reminiscences, and disagreements. As with the figure of the fan and the idea of a time of one's own, the body is insistently present, but not specified or biologically defined. The feminist chorus is another way to explore the experience we have of historical material in a particular moment of time, with a particular group of people, and how that informs our sense of identity.

I have taken part in a number of the works discussed in this chapter, which include artworks, reading groups, and public events. They took place within feminist communities in London and the United Kingdom, although some extend to different geographical contexts. The beginning examples are two artworks that respeak material from feminist archives and libraries: Clare Gasson's *The River* (2011) and Lucy Reynolds's *A Feminist Chorus* (2014–ongoing). The implications for these different modes of feminist chorus are contextualized by the use of the chorus as a political tool in Weimar Germany, picking up on its Brechtian links to the learning-play explored in chapters 2 and 3. In the second half of this chapter, which focuses on the forms of dialogue that take place alongside this respeaking, I explore an ongoing artwork that "translates" Zoe Leonard's text "I Want a Dyke for President" (1992) and, in particular, a version made for the UK elections in 2015. The conversations that fed into this work lead to a consideration of how consciousness-raising and small group work in the 1970s often used scripts or scores that could be taken up by other feminist groups. These tactics are being revived, particularly by artist-run reading groups, using feminist archival material as a starting point for small group work. One particular group, the Women of Colour Index (WOCI) Reading Group, is examined as part of a wider move for women artists of color to be more fully represented within feminist and mainstream art-world communities. The title "a feminist chorus" is taken from Reynolds's ongoing project, as well as from the chapter 3's opening evocation of books in a library, unified by their dark green Virago Classic covers, visually presenting as a feminist chorus.

This idea of the feminist chorus, both literally and as a methodology, takes up the concept of "recitation" found in Clare Hemmings's influential book *Why Stories Matter*.[1] Hemmings asserts that stories about Western feminist theory have been created through the citation of various authors and their intellectual histories that flattens how different tendencies within feminist thought are understood. In the chapter "Citation Tactics," she uses the work of Judith Butler and, in particular, their book *Gender Trouble* (1990) as a case study. She explores how Butler often stands in for a turn from feminist to queer theory, with Michel Foucault being cited as their intellectual predecessor, ignoring the feminist work that Butler themself cites. Hemmings proposes that Butler's legacy and position within feminist histories would shift if their intellectual debt to the lesbian feminist theorist and writer Monique Wittig, rather than to Foucault, was foregrounded. What occurs in Hemmings's text is a humorous, but nonetheless instructional, experiment with recitation, which she frames as changing citational practices to perform feminist histories that have been marginalized or repressed. She gives this definition of recitation: "*reading aloud of something; reciting of something, from memory; revisiting material previously encountered (review); un-forgetting.*"[2] She explains her use of the term as "not the telling of a new story, but a renarration of the same story from a different perspective."[3] She employs this technique to "un-forget" a history of lesbian feminist thought around the category of "woman," which is often obscured when a Foucauldian lineage is privileged for Butler's theory of gender performativity. Hemmings is clear that this is not a process of substitution—in this case, Wittig for Foucault. Instead, she wants to highlight what has been marginalized or edited out—often lesbian, Black, and postcolonial feminist perspectives—and think about the political implications of this. She says that recitation "operates as a breaking open of the presumed relation between the past and the present, rather than an instantiation of a new, fixed relation between the two. I visualize recitation, then, as an intervention, a mode of engagement that values the past by understanding it affectively and politically rather than in terms of finality."[4] This process of "recitation" as an intervention is taken up by the artists and artworks explored in this book.[5] It joins with my own initial thoughts about reenactment being a process of "embodied quotation," which allows for the idea of "recitation" as operating in a broader, more embodied register than Hemmings's textual substitutions, a register that looks at the potential of recitation as "reading aloud" and joins this with the "revisiting" and "un-forgetting" that Hemmings's work underlines.[6]

TWO FEMINIST CHORUSES

I'm standing next to someone reading a completely different text from mine. We are all asked to start to read at the same time, producing a cacophony of sounds, with our own voices individually experienced as the clear line through.

I've been given a section from Susie Orbach's book *Fat Is a Feminist Issue* (1978). A color photocopy of a page picks out a section of the text, including a part entitled "Food Is for Others." I read this incomplete text—beginning and ending in mid-sentence—and the words become strangely physical as I speak them out loud, feeling that I am both reading to myself and proclaiming to the group, a proclamation they won't be able to hear due to their own and other voices.

This is not what I expected when Lucy Reynolds told me she would perform her *Feminist Chorus* as part of an event at Chelsea College of Art in London.[7] I had imagined a score for music, a structured lyric drawn from the archival sources to be sung, and had been apprehensive about having to take part. As it happened, the reality of Reynolds's *A Feminist Chorus* was a very simple, almost raucous-sounding affair. At the all-woman event, the mass of voices speaking out provided a moment of humor, as the different timbres, speeds, and volume levels produced an atonal soundscape. Reynolds has described how she wants to create a loose structure that will allow participants to take "ownership of the process and . . . interpret their reading as they wish."[8] For her, the pleasure of the work is in taking up space and making noise, an assertion of a feminist community that is heard and felt by the group and the audience alike. She describes this as a "cacophony of feminist noise" that incorporates "the sound of epiphany, revelation, anger, doubt, all embodied in the sound where you can't hear any words."[9] Here recitation becomes an abstraction, an assertion of sound rather than a particular quotation. Each of the speakers can hear the text she is speaking, and fragments can be picked up by the audience. The feminist chorus asserts an archive of texts that is too various to be heard as a single narrative.

The iteration of *A Feminist Chorus* that I took part in was a practice for a series of performances and installations at Glasgow International in April 2014.[10] It was divided into three parts: texts chosen from the Glasgow Women's Library; documents from the Glasgow Society of Lady Artists (an organization that operated from 1882 to 1971); and registers from the Glasgow School of Art, edited to include only the women students, from 1886 to 1901. The three sections of the score were performed and filmed at Glasgow Women's Library, then installed within the library itself (figure 4.1).[11] At the event in which I took part, the selection from the library had been Reynolds's choices, but for the recorded version she asked a group of women with connections to the library each to choose a text, which they would then perform. This final range of extracts is diverse, reflecting the different communities who use the library, including library volunteers, a theater group, and literacy group for refugee women. The range of texts chosen are described in the book that accompanies the performances as including "fiction, poetry, feminist theory, exhibition, knitting" (figure 4.2).[12]

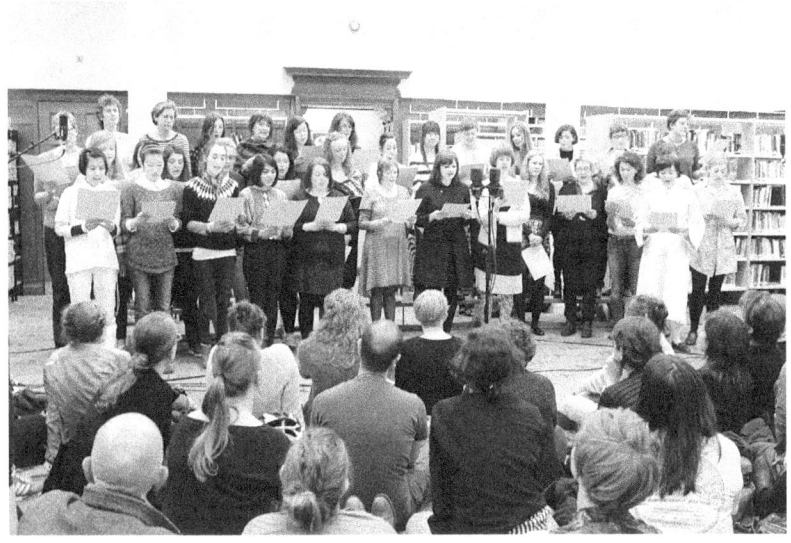

FIGURE 4.1. Lucy Reynolds, *A Feminist Chorus*, Glasgow Women's Library, 2014. Photograph of the performance at Glasgow Women's Library, part of Glasgow International 2014. Courtesy of the artist and Glasgow Women's Library.

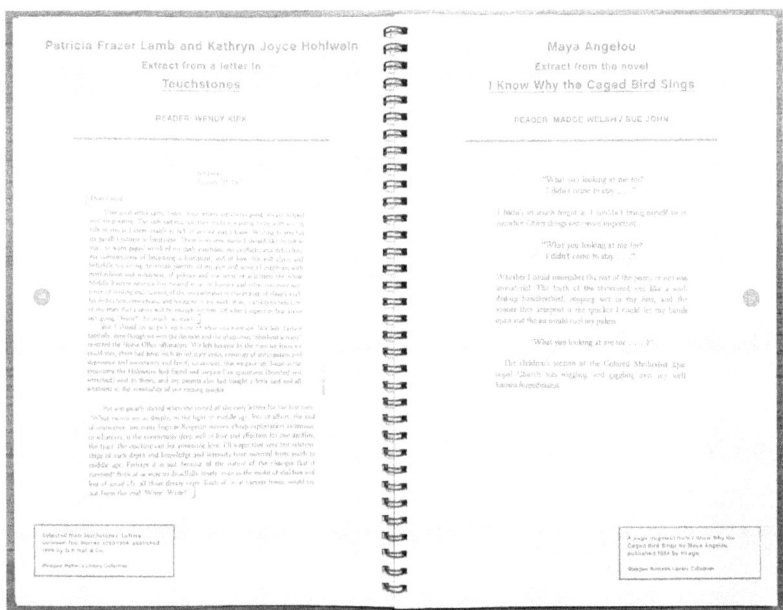

FIGURE 4.2. Lucy Reynolds, *A Feminist Chorus*, 2014, exhibition catalog showing texts read at the Glasgow Women's Library. Photograph by Catherine Grant. Courtesy of the artist.

For the other two sections of the score, Reynolds asked current Glasgow School of Art students to perform the registers from early in the school's history and a range of artists working in the city to perform documents from the Glasgow Society of Lady Artists.[13]

A few years earlier, I had attended a performance created by another London-based artist, Clare Gasson. This piece, *The River* (2011), was a very different kind of feminist chorus, with eight vocalists performing an intricate score consisting of every name in the Women's Art Library collection.[14] Gasson says that the vast list of names (about twelve thousand) was turned into a minimalist composition through a collaboration with the musicologist Huw Hallam.[15] For Gasson, *The River* is not explicitly feminist, and while she did not refuse my contextualization of the work, she personally foregrounded its minimalist qualities and the experience of the live performance. These qualities inform what can be done with bodies speaking or singing together and point to the difficulty of representing the sonic and embodied experience of this work, as well as the others explored in this chapter.

The composition was derived from a set of instructions that divided the list up into sections, starting with the names being whispered, followed by a range of instructions that included "staccato and random" and "with the energy of no compromise" (figure 4.3).[16] At the performance at the South London Gallery, the vocalists were placed around a darkened room, allowing the audience to walk around them (figure 4.4). This spatiality created an experience of the vocalizations as shifting, depending on where you stood in relation to the performers. Gasson describes the staging this way: "The vocalists (men and women of all ages—this was important) were standing in the round on the edges of a low rectangular stage which was set on a diagonal across and in the middle of the space. It meant that the audience could get very close to them and hear the names and their breath."[17]

This version of a feminist chorus included the audience in a different way: rather than joining in with the recitation, each audience member was enveloped in the flow of names, picking out individual women artists from the soundscape that was literally all around. The darkened space and the vibrancy of the score lent this performance a sacred air that held the audience for its duration of more than an hour. Gasson had found a way to bring to life one of the most basic structures of the Women's Art Library—a list of all the artists to be found within it— and turn what would normally be dry, archival overload into a physically palpable representation of this archived community. Her title, *The River*, evokes this list as a flow that is continuing and is available to the viewer in only a partial manner. She describes the vocalization of these names as a kind of man-

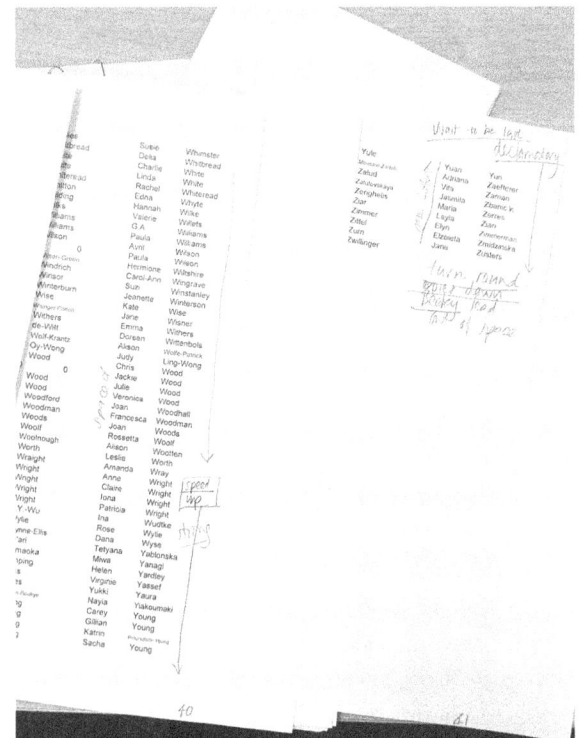

FIGURE 4.3. Clare Gasson, *The River*, 2011, performance at South London Gallery, pages from performer Amy Cunningham's score, Women's Art Library, London. Photograph by Catherine Grant. Courtesy of the artist and the Women's Art Library, London.

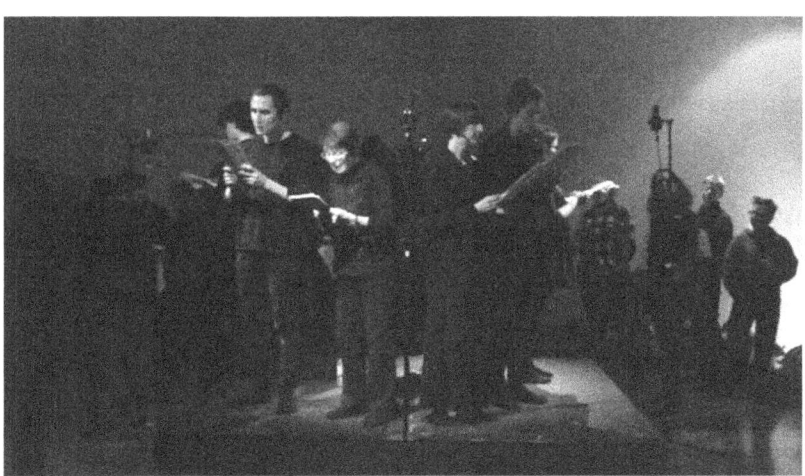

FIGURE 4.4. Clare Gasson, *The River*, performance at South London Gallery, London, 2011, video still. Performers: Barbara Alden, Amy Cunningham, Robin Dann, Huw Hallam, Becky Hardwick, Lara Karady, Toby O'Connor, Portia Winters. Courtesy of the artist.

tra, producing a state of reflection.[18] In the press release for the performance, this flow is evoked on the page: "The River—a mix of voices—raining names down pages—splitting rhythms and text—voices—working—horizontal and vertical—weaving—expanding—contracting—intermingling currents—forming The River."

The two feminist choruses described here present the two poles between which this idea is suspended. The delicately choreographed performance by Gasson was nonetheless one in which the audience was drawn, finding their own line of names through the sound. In Reynolds's event, the orderly nature suggested by the work's title, *A Feminist Chorus*, is undone by the improvised nature of these groupings, which can be awkward, uplifting, humorous, or ener-vating. In these two choruses, the emphasis is on making archival material pres-ent, a group experience of recitation that insists on the power of these names and texts. The experience of both these works was that the histories of women artists and activists are present but often silent or invisible. In the examples of feminist choruses in the rest of this chapter, I explore variations on the chorus form and think about the ways in which recitation is joined with dialogue: both between a group that is physically present and between moments in history. Be-fore turning to this aspect of the chorus, I explore how the chorus historically has been used for learning and community making.

THE CHORUS

A chorus indicates a group speaking, singing, standing together. A chorus is also the song being sung or spoken by the group.[19] In its original Greek context, the chorus indicated dancing as much as singing, as H. P. Kitto has described: "The Greek verb *choreuo*, 'I am a member of the chorus,' has the sense 'I am dancing.'" He continues: "The 'orchestra' in which the chorus had its being is, literally, a dancing-floor."[20] This dancing was a way to embody elements of the poetry they were performing, with scholars arguing for a broader definition of dancing than we would understand today, so that dancing indicates the use of gesture, pose, and attitude.[21] What these gestures and movements might have been has been lost, but the function of the chorus has continued in drama to the present day. In my version of a feminist chorus, this etymology pays at-tention to the chorus as bodies gathered together so that the chorus is both a physical and a sonic taking up of space, a gathering together of bodies and voices.[22] These bodies are not necessarily choreographed; instead, the experi-ence of being one body among many is activated through the speaking or sing-ing that takes place communally.

The Greek chorus was central to religious festivals and dramas, with chorus members drawn from the general population of Athens. Peter Arnott argues that the chorus onstage both reflected and was an extension of the audience watching. Rather than a passive audience, an Athenian audience would have been in active partnership with the performers onstage, and many of the audience members would have taken part in choruses themselves. Here the lines between audience and actor are bridged or blurred through the presence of the chorus, who are used as both performers within the narrative structure of the plays and narrators who can stand outside of the play. The instructional nature of the chorus, as a form of learning together that is performed in a group, is key to my idea of the feminist chorus. The chorus can explain, comment on, and disagree with the action onstage, moving between a place of identification for the audience and part of the drama unfolding. Arnott describes the function of the Greek chorus in a manner that echoes many of the reenactments of feminist histories, as well as Hemmings's concept of "recitation": "The chorus may enlarge upon information already received; it may reflect upon it, and color it. But it does not originate it."[23] In a feminist chorus, this information can be transformed through its embodied quotation: rewritten or recited in the present.

Continuing the reimagining of the learning-play in previous chapters, the chorus's ability to be both inside and outside the dramatic universe is something that Brecht drew on in a number of his learning-plays. His writings and the historical circumstances of his use of the chorus form an important precedent for the contemporary works explored here. They also show how techniques of learning found in the chorus are brought together from inside the classroom, on the stage, and, one hopes, as a way to inform life. In "Theatre for Learning," he describes how "choruses informed the audiences about facts it did not know."[24] Elsewhere he has explained that, in the learning-play, choruses were used to "vivify" the action.[25] Here he draws on the Greek chorus's role in providing a point of identification for the audience, performing observations as well as taking part in the dramatic action. However, this information was not simply imparted by the chorus onstage to the audience listening. The use of the chorus also allowed for Brecht to draw the audience into the play, something he experimented with in radio broadcasts that could be followed by children in their classrooms in his early learning-plays and the use of workers' choirs. When discussing one of his first learning-plays, and how it had to be employed as "an *object of instruction*" and not simply as a performance to be watched, he explains how the lead character, the aviator Charles Lindbergh, must be sung by a chorus: "Only *collective I-singing* (I am Charles Lindbergh, I am setting forth, I am not tired, etc.) can salvage some of the pedagogical effect."[26] In his experiments with radio, he extended this collectivity by including the audience as participants, which would inform his theory of the learning-play as blurring or dispensing with the distinction between the role of actor and audience. Or, as Reiner Steinweg puts it, the learning-play "recognizes actors who are at the same time students."[27] Being both a student and an actor also requires a dialogic approach to the script in hand, so that, as Nicholas Ridout describes, "The text is not a finished text but an open field for a process of improvisation, rewriting and discussion."[28]

The feminist chorus produces a way of thinking about this blurring or merging of the roles of actor and audience, imaging its participants as students, as well as performers. Taking part in a chorus means joining together with a group and brings to mind the experience of speaking a shared text in a process of being educated or enlightened. Think of the act of communal prayer or singing songs as children. This experience also points to the fact that the feminist chorus is not tied to a particular space. One can experience it in a gallery, out on the street, or in a seminar room. The Greek chorus was also seen as a part of a moral, religious, and political education.[29] Brecht's use of the chorus came out of this tradition, influenced by the huge range of workers' choruses active in Weimar Germany. Richard Bodek argues that workers' choruses were an important way to create a sense of proletarian community, history, and culture.[30] He explores the hundreds of active choruses during this period and the influence that they had on Brecht's theater. Alongside the use of choruses at large festivals, Bodek investigates the numerous agitprop troupes in Berlin that took up the ideas of Soviet groups who performed as "living newspapers."[31] Brecht's concept of the learning-play can be seen as having come out of these political uses of choruses and improvised theater. The agitprop troupes wrote scripts quickly in response to the local political situation, designed as forms of participatory education and entertainment, something that is borne out in the rewriting and discussion that is foregrounded in the examples later in this chapter.[32] The workers' choruses sang a range of classic songs and new, explicitly political songs, with the intention of creating a new proletarian tradition. This is also found in the use of archival material in the feminist choruses explored in this chapter, linking to a longer history of feminist art and activism, particularly during the Women's Liberation Movement, that seeks to bring women's histories and communities to life.

For Brecht, learning was central to his concept of epic theater in general as well as to the learning-play. In "Theatre for Learning," he argues that learning can be "thrilling," proposing a "joyous and militant learning," which echoes Bodek's descriptions of both the choruses and agitprop troupes in Weimar Berlin.[33] Brecht talks about learning beyond the school environment, proposing that learning done by "people who have not yet 'had their turn', who are discontented with the way things are, who have an immense practical interest in learning, who want orientation badly, who know they are lost without learning—these are the best and most ambitious learners."[34] This is the kind of learning that Bodek explores in his account of workers' choruses and agitprop groups, and this is the kind of learning that can take place as part of a feminist chorus, with an interwoven relationship between the politics and the lived practice of feminism.

Before I continue to explore artworks and events that can be seen as performing this kind of feminist chorus, I want to address the negative consequences of taking part in a chorus—or, as Roswitha Mueller puts it in relation to the learning-play, "questions about the *Lehrstück* as a possible instrument of indoctrination."[35] What is useful in Mueller's discussion of these questions is how she argues that Brecht saw the learning-play not as communicating political truths, but as a structure that could be altered as needed: "While Brecht departed from and made use of current political theories, he approached them undogmatically. Aware of their *faulty and time-bound character*, he opened them up for discussion. Brecht expressly pointed out that the commentary may be changed at any time: 'It is full of mistakes with respect to our time and its virtues, and it is unusable for other times.'"[36] If we transpose these comments about the learning-play to the idea of the feminist chorus, we can imagine it not as a vehicle for simply repeating the lessons of the past but as an active grouping through which these lessons can be interrogated for the present. As in Hemmings's concept of recitation, there is a return to the material at hand that does not simply substitute one political truth for another, one feminist history for a different one. Instead, the past is understood "affectively and politically" and has to be taken up alongside our own histories, bodies, and desires within it.[37]

I WANT A DYKE FOR PRESIDENT

This sense of current political theories' "faulty and time-bound character" came to the fore in my third example of a feminist chorus, one within an explicitly political, public context: the UK General Election in 2015. Performed in Trafalgar Square, two versions of Zoe Leonard's "I Want a President" (1992) were read over and over again by a group that had gathered on the eve of the election. Organized by the writer and curator Laura Guy, this was an iteration of the open-ended project "I Want a President" begun in Sweden by Malin Arnell, Kajsa Dahlberg, Johanna Gustavsson, and Fia-Stina Sandlund in 2010.[38] Whereas previous versions of the project had translated Leonard's text into the language of the country where it was being read out, for this reading the text

I want a dyke for president. I want a person with aids for president and I want a fag for vice president and I want someone with no health insurance and I want someone who grew up in a place where the earth is so saturated with toxic waste that they didn't have a choice about getting leukemia. I want a president that had an abortion at sixteen and I want a candidate who isn't the lesser of two evils and I want a president who lost their last lover to aids, who still sees that in their eyes every time they lay down to rest, who held their lover in their arms and knew they were dying. I want a president with no airconditioning, a president who has stood on line at the clinic, at the dmv, at the welfare office and has been unemployed and layed off and sexually harrassed and gaybashed and deported. I want someone who has spent the night in the tombs and had a cross burned on their lawn and survived rape. I want someone who has been in love and been hurt, who respects sex, who has made mistakes and learned from them. I want a Black woman for president. I want someone with bad teeth and an attitude, someone who has eaten that nasty hospital food, someone who crossdresses and has done drugs and been in therapy. I want someone who has committed civil disobedience. I want to know why this isn't possible. I want to know why we started learning somewhere down the line that a president is always a clown: always a john and never a hooker. Always a boss and never a worker, always a liar, always a thief and never caught.

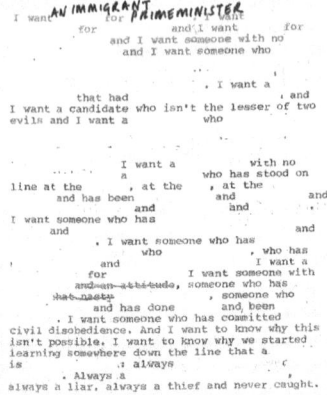

A COLLECTIVE READING ORGANISED BY
ARTISTS TO COINCIDE WITH THE ELECTION
6·15 pm FOR 6·30 pm START
6 MAY 2015, TRAFALGAR SQUARE STEPS

WE WILL READ ZOE LEONARD'S TEXT
I WANT A PRESIDENT... AND AN
UPDATED VERSION OF THE TEXT
WE WILL READ FOR 1 HOUR

FIND US ON FACEBOOK: I WANT A PRESIDENT

FIGURE 4.5. Flyer for *I Want a President*, organized by Laura Guy, London, Trafalgar Square, 2015. Courtesy of Laura Guy.

was translated to reflect conditions in the United Kingdom in 2015 (figures 4.5–4.6). Guy has written about what she describes as "the time of the manifesto" in relation to this piece and how the act of rewriting Leonard's text was a collective translation.[39] For Guy, the time of the manifesto is a combination of "the past, present and future tense" that "allows persons or groups to stake a claim to forms of political subjectivity."[40] Like Hemmings's framing of recitation as an intervention, Guy worked with a group of collaborators to think through what of kind of recitation would go beyond a nostalgic or aestheticizing presentation of Leonard's visceral text, which was initially written and handed out a rally during the US presidential primaries and was part of Leonard's work with the activist group Fierce Pussy.[41] The resulting "translation" begins with the words, "I want a dyke for prime minister. I want an immigrant for prime minister and I want someone with AIDS for prime minister and I want someone who has debt and I want someone who watched their council estate bulldozed and replaced with luxury flats."[42]

In the UK version, the performance of the two texts—Leonard's original and

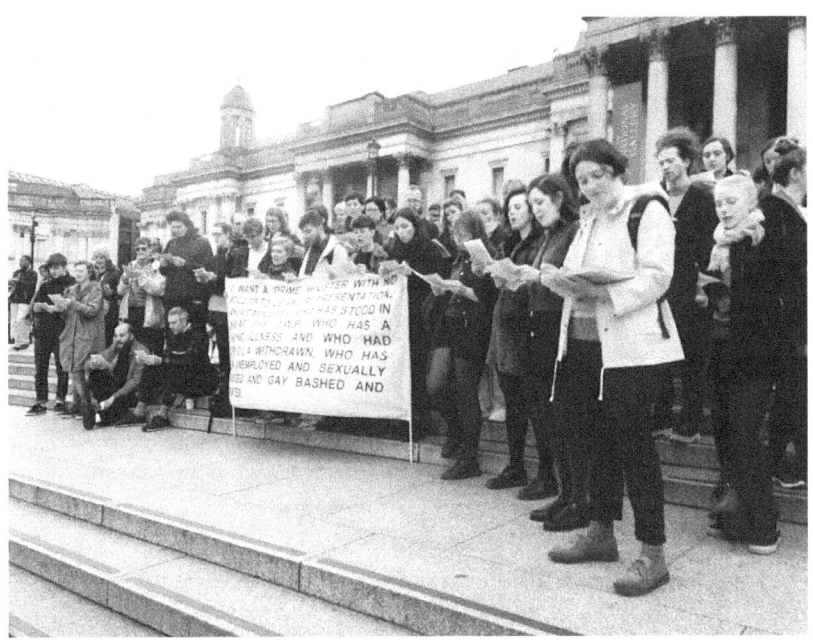

Figure 4.6. *I Want a President*, organized by Laura Guy, banner made by Nicola Guy, London, Trafalgar Square, 2015. Courtesy of Laura Guy.

the translation that reflected on the situation in the United Kingdom in 2015 — highlighted the need to engage in detail with historical material to understand our present. Here, recitation is a respeaking and a remaking, a citation that does not need to stay completely bound by its origins. The power of Leonard's piece was honored but not enshrined — an important aspect of a feminist chorus as the needs of our moment change. The flow of the text, in both Leonard's version and this collective translation, with its insistent chorus of "I want . . . ," is broken only near the end with the sentence, "And I want to know why this isn't possible."[43] When I've read this text, this line has always come as a shock, a moment of sadness, with the repetition of readings not lessening the keening felt. The resilience, anger, and humor that draw together the different experiences of marginalization are broken, and a limit point is reached. "And I want to know why this isn't possible" is a call to find out why, to learn from the excessive nature of the emotions that drive this text, and to not settle for something less. Through a text spoken together, questions are raised that are not answered by this act of recitation but demand further discussion and action.

In the line, "And I want to know why this isn't possible," there is also the echo of consciousness-raising, the group activity that fueled much of the early Women's Liberation Movement, a process based on asking questions and sharing experiences as a basis for further action. I explore the practice of consciousness-raising and the importance of the small group as a way into the second aspect of the feminist chorus on which I want to focus: the dialogue and conversations that it can hold. As mentioned in chapter 3, consciousness-raising shares elements with the learning-play, and I see it as part of a tradition of radical pedagogy. In the Women's Liberation Movement, consciousness-raising sessions were a way to craft a political consciousness through women speaking with one another. Juliet Mitchell gives a concise description in *Woman's Estate*: "The process of transforming the hidden, individual fears of women into shared awareness of the meaning of them as social problems, the release of anger, anxiety, the struggle of proclaiming the painful and transforming it into the political—this process is *consciousness-raising*."[44] Mitchell explores how consciousness-raising was often dismissed as group therapy and instead explains it as "the re-interpretation of a Chinese revolutionary practice of 'speaking bitterness.'"[45] She examines the transposition of this practice from Chinese peasants to "Women's Liberation Movements in the advanced capitalist countries," arguing that the process allows for "speaking the unspoken" as a necessary step in understanding oppression.[46]

Instructions for setting up consciousness-raising groups were circulating widely in the late 1960s and '70s, with the earliest being Kathie Sarachild's "A Program for Feminist 'Consciousness Raising'" from November 1968.[47] Consciousness-raising informed the idea of the small group as the key structure for many feminist groups during the 1970s. These two structures—consciousness-raising and the small group—are both important for my concept of the feminist chorus. The feminist chorus reengages with the energy and interaction the small group allowed while also being attentive to the tensions inherent in its structure. As Shelia Rowbotham writes, "In the early feminist groups there was a relatively straightforward assumption that if women talked long and intimately enough their real desires could be detached from those with which they had been lumbered by men or capitalism."[48] She goes on to say that this optimism was not always borne out: "Consciousness-raising could illuminate and reveal, but it could also stifle and steer." She continues, "Two stark emotions loomed persistently: betrayal and coercion. The small group sought a consensus which had ramifications within the politics of the women's movement."[49]

This tension between transformation and coercion echoes Mueller's comments about the potential of indoctrination in relation to the learning-play. As feminist ideas were elaborated and communities grew in the late 1960s and early 1970s, what was possible in terms of a feminist politics was hotly debated. Collaborative, dialogic structures grounded in consciousness-raising led to study groups, "zap actions," collectively written texts and publications, and a desire to operate without leaders or hierarchies.[50] While there is a growing literature on the impact of these organizational structures for activism and our sense of feminism in the present, there has been less reflection on what this meant for art practices coming out of feminist communities and the actual experience of consciousness-raising.

In the recent surge of writing about the Women's Liberation Movement, most works focus on the US context.[51] While there is a large body of literature on art influenced by feminism, there is less in-depth scholarship on how small group work and consciousness-raising informed collaborative practices beyond a few key examples, such as Judy Chicago and Miriam Shapiro's *Womanhouse* (1971). This is beginning to be addressed by recent publications that focus on UK activism and art, such as Siona Wilson's *Art Labor, Sex Politics*, and ongoing research by a number of scholars.[52] What is notable is that this area is being explored by a growing number of curators, activists, and artists who are engaging with the forms of consciousness-raising and small group work to create new feminist communities today. Limiting my examples to London, they include the Feminist Duration Reading Group set up by Helena Reckitt, which has explored (among other things) the Italian version of consciousness-raising in relation to Alex Martinis Roe's artwork and research; X Marks the Spot, a collective that has worked on the Jo Spence archive and has an ongoing exploration into the Women of Colour Index at the Women's Art Library (one of the founders is Ego Ahaiwe Sowinski, discussed in chapter 2), which is also the focus of the WOCI Reading Group set up by Samia Malik, Michelle Williams Gamaker, and Rehana Zaman at the Women's Art Library, as discussed later; exhibitions such as Raven Row's *56 Artillery Lane* (2017), which included research into the early collaborative project *A Woman's Place* (1974), by Amy Tobin, and *The Sun Went In, the Fire Went Out: Landscapes in Film, Performance and Text* (2016), an exhibition curated by Karen di Franco and Elisa Kay.[53] As I've worked on the idea of the feminist chorus, I've drawn on this range of events, exhibitions, activism, and scholarly research in my immediate orbit, knowing that this is only one nodal point in an international network. In the space of the reading group, the exhibition, the symposium, and the study group I have learned about these different feminist histories that foreground collaboration. The format of these events echoes the earlier work they explore, creating spaces for groups to meet together and draw on these histories in the present. For example, Reckitt's Feminist Duration Reading Group explains its process this way: "The group has evolved a style of reading out loud together, in order to make these texts and ideas present in the room. Formats including performance and film screening, listening and writing exercises, are regularly included."[54] The impact of reading together when I have attended this reading group has produced an effect similar to that of taking part in Reynolds's *A Feminist Chorus*. Reading out loud becomes a simple way to bring all of the participants' voices into the room, breaking the barriers among the individual members and producing a sense of coming together, which can lead to conversation and analysis.

These events, exhibitions, and reading groups reimagine the constellation of feminist groups loosely linked with one another during the late 1960s and 1970s. Equally important during this earlier period are the various methods of distribution, publication, and art practice that came out of these small group meetings. Using a variety of creative forms, the Women's Liberation Movement found ways to pass on models, ideas, manifestos, and a sense of solidarity, both in person and through remote communications, a sisterhood understood as both an imagined and an embodied community. These formats are being reprised by contemporary artists, writers, and curators to create an embodied community in the present that touches these historical networks and materials. As in Sharon Hayes's film *In My Little Corner of the World, Anyone Would Love You* (2016), discussed in the introduction, feminist publications in the 1960s and '70s acted as a more diffuse form of consciousness-raising, with texts often explicitly addressed to other women and the letter form being used as a way to address a community that was not physically present but viscerally engaged with.[55] Alongside movement publications, edited collections employed a variety of direct addresses to the reader and presented material literally to be taken up. The "Historical Documents" section in the famous collection *Sisterhood Is Powerful* includes songs alongside poems and hexes created by the collective WITCH, providing material for a feminist chorus at any time in the future—a script or score that can be picked up by feminists in a different geographical location or historical moment.[56]

WOCI READING GROUP

This idea of a script or a score that can be picked up is found in many reading groups and creative projects that have been set up by artists in response to archival feminist material. They may not seem to fit easily into the idea of a feminist chorus, but they are an important element of my thinking around what it means to learn with a group of others through acts of recitation and discussion. While reading groups are not public performances in the way that Reynolds's, Gasson's, and Guy's projects were, they also invite a coming together that does not have an explicit division between audience and participant. A number of reading groups—particularly those run by artists and curators—use communal speaking as a way to bring the set text to life in the reading group, rather than in a traditional manner in which participants would read on their own at home (although this can accompany the reading together in the group). I have already mentioned Reckitt's Feminist Duration group, which has sought numerous ways to make the archival material "present in the room."[57] While I researched this chapter, a reading group that focuses on the need to "un-forget" histories of women of color in feminist archives gained traction. The WOCI Reading Group was set up by Samia Malik, Michelle Williams Gamaker, and Rehana Zaman at the Women's Art Library in 2016. Their starting point was archival material from the Women of Colour Index (WOCI), which was created by Rita Keegan in 1987 (figure 4.7).[58] Malik had first discovered the WOCI in 2015 at the Women's Art Library, also the location of Gasson's residency, which had resulted in *The River* five years earlier.[59] What was meant to be a temporary series of reading groups has expanded into an ongoing and evolving series through invitations from various institutions outside the Women's Art Library itself.[60] One of the formal characteristics of the WOCI Reading Group is that the set text is fairly short (often a text by one of the women in the index) and is read aloud by the group. In this reading aloud (with individuals reading a sentence apiece when I attended) there is a heightened feeling of one's own body and vocality in the room, something that is not often experienced when one reads silently alone. As I found while taking part in *A Feminist Chorus*, the words have a physicality when spoken aloud; they are given a presence that demands the groups' attention. This is mirrored by the experience of holding photocopied material from the archive, normally one or two pages. These pages become physical traces of the words of the artists held in the WOCI, and as one participant noted, they become talismans for members of the group as they are taken away, pinned up, referred to in people's private spaces.[61]

For its three founders, the WOCI Reading Group has become an important platform for communities of color within the art world, as well as a champion for the often hidden work of the women of color in the index. When I spoke to Zaman about the group, she emphasized that it explored connections between the historical material and contemporary conditions for people of color in the art world. Part of its popularity has come from the fact that it creates a

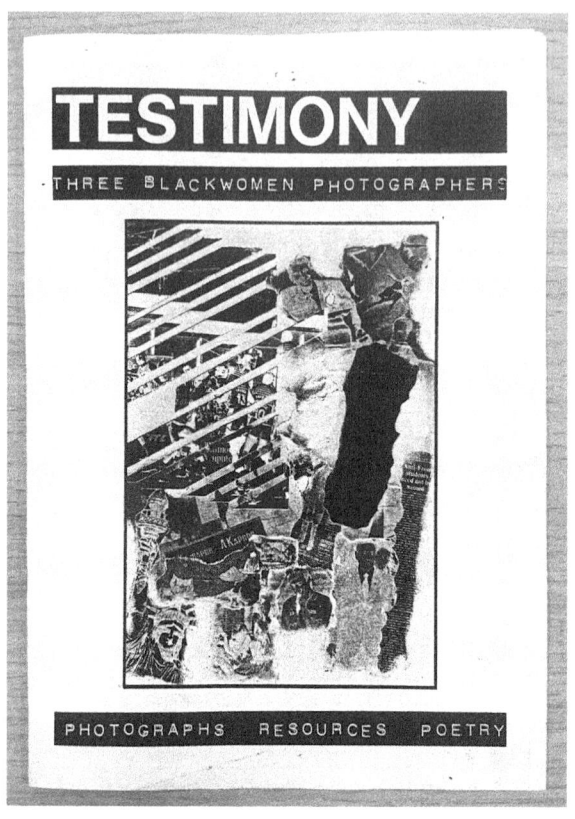

FIGURE 4.7.
Booklet from the
exhibition *Testimony:*
Three Blackwomen
Photographers,
Camerawork, London,
1987, part of the Women
of Colour Index, Women's
Art Library, London.
This was the material
discussed at the first
WOCI. Reading Group,
organized by Samia
Malik, Michelle Williams
Gamaker and Rehana
Zaman, October 10, 2016.
Photograph by Catherine
Grant. Courtesy of the
Women's Art Library,
London.

space to discuss histories and strategies for survival in relation to racial politics, feminism, and the arts. The sessions often start with a group reading of a text taken from the WOCI, then move into wide-ranging discussions about race, gender, and art practice. Zaman discussed the resonances between conditions for women of color described in the archival material and now, explaining how the group provides space to think about this in the present. On a practical level, she continued, it "makes a very clear and visible network of people who are of color and working in the arts."[62] This sentiment was echoed by another of the organizers, the artist Michelle Williams Gamaker, who explained that the group is "about self-defense or preservation" and that she realized, "If I don't fight/talk and raise awareness about the practices of women artists of color, my future is as precarious as the artists in the WOCI archive."[63] Williams Gamaker's use of metaphors of "self-defense" and the combination of "fight/talk" point to the urgency felt by women artists of color, who are still often relegated to the margins of (feminist) art history or who exist as a single individual, a token presence. Williams Gamaker concludes: "There is something deeply troubling that we find ourselves having to do this work of discovery and remembering today, given so many women before us strove for visibility and parity."

Samia Malik explained her experience of discovering the WOCI in similarly charged terms: finding the work in the index was "exciting and restorative," but her realization that these artists had been left out of mainstream art histories was traumatic.[64] Malik expressed anxiety and anger at not having heard of these artists during her art education, and this fueled her desire to continue the WOCI Reading Group as a vital platform for students, artists, writers, and curators. Here the feminist chorus is heard from the archive: a chorus of women of color who are barely represented in mainstream art histories, along with the participants of the WOCI Reading Group, who work together alongside the archival material. This feminist chorus is heard literally, through the recitation by members of the reading group of the archival material, often texts written by the artists in the index, and metaphorically, through a focus on networks of women artists of color who were and are in conversation with one another while often marginalized in the mainstream art world.[65] The ways in which the WOCI Reading Group can combat feelings of isolation for people of color in a mostly white art world was brought up by all three of the founders, as was the emotional labor running the group required. While the reading group is open to all, the sessions often have a majority of artists, writers, and students of color, something that is still unusual in university art departments and art galleries and that points to the importance of the group in the present moment.

The WOCI Reading Group reflects a broader move within feminist art history and curation to spotlight the continuing marginal status of women artists of color. For example, in the United States, ten years after the founding of the Elizabeth A. Sackler Center for Feminist Art at the Brooklyn Museum and the "Year of Feminism" in 2007, the Brooklyn Museum staged *We Wanted a Revolution: Black Radical Women 1965–85*.[66] Part of the yearlong celebration of the Feminist Art Center's first decade, it was also part of a growing demand for women of color to be put center stage in the context of a renewed intersectional feminist movement. With the political situation in the 2010s increasingly divided and bitter across political, racial, national, and gender lines, feminism was both more visible and more under threat in the United States, particularly after the inauguration of Donald Trump as president in 2017, alongside growing police violence, inequality, and unrest, which was highlighted through the Black Lives Matter Movement. In Britain, the vote to leave the European Union in 2016 left many people profoundly shocked by the xenophobia and rising right-wing rhetoric that this endorsed, both in the United Kingdom and across Europe. In this broader political context, small group work such as the WOCI Reading Group is both a response to the need to hear the voices of women of color within feminist communities and a broader move to decolonize cultural structures, histories, and institutions in the face of right-wing racism and divisive austerity politics.[67]

Rather than the celebratory air that had circulated around the revival of feminism in the mainstream art world in 2007 that forms the backdrop to chapter 1, ten years later there was a sense of embattlement in the political climate, as well as continuing urgency that these histories were sorely needed in the present. Alongside *We Wanted a Revolution*, a number of exhibitions returned to artists of color from the 1970s and '80s in both the United Kingdom and the United States. Often using shifting past and present tenses—as in the title *We Wanted a Revolution*, which matched early Black radical practices with current desires for change—the sense of these histories' importance for the contemporary moment was strong. Walking around *Soul of a Nation: Art in the Age of Black Power* at the Tate Modern in London, I felt a sense of sadness and anger that I did not know many of the women artists in the exhibition—including artists who were part of the Where We At collective, which had been featured in *WACK!* ten years earlier.[68]

This focus on cyclical time and the need to foreground women of color's histories also came through in the exhibition *The Place Is Here* (2017), which explored the "Black Arts Movement" in the United Kingdom.[69] The title is taken from a cutout work by the British artist Lubaina Himid, who won the Turner Prize in 2017 after decades of work as an artist, curator, and lecturer. In the exhibition, my attention was held by a map of her fellow artists that Himid produced in 2011 for a display at Tate Britain to mark her curatorial work from the 1980s.[70] In it, she includes exhibitions, institutions, publications, and universities in a format that echoes the London Tube map (figure 4.8). The work is entitled *Thin Black Line(s)*, a play on the title of her earlier show *The Thin Black Line* (1985). The map presents a network of women artists of color embedded in the galleries and exhibitions that showed their work; the educational institutions at which they studied or worked; and the publications that championed their practice, along with other artists of color who form a loose but vital community. When I saw this work, I interpreted it as a mapping of a feminist chorus. A map might be thought of as similar to a script or score, but in this case it traces the networks of a community to keep them present beyond their lived reality. In the next chapter, I explore various forms of mapping to describe and document feminist communities, taking up Himid's practice as a writer, artist, archivist, and curator. Like the relationship to the past that I am trying to de-

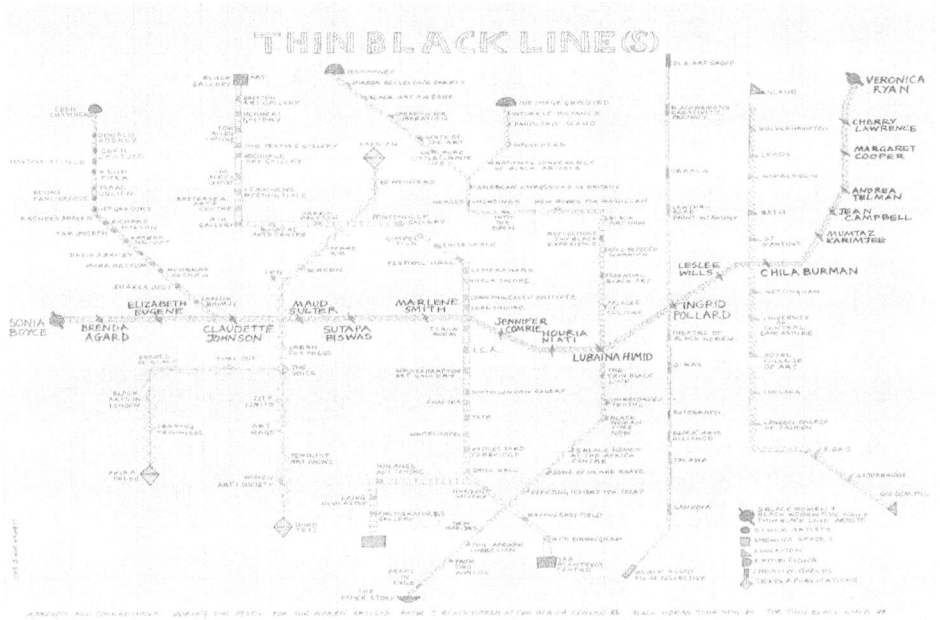

FIGURE 4.8. Lubaina Himid, *Thin Black Line(s)*, 2011 (originally titled *Moments and Connections*). Courtesy of Tate, Hollybush Gardens, London, and the artist.

scribe with the notion of the feminist chorus, Himid's map is not only an important way to "un-forget" but also a way to start on a new journey.

To conclude, I return to the different modalities of feminist chorus that I've outlined here. In all of the works there is a bringing together of the chorus and audience with archival material imagined as a script or a score. The ways in which the chorus is outlined is different, however. In Gasson's work, the chorus is a group of trained vocalists whose work in setting out the names of the thousands of women artists in the Women's Art Library is experienced as an almost spiritual experience. The work's title, *The River*, evokes an ongoing flow of women artists' work, a combination of the unknown and the famous, woven together in an act that refuses to select from its ranks. Reynolds's *A Feminist Chorus* also abstracts its source material, but with the opposite effect: rather than a haunting vocal piece or an instructive narrative, the chosen texts are experienced as a chaotic taking up of sonic space. What we learn from Reynolds's chorus, I would argue, comes from the experience of speaking as one person within a group of others. We learn to embody the experience of being together but separate; to present a feminism that is not homogeneous but awkward, various, and impossible to describe in a linear history. Like Gasson's lists of names, Reynolds's selection of texts from feminist libraries embodies and vocalizes the feminist histories that so often are forgotten in archives and on shelves.

In contrast to Gasson's and Reynolds's works, which are designed for the gallery space or the seminar space, the ongoing work "I Want a President" is designed for public, civic spaces; it is artwork as public protest. Leonard's 1992 text is the starting point for a chain of translation and discussion. Although the European versions of this project have been less publicly acknowledged than the wave of readings and responses that Leonard herself organized on the eve of the 2016 US presidential election, the focus of these early pieces on translation is key.[71] The process of a feminist chorus also being a conversation is foregrounded in this work, as the working group for the UK version debated the various ways translation of different historical and geographical moments could be managed to make the work active in the present. This need to recite and reimagine is emphasized in the reading groups set up to explore feminist histories, such as the WOCI Reading Group. There the process of discussion around the archival material is the focus, taking up some of the aspects of consciousness-raising but using a pedagogical format that allows for the archival material to work as a script from which to begin. In all of these works, there is an understanding that coming together to recite, read, and discuss is a powerful act of community building.

These various feminist choruses strive to keep feminist histories alive in the present and felt across bodies, across time. The sentiment of "un-forgetting" is joined by various forms of realization and, in particular, the ability to realize oneself as a feminist now, connected to the past through the act of respeaking or listening to others speaking, joined to the act of discussing, arguing, making new. As in Brecht's concept of the learning-play, taking part in a feminist chorus is not meant as a form of indoctrination about feminist histories. Rather, it is a form that encourages learning that takes place through the body and alongside others; that draws on the feminist practices of consciousness-raising and small group work. This learning often leads to conflict and disagreement but aims to provide a space in which feminists can listen to one another and learn from the material that we want to bring to life in and for the present moment.

5

Conversations
and Constellations

This chapter brings together two figures who have been influential to the artists and cultural practitioners featured in this book: Lubaina Himid and Mary Kelly. Whereas most of the artworks discussed so far return to histories of feminism that are outside of the individual experience of the participants, this chapter explores how these two artists have returned to their own pasts, representing and reflecting on the networks of which they have been part. There is awkwardness to putting Himid and Kelly alongside each other, as their artistic and biographical trajectories touch only tangentially. However, as I researched their approaches to keeping histories alive, particularly the histories of their own feminist communities, I realized that both were strongly invested in the notion of artistic practice as a project that stretches across their work as educators, writers, mentors, and, in Himid's case, curator.

Since Himid won the Turner Prize in 2017, the first woman of color to do so, her work has been visible in a manner that it rarely enjoyed previously, despite the decades of important curation, writing, and art making.[1] Her work has kept a feminist chorus that foregrounds the work of women of color in the United Kingdom during periods when there was little interest in the major centers of the power.[2] As Himid has described her practice: "I am a political strategist who uses a visual language to encourage conversations, argument, change."[3] Himid became well known for her artwork and curation in London in the 1980s before moving to Hebden Bridge and then to Preston, where she has lived and taught ever since. She set up the Making Histories Visible archive in 2005 with Susan Walsh. Kelly is just over a decade older than Himid and became known for her artworks and activism in the late 1960s and 1970s in London before moving to the United States in the late 1980s.[4] Both Himid and Kelly are professors at art schools, as are many of the artists featured in this book, with pedagogical approaches that, I argue, grow out of their politicized art practices. Kelly has been influential as a writer and a teacher with various programs, including the Whitney Independent Study Program (ISP) in New York and the Interdisciplinary Studio Program at the University of California, Los Angeles (UCLA). Her influence on a number of artists in this book has been considerable, and I first started thinking about this chapter as a way to map the network of her peers and students to explain these feminist constellations. However, as I was doing this research, a parallel constellation emerged that centered on Himid, foregrounding women artists of color in the United Kingdom and more accurately contextualizing projects such as the gravestones at the British installation of *Killjoy's Kastle* and the Women of Colour Index Reading Group. The overlapping but mostly separate feminist networks represented and supported by, but also surrounding and influencing, Himid and Kelly tell a story of the tensions among feminist communities as well as of the points of connection and commonality. Himid's network centers on women of color in the United Kingdom across four decades, whereas Kelly's network connects to an international range of artists centered in the United States, anchored by her formative feminist communities in London in the late 1960s and 1970s.

Both Kelly and Himid engage with the networked forms of history making that this chapter highlights: conversations and constellations. Their recent individual projects, which look back across their political and personal histories, continue the discussion of Kelly's *Love Songs* from chapter 1 and Himid's *Thin Black Line(s)* from chapter 4. I explore the tensions and commonalities found in their depictions of networks and feminist histories, focusing on racial politics, art-world success, and geographical visibility. This begins with a discussion of the launch event for the well-known publication *Framing Feminism* in 1988 in which Himid discusses issues of whiteness, art-world success, and feminist networks in a conversation with the art historian Griselda Pollock at the Institute of Contemporary Arts (ICA) in London. These issues, particularly those around whiteness and feminism, continue into the present moment and are crucial when thinking about how to represent histories of feminism in contemporary art. I then turn to Himid's famous *Revenge* series and the central role of conversations within it, followed by an exploration of her use (and rejection) of maps to show how she has sought to combat the invisibility of women of color by continually reasserting their presence. I argue that what Himid creates are constellations, which I theorize through Giorgio Agamben's reworking of Walter Benjamin's model of history, as well as through contemporary uses of constellations as a way to represent networks of influence, friends, and chosen family, particularly within queer communities. This leads into discussions by contemporary US artists about Kelly's position within their constellations and her definition of "project-based work" as being grounded in her experiences of feminist groups in London in the late 1960s and early 1970s, concluding with Kelly's extended written conversation that documents her artistic and political communities across the decades. Joining these individual projects is the importance for both Himid and Kelly of their own foundational feminist communities, as well as their commitment to continuing and expanding on the legacies of these early groups as a crucial resource for artistic communities across the decades of their practice.

FRAMING FEMINISM

In a conversation staged to launch Griselda Pollock and Rozsika Parker's *Framing Feminism: Art and the Women's Movement, 1970–85* in 1988, Himid discusses her impression of Mary Kelly as a famous feminist artist.[5] She says, "I wouldn't know what she looked like" and that she has "little patience with a movement where I don't know where the key people are." Kelly becomes a symbol of feminist mainstream success—not so much the actual person, but as a way to represent the estrangement Himid feels from both the broader culture and feminism. She gives a searing critique of white feminists' blindness to Black culture and history and says that she sees Black women having to pump life blood into a feminist movement that is of their creating while being presented as a new phenomenon.

What follows among Pollock, Himid, and members of the audience (who include Maud Sulter) is a viscerally felt, painful conversation about feminism, history, race, visibility, politics, and activism. In the questions, Sulter asks white feminists to address their racism and accuses the feminist press that published Pollock and Parker's book of withdrawing support for her own publication on Black women's creativity. In this one recorded conversation, the moments of dialogue, as well as the conflicts and distrust over the unacknowledged whiteness in feminism and the exclusion of women of color and their histories, is laid bare. As I have been writing about the feminist communities that figure in this book, I've been thinking about how to represent these fissures, or moments of conflict, that are central to the continuing dialogue on feminist thinking and politics. Thirty years ago, Pollock was also trying to create a space for them. In her opening remarks, she asked that the book she had edited with Parker, *Framing Feminism*, be seen as making available material from the Women's Liberation Movement that went beyond people who were involved in it, saying that she and Parker had provided a "sense of meaning" for the documents. She said that the book was not meant as a definitive history but was, instead, born from a "growing necessity for history" to be written about the Women's Liberation Movement. As she went on to introduce Himid into the conversation, she discussed how the notion of sisterhood had been contested and how differences needed to be acknowledged, whether along lines of race, class, age, or culture. "Black women have a powerful charge to put against white feminism in its failure to acknowledge the difference and specificities of peoples' lives," she said, and called for discussion rather than ending up in communities that didn't speak to one another. This conversation between Pollock and Himid is one that needs to continue in the present day, and it is staged here through the differing constellations around Himid and Kelly as powerful figures or nodal points in feminist art networks.

As Pollock talks with Himid in the recording, their conversation theorizes and expresses deep feelings about questions of racism and Eurocentric accounts of art, creativity, and feminism. There is respect between Pollock and Himid but also tension and differing perspectives, not just as white woman and Black woman but as artist and art historian, professor and freelance curator. In the concluding questions, Himid says that she is interested in "talking about history" and that her own art practice has been helped through her organization of exhibitions of works by other Black women artists. She also asks, "Why aren't we writing the books, making the television programs?" Pollock grapples with questions from the audience, but often it is Himid's sighs, exasperation, and repeated calls that hold the listener.[6] Speaking at age thirty-three, Himid holds the position that she will not be seen as "the new" but, instead, wants the influence and histories of women of color to be acknowledged.

While Kelly becomes a symbol of the successful feminist artist in this conversation, I would argue that both Himid and Kelly have employed similar techniques to keep conversations going across their long careers. They have both grounded their individual practice within their earliest community of women artists, beginning in the late 1960s and 1970s (for Kelly) and the 1980s (for Himid). They have reflected on their broader roles in creating communities across their careers, with their work being embedded in a political sense of what it means to be an artist and to affect a cultural landscape. Rather than keep their constellations of friends, lovers, students, and historical influences separate, I put them together in this chapter to show how two artists who were active as feminists in the same time and place (London in the 1980s) could still have very separate communities and politics. This is a simple point but one that often gets elided when writing histories; it is also something of which I was keenly aware when I chose networks of artists and artworks to trace the constellation of this book (although it sometimes felt as if I was found by them). In this chapter, the models of "conversations and constellations" are there to show points of discussion that can lead to an ongoing network of figures who are engaged with the histories of feminism in their work. Nonetheless, the questions and tensions raised in the conversation between Himid and Pollock are not resolved three decades later, although networks of women of color are becoming increasingly visible and central to histories of feminism. As Sara Ahmed comments, "Feminist histories are histories of the difficulty of that *we*, a history of those who have had to fight to be part of a feminist collective, or even had to fight against a feminist collective in order to take up a feminist cause."[7] For Ahmed, feminism has to be intersectional, and becoming a feminist is done in dialogue with others, even when that dialogue is fraught.

REVENGE

> Planning always planning. Listening to the voices; they sometimes argue with them and listen to each other instead.
> —LUBAINA HIMID, artist's statement, in Sulter, "Without Tides, No Maps"

The 1991 painting *Five*, by Lubaina Himid, shows two Black women seated at a table, with a representation of the Middle Passage from Africa to America depicted on the plates and bowls between them (figure 5.1). This painting, taken from her series *Revenge: A Masque in Five Tableaux* (1992), stages a conversation, which is complicated by Himid's description of the pair listening to other voices from the past in order to think about strategies for the future. As with the others in the series, the painting is accompanied by a short text that invites us as viewers to imaginatively take part, too, so the paintings and texts can be seen as prompts for a theatrical scene. The short text labeled "Five" (the same title as the painting) is paired in the exhibition catalog with the double canvas *Act One No Maps*, while the text itself describes all five main paintings in the *Revenge* cycle (figure 5.2). While there has been much art-historical analysis of the painting *Five*, here I want to focus on the exchange between the two women, Himid's textual description, and how these continue the idea put forward in the

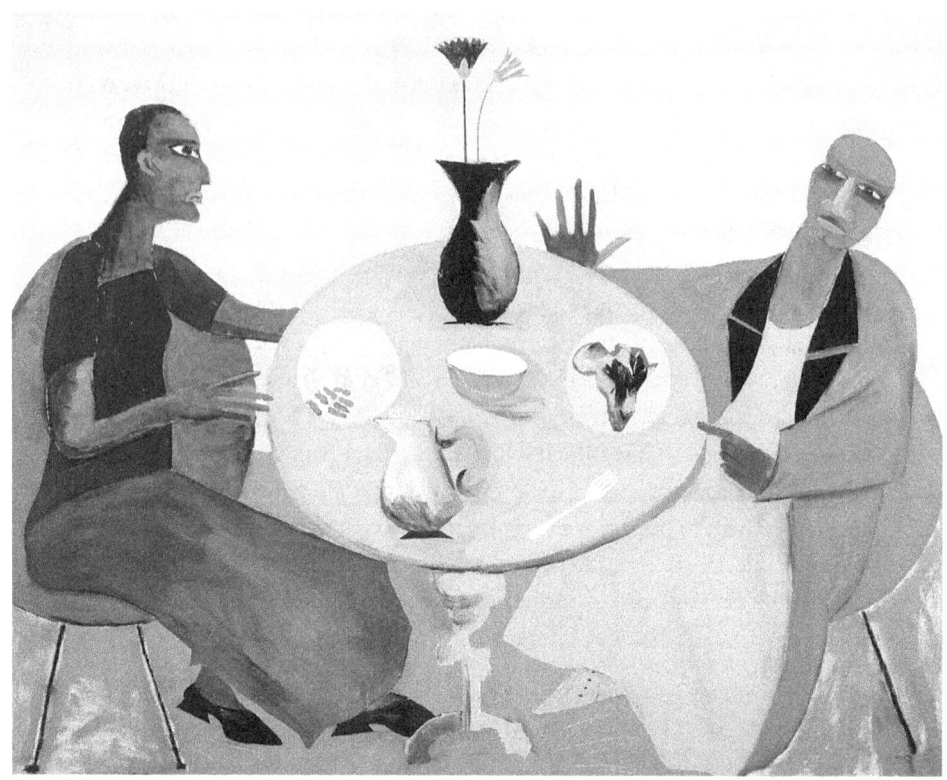

FIGURE 5.1. Lubaina Himid, *Five*, 1991, from the *Revenge* series, 1992, acrylic on canvas, 48 × 60 in (122 × 152.5 cm). © Lubaina Himid, image courtesy of the artist, Hollybush Gardens, London and Leeds Art Gallery.

previous chapter of a feminist chorus, particularly a chorus that pays attention to marginalized voices both within and outside feminism.[8] A feminist chorus is a way to think about reciting histories and the experience of coming together to discuss our relationship to them. Here, the model of the chorus is moved into spaces of conversations and constellations—ways to present and interrogate history in nonlinear forms.

In an artist's statement about the series *Revenge*, Himid gives an extended gloss on what is taking place in the paintings: "The women are always talking, sometimes to each other. The women do things together not always in the same way, but usually for the same reasons."[9] Published in the exhibition catalog for the series, the statement is embedded in an essay by Sulter, who at the time was Himid's partner. The catalog becomes an important site to extend the conno-

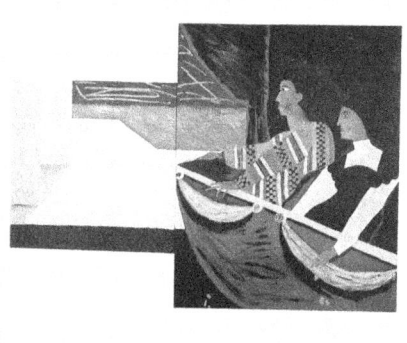

Five

Two women standing ankle-deep behind banners in front of cloths shredding maps; fragments float away. Two women sit in a small boat tearing up navigation charts; how many died crossing the water. Two women sit in a theatre box ripping up maps; can the past be replayed. Two women sit at dinner forming strategy; can the future be different better. Two women sit on rugs reliving the history and planning the future; magic carpet fly.

Act One No Maps

FIGURE 5.2. Lubaina Himid, page spread from exhibition catalog *Revenge: A Masque in Five Tableaux*, Rochdale Art Gallery, 1992. Courtesy of Hollybush Gardens, London, and the artist.

tations of the work, literalizing the images of two women talking in a textual form. Himid and Sulter were the models for the pair of women in the painting *Five*, as well as for others in the series, although this was not articulated at the time.[10] In 1992, lesbian visibility in the mainstream art world was still minimal, although the *Revenge* series coincides with an increase in writing about, and curating around, the newly formed notions of queerness and queer art. This was compounded by the lack of mainstream visibility for women of color. This series is absent from most accounts of British art in the 1990s, except in the work of a number of feminist art historians, who performed detailed and subtle analyses but rarely touched on the theme of lesbian relationships and communities that are a constant in Himid's work.[11]

In an often quoted section of her artist's statement for the series *Revenge*, Himid says: "The women take revenge; their revenge is that they are still here they are still artists, that their creativity is still political and committed to change."[12] She evokes a flexible, cyclical sense of time and place, saying that the women were in Paris in the early twentieth century, in Milan watching the opera, and sailing on the high seas. Importantly, she says: "[They were p]lanning always planning. Listening to the voices; they sometimes argue with them and listen to each other instead."[13] In writing about this listening to the voices, as well as by arguing with them and turning to one another, Himid captures something about how artists are drawing on histories of feminism, which in her series are intertwined with histories of colonial violence and racism. As Dorothy Price has explained: "A project to memorialise the horrors of the Middle Passage . . . is conceptualised as part of a political imperative for a different set of future relationships between Africa and Europe in which Black women will be agents for remembering, interrupting and changing the course of events."[14] Parts of the series explicitly reference the slave ship *Zong*, whose captain disposed of enslaved people overboard to claim insurance on them.[15] This incident has been memorialized in an 1840 painting by J. M. W. Turner, and motifs from his work are picked up in Himid's series, evoking the experience of the enslaved people in the water and putting them alongside images of two women ripping up maps (in *Ankledeep* and *Act One No Maps*) and navigation charts (in *Between the Two My Heart Is Balanced*). These women are cognizant of what came before but also keen to find something beyond. These acts of tearing up are joined with abstracted images of magic carpets—of travel to unseen spaces, providing a counter-imaginary to the overwhelmingly traumatic evocation of the Middle Passage, part of what Christina Sharpe has theorized as "wake-work."[16] Here I am not going to explore the rich imagery that draws on Turner's painting of the *Zong* that Himid mines in the series but, instead, turn to the ways in which her interrogation of this colonial history is done through her imaging of Black women together. Himid seems to say to the viewer that attending to these histories is not enough. Recitation has to be joined with discussion. The planning, listening, and talking found in this series is not easy, and it does not result in a homogeneous sense of purpose.

In a statement quoted by Price, Himid sketches out how the series takes up the "theme of re-writing history" and states that in all of the *Revenge* paintings "we are arguing," concluding, "In our house we are arguing."[17] In a recent conversation with Marlene Smith, Himid describes the series as being about two women discussing strategies: strategies for how to change British art and strategies for how to live together under the same roof while arguing all the time.[18] When I read this phrase, "In our house we are arguing," it was resonant as a description of a moment in the late 2010s when feminism was both much more visible in mainstream culture and often felt to be contentious, particularly around issues of race. It also confirmed my sense that this series articulates scenes from Himid's relationship with Sulter, presenting their collaborative creative and romantic partnership as a politically active, if contentious and painful, space. Here their relationship is depicted but also stands in for a wider feminist community.[19] "In our house we are arguing" can also be seen as articulating the part of consciousness-raising that is the most difficult: managing conflict. To join together as feminists, there is also a need to go beyond a sense of sisterhood as a utopian space and to stop the sense of being policed by one another, what Sheila Rowbotham has described as "betrayal and coercion."[20]

Maps often appear in Himid's artwork, and she has described how important they are to her. Talking about the *London A–Z Map*, she describes how she "learned early that no two maps are the same (I love that) that maps are a guide for you to learn to discard really."[21] As introduced in the previous chapter, my way into Himid's work in recent years was through the map drawn to capture the networks around the women artists of color who took part in her exhibitions *5 Black Women* (Africa Centre, London [1983]), *Black Woman Time Now* (Battersea Arts Centre, London [1983]), and *The Thin Black Line* (ICA, London [1985]). Originally titled *Moments and Connections*, this map, which looks like a subway or train map, shows the artists from the three exhibitions, intersected with lines that show "other artists," "showing spaces," "education," "exhibitions," "creative groups," and "texts and publications" (see figure 4.8).[22] Himid has said that the map was made to fill in the gaps that were necessarily left when curating a display at Tate Britain that showed a selection of artworks by these artists from the 1980s, called *Thin Black Line(s)*. In light of the constraints of the wall text and range of artists' meanings, the map indicates the broader constellation within which the display should be understood. She says, "The map is my gift to curators, academics, artists, interested collectors and scholars to take the information offered and do something with it (to be spoken in a loud voice)."[23] Like the ongoing conversation that the painting *Five* indicates, Himid's map asks that a conversation be continued "in a loud voice," looping from her exhibitions in the 1980s, to the display at Tate Britain in 2011–12, to the present of the viewer looking at her map and using it as a starting point alongside the texts, images, and conversations that she has carefully documented and archived both online and at the research center Making Histories Visible at the University of Central Lancashire.[24]

I saw the map at the exhibition *The Place Is Here* at the South London Gallery in 2017. I was struck by the careful detail that was held within its modest confines, a world of people, places, books, magazines, events—some known; many not. It stood out to me as I was trying to find a way to draw out the network of artists, writers, organizations, publications, and exhibitions that structure this book and my research into contemporary artists engaging with histories of feminism. Rather than Himid's neat, precise "Tube map," my network was a scrawled series of nodal points, too layered to reproduce easily on a piece of paper and so eventually discarded. Rather than a tube map, my model had been the whiteboard-written, endlessly added-to chart in the series *The L Word* (2004–2009)—a famous mapping of the fictional lesbian universe that shows which character had slept with whom. My nodal points weren't dictated only by romantic relationships; they also included educational influence, curatorial focal points, and organizations on which feminist art that dealt with history and reenactment centered.

As I mapped out the artists in this book, it became clear to me that I was trying to describe a particular constellation of a feminist community—one focused on queer and lesbian identities and histories. Key geographical points were focused on university programs, as well as on cities with a strong queer scene. The key cities of London and New York are linked across other British, European, and North American locations, threaded through with sites of concentrated activity through various means, including symposia on key feminist texts, feminist organizations, galleries or commissioning agencies, and educational programs with key feminist teachers. The range of artists often were taking part in an extended conversation of which I hadn't been aware at first, so I would realize that an artist had studied with another in the book or that a particular music scene provided the background to numerous friendships across geographical locations. Both Himid and Kelly recurred as key nodal points of influence on artists, writers, and curators featured in this book, not only through their work as artists, but also, as noted earlier, educators, writers, and curators.

NO MAPS

In my attempt to map, I realized that I wouldn't be able to create an adequate visualization of the networks that I wished to represent. This sense of limitation, as well as the necessity to try, is also found across Himid's practice. She returns to the metaphor of mapping as well as to the necessity of leaving maps behind or finding new representations of family and history. I would argue that what she comes up with instead are forms of constellations and conversations. An early essay is titled "Mapping: A Decade of Black Women Artists 1980–1990," whereas the editor's letter for her coedited issue of *FAN* (with Maud Sulter) signs off with, "Diasporan blues may appear on the horizon but our course is self-determined. As Family. No Maps."[25] In her artworks and curated exhibitions from the 1980s, constellations of historical and contemporary communities of color abound, depicted through collage, compilation, and textual invocation. In her foundational exhibition *The Thin Black Line*, a collage of

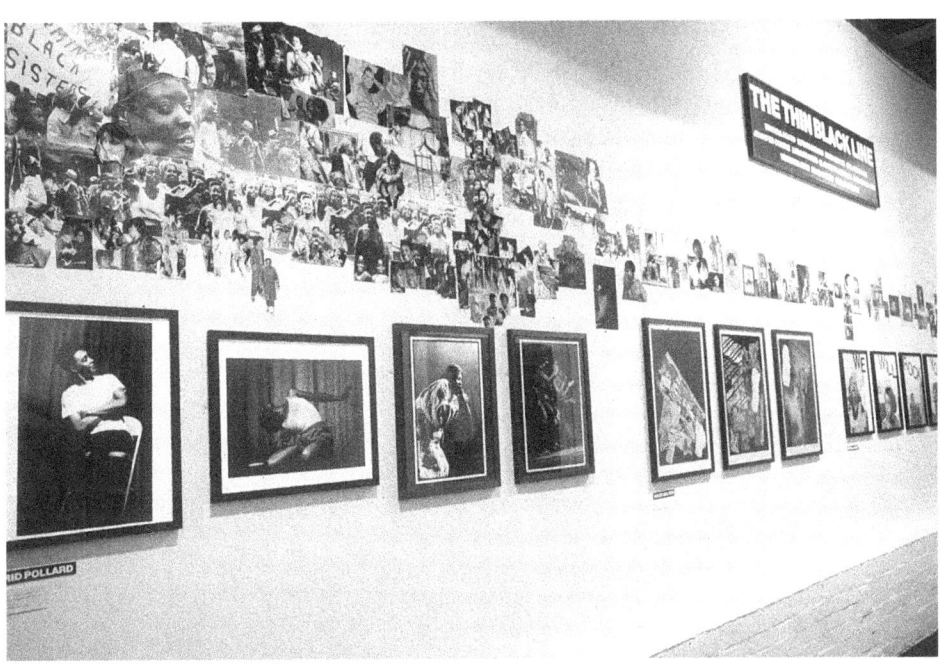

FIGURE 5.3. Installation view of *The Thin Black Line*, Institute of Contemporary Arts, London, 1985, curated by Lubaina Himid. Photograph by Denise Swanson. Courtesy of Hollybush Gardens, London, and the artist.

photographs is threaded across the space, which Deborah Cherry describes this way: "Above the exhibits . . . was a 'thin black line' of archival, found, family, personal and media photographs that stretched the length of the long wall."[26] This "thin black line" is a form of map, but one that pinpoints only a few people to indicate a bigger community—just as a constellation of stars picks out only a few from the sky (figure 5.3). Himid explains to Cherry: "We wanted to bring our 'community' 'heroines' 'sisters' into the space with us for company and to provide the context and the 'soundtrack' for the show. Everyone brought images and we installed them on the 'photo' wall together.'"[27] Like the map Himid drew almost thirty years later, these pictures represent a history and a community that stretches out in time and space. As Ella Mills has proposed in relation to Himid's later exhibition, "*Thin Black Line(s)* simultaneously dismantles a singular narrative and instead, through signifiers of networks and plurality, rebuilds a 'common' and/or shared art history."[28]

This collaborative effort to assert the presence of women of color in the present, and to place them within a continuum, is also found in early work by

Himid: *We Will Be* (1983 [figure 5.4]). A cutout figure shows a woman with a full skirt covered with photographs, bits of wool, playing cards, and marker-printed text, and a bodice made of shining drawing pins, her arms folded and her gaze looking off to the right, absorbed in thought as the viewer takes in the rich display on her outfit. Himid has described how she made this work collaboratively with housemates.[29] The poem on the skirt is a declaration of presence in which the words *here* and *now* are repeated over and over, along with the words *we want*:

> We will be
> who we want
> where we want
> with whom we want
> in the way that we want
> when we want
> and the time is now
> and the place is here
> + there and
> here + there
> + here
> now now
> now now
> now now
> here here now
> here here now + now here
> now now

Reading this poem, the here and now of Himid's 1983 is also the here and now of the viewer looking at the work. This piece was first shown in the exhibition *Black Woman Time Now*, with its title's equally firm call. The sense of Benjaminian now-time is evoked in both the artwork and the exhibition title, as well as in Julia Kristeva's famous essay "Women's Time," with its evocation of feminist generations as a structural space, as explored in chapter 3.[30] Himid insists on this community stretching across time and being activated in the now. In a number of her texts (as well as in Sulter's), there is an emphasis on a history of women artists of color, so that she/they refuse their position as the token Black woman or the beginning of a Black history. In the opening paragraph of her essay "Mapping," Himid states: "If we really believed that we were the first black women to call ourselves artists we would have an excuse to give up, we were not,

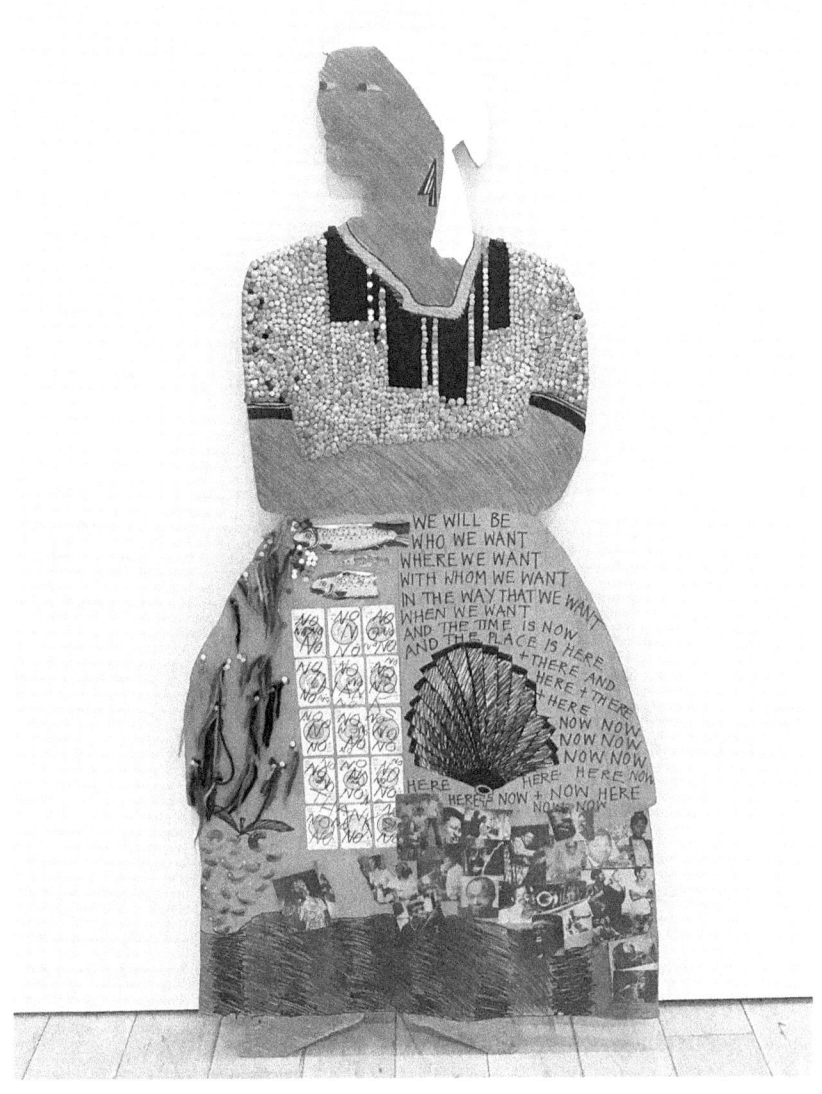

The artwork contains the following text within it:

WE WILL BE
WHO WE WANT
WHERE WE WANT
WITH WHOM WE WANT
IN THE WAY THAT WE WANT
WHEN WE WANT
AND THE TIME IS NOW
AND THE PLACE IS HERE
+THERE AND
HERE +THERE
+ HERE
NOW NOW
NOW NOW
NOW NOW
HERE HERE NOW
HERE + NOW + NOW HERE
NOW NOW

FIGURE 5.4. Lubaina Himid, *We Will Be*, 1983. Courtesy of Walker Art Gallery Liverpool, Hollybush Gardens, London, and the artist.

we are the continuum. We are part of an enormous international movement which stretches far back in time."[31]

More than thirty years after *Black Woman Time Now*, the title and poem on the skirts of Himid's figure in *We Will Be* still resonate in a present in which racism, misogyny, and homophobia are felt strongly, linking with contemporary communities of women of color at the forefront of activist and artistic political art and organizing.[32] Ironically, *Black Woman Time Now* exists mostly in name and description, as it was not documented.[33] When one reads across the many texts, interviews, and talks that Himid has written and given, there is a constant sense of her re-presenting her own history as an important one that must not be made invisible again. Her presence as both a contemporary and a historical figure was felt strongly in 2017 as the 1983 work provided the title for the exhibition *The Place Is Here*, with her 1986 installation *A Fashionable Marriage* feeling queasily relevant to the political situation as Donald Trump came to power as US president.[34] A younger generation of artists has found much to draw on in Himid's multidisciplinary practice, with one example being the collective Thick/er Black Lines. Working with Himid's map for the *Thin Black Line(s)* exhibition, Thick/er Black Lines has produced a new version of this mapping that shows the vibrant network of "Black British women/femme artists and cultural workers" during the 2010s.[35] Entitled *We Apologise for the Delay to Your Journey* (2017), this new mapping is part of a series of projects and events that centralize artists of color within the British art world (figure 5.5).[36]

A CONSTELLATION

Through these various strategies, Himid creates constellations that are meant to resonate in the present. A constellation describes the mapping of stars in the sky as well as a grouping of similar objects or people. Differently from a map, a constellation is seen in relation to the viewer's position rather than that of the omnipotent viewer.[37] This position of the viewer is turned from a spatial phenomenon into a temporal one in Agamben's essay "What Is the Contemporary?" as he uses the example of stars in the sky as a way to imagine the complicated time sense of the contemporary that he wishes to put forward. As explored in the introduction, Agamben reshapes Benjamin's theses on history into a provocative contemplation of now-time thought as "the contemporary." Benjamin's use of the term *constellation* is described most clearly in fragments in *The Arcades Project*, where he describes his concept of the dialectical image: "It is not that what is past casts its light on what is present, or what is present its light on what is past; rather, image is that wherein what has been comes to-

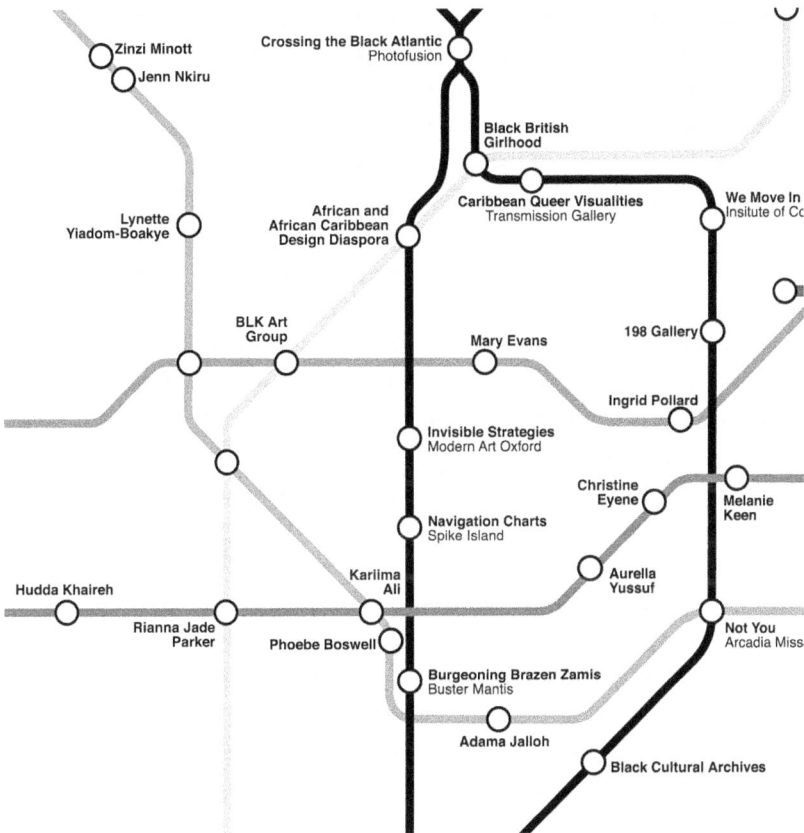

FIGURE 5.5. *Thick/er Black Lines* (Rianna Jade Parker, Aurella Yussuf, Hudda Khaireh and Kariima Ali), crop of *We Apologise for the Delay to Your Journey*, 2017–19. Courtesy of the artists.

gether in a flash with the now to form a constellation."[38] Rather than focusing on Benjamin's notion of flash or shock, Agamben, along with a number of queer theorists such as Elizabeth Freeman and Carolyn Dinshaw, has taken up the constellation as a model of history that refuses the linear and points to the ways in which making a constellation (in terms of stars in the sky) depends on the viewer's particular position. It involves bringing together elements that are light-years apart and may never actually exist in the same time as us or one another but that are nonetheless important. Agamben inverts Benjamin's image of the constellation by describing the experience of staring at the darkness between the stars. He says, "What we perceive as the darkness of the heavens is this light that, though travelling towards us, cannot reach us, since the galaxies from which the light originates move away from us at a velocity greater than the speed of light." He continues: "To perceive, in the darkness of the present, this light that strives to reach us but cannot—this is what it means to be contemporary. As such, contemporaries are rare."[39] In this passage, Agamben rewrites Benjamin's conception of historical moments coming together in constellation to form moments of insight, moments that occur at points of pressure and political urgency. Instead of a flash, Agamben pictures this act of being contemporary as perceiving in the dark, an obscure reckoning with the almost visible—or, as Himid, has put it, "Inside the Invisible."[40]

This notion of the constellation has also been brought up in recent attempts to create queer lineages for artists, as in the exhibition at the New Museum in New York *Trigger: Gender as a Tool and a Weapon* (2017). As part of the exhibition catalog—like Himid's statement within Sulter's essay or the "thin black line" above the artworks at the ICA—there is an attempt to represent support structures that are not always visible. In a section titled, "Chosen: Constellations of Influence," the exhibiting artists present visualizations of their "influences and support structures" to represent the conversations that the curators had had with the artists about the "dimensions opened up by others—some they call friends and others they know only through books and stories."[41] These constellations, and the title of the section, "Chosen," point to the idea of a "chosen family." Often within queer communities, kinship is refigured through friendship in the face of homophobic relations; recall Himid's desire to present heroines and sisters alongside the work of the artists in *The Thin Black Line*. In "Footnotes on Genealogy," the artist Sharon Hayes uses a series of footnotes to put forward her thoughts. She moves through the naming of her daughter to the influence of New York in the 1990s on her life and art and her working practice, about which she says: "It turns out that I spend a lot of time reading, seeing, watching things in libraries or archives or collections. Sometimes the things I encounter in these one-way relationships change what I do, how I act, who I think I am, what I understand to be possible. If these encounters are a genealogy, then my kinship is not a fact but a request. Who am I to these encounters? A fan?"[42] Later, she says that her "ideal organization of this genealogy would actually be a pile, a stack."

Alongside the influence of 1990s New York, Hayes cites two other key moments: studying with Mary Kelly at UCLA in the late 1990s and her current relationship with her students at Cooper Union and Penn State University. Here constellations of teachers and students are put alongside friends, lovers, performers, writers, and activists. She says: "So much that is important to me to know about art, I learned from Mary Kelly," and she notes "the curious experience wherein I inherit influences from my students. . . . [A] temporal hiccup where I see or understand something, where I take something in that is out of time with my own generational lineage."[43] Kelly has also been reflecting on this back and forth between herself and her students over the past decade, begun by the project *Love Songs* explored in chapter 1. She starts an essay about the project by saying: "Artists generally think of themselves first of all as practitioners and then, perhaps reluctantly, as educators. But, over the years, I have found the two practices more deeply imbricated than I could ever have imagined, not by an institutional imperative, but as a consequence of lived experience."[44] To explain this dialogue, she draws on Benjamin's theses on history, discussing his quote "a secret agreement between generations" and employing the same quotation as I do earlier in the chapter to describe a dialectical image.[45] She proposes to shift the understanding of the dialectical image: "Where he states that the relation of the what-has-been to the now is dialectical, I might say instead, or more cautiously, in addition, that it is dialogical. Moreover, that it is not only figural, but also performative."[46] This sense of the performative quality of the dialectical image is one that underpins my use of the constellation here. Kelly also draws on Benjamin's description of a constellation in a number of texts in which she describes her concept of generational consciousness. In her work of the past decade, she has turned to numerous strategies to think through the ways in which histories can be brought back to life in the present and how to present the back-and-forth between historical moments, captured through exchanges between teachers and students, friends, idols.

A FEW PEOPLE . . .

To explore Kelly's strategies further, I turn to an online conversation published as a continuation of her series *On the Passage of a Few People through a Rather Brief Period of Time* (2014). Here I return to the theme of conversations begun in relation to Himid's painting *Five* and the discussion between Himid and Pollock at the ICA, with this conversation opening out to a large group of people, addressing numerous moments in time across Kelly's career since the late 1960s. This conversation also provides a way to think about the networks that thread across the artists and artworks included in this book. The conversation, which took place by email over a number of months in 2015 and is now published on the Tate Modern's website, is a fairly obscure part of a project that is known as a series of large lint works commemorating various key moments across Kelly's lifetime, from World War II to the Arab Spring (figure 5.6).[47] In a statement outlining her reasons for beginning the project, she says she wanted to "ask what

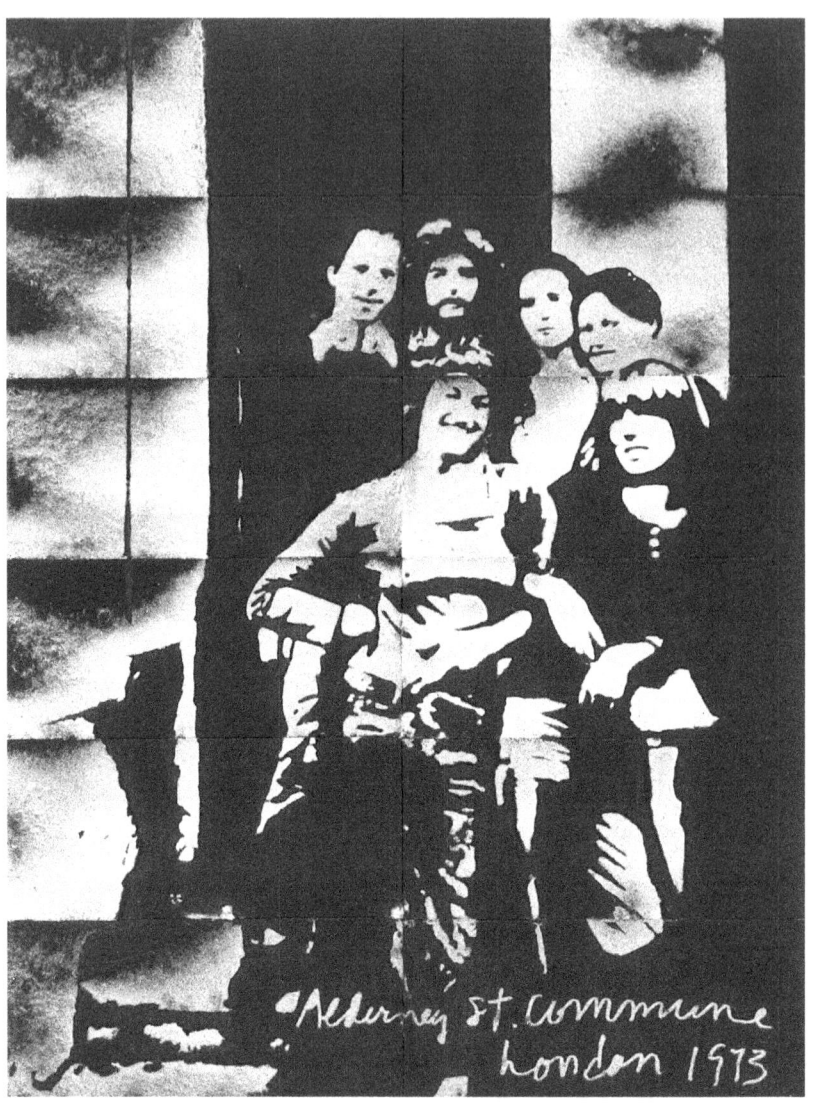

FIGURE 5.6. Mary Kelly, *Alderney Street, 1973*, from the series *On the Passage of a Few People through a Rather Brief Period of Time*, 2014, compressed lint, 30 × 23 in, (76.2 × 58.4 cm). Courtesy of Pippy Houldsworth Gallery and the artist.

defines an era, and for whom, not only as political discourse, but also as trace, or residue, of the personal lives that were defined by it."[48]

As has been well documented elsewhere, Kelly was active within the New Left and the emerging women's movement in London, which provided the background for her early projects.[49] In the online conversation she invites members from the History Group, set up in 1969 as a study group that was part of the wider London Women's Liberation Workshop, to reflect on this moment (figure 5.7). The online conversation then moves through other key moments and places in Kelly's artistic and political development, ending with a number of artists she taught on the Whitney ISP and her Interdisciplinary Studio program at UCLA, including a number of artists featured in this book, such as Hayes and Wu Tsang.[50] The Whitney ISP and the Interdisciplinary Studio Program have been key in developing Kelly's reflections on her own history and that of her students, particularly in what she has described "the discursive site" to focus project-based work.[51] In the online conversation, Tsang describes Kelly's pedagogical approach: "I remember during our first studio visit you told me that a 'project' was precipitated by the intersection of a subjective political investment and historical events."[52] As with Himid, the conversations started with peers open out into a pedagogical practice. Kelly's recent works and texts have focused on publishing elements of this lived practice as well as on their structural and political implications.

Kelly has set out the discursive site for herself as being the women's movement of the late 1960s, describing the core of *On the Passage of a Few People*:

> I would describe the discursive site for this project as London in the early 1970s at the moment of an emerging women's movement, but my focus has not been on feminism alone. Rather, my inclination has been to frame a wide-angle view of that period of time, stretching from the end of World War II to the beginning of the Arab Spring. My starting point was to document the passage of a few women, who formed the History Group in 1969. I was part of this Group and, clearly, it determines my personal recollection of the past. Yet, it became apparent in the discussion of the first exhibition of *Circa 1968* in 2004, that not only what takes place, but also, what is thought, defines an era, and in this respect, the consequences of the "events of 68" are intergenerational.[53]

In the conversation that follows, as already set out, she invites key collaborators, including her students, to reflect on their own relationship to historically and geographically specific moments, moving from the collectivity of the Women's Liberation Movement in London to the psychoanalytically invested pub-

1. Anna Murray
03-26-2015
10:01 AM ET (US)

Welcome to the conversation – 'On the Passage of a Few People Through a Rather Brief Period of Time.'

2. Mary Kelly
03-26-2015
08:45 PM ET (US)

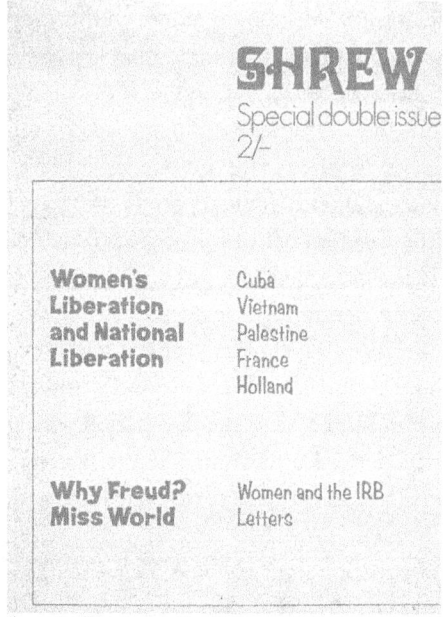

Shrew cover, 1970

'On the Passage of a Few People through a Rather Brief Period of Time,' was a response, in the form of an exhibition, to a suggestion that the era associated with the events of 1968 had ended. I began with a rather broad question: What defines an era and for whom? Certainly, for many, May 1968, is simply an event in the political history of France, but for some, it has come to mean the beginning of an era characterized by new social movements, which have been transformed over time, but by no means ended. The women's movement is one of the most prominent among these, and ultimately, it's why I'm interested in having this conversation. But, I would like to start by narrowing down the unwieldy topic further by focusing on the London Women's Liberation Workshop, in particular, the History Group, and recollections of events I shared, as a member of the Group, with Sally Alexander, Rosalind Delmar, Juliet Mitchell and Laura Mulvey.

When I arrived in London in the fall of 1968, to do post graduate work at St. Martin's School of Art, many of the art schools were occupied and the repercussions of recent events in France were palpable. In just a few months, I found myself marching in the largest anti-Vietnam war demonstration that had taken place in Britain up to that time. Then, the London Women's Liberation Workshop was formed in 1969. This, as I remember it, is when Branka Magas brought me to a meeting of the History Group at Mary Kennedy's, I think, and quite simply, it changed my life.

Before coming to London, I had been living and working in Beirut, Lebanon. As part of a community of new left intellectuals, mostly educated in France, my introduction to politics was Fanon's "Wretched of the Earth," Sartre on

FIGURE 5.7. Mary Kelly, *On the Passage of a Few People through a Rather Brief Period of Time*, 2015, first page of PDF published on the Tate Modern website. Courtesy of Pippy Houldsworth Gallery and the artist.

lications, exhibitions, and teaching in the late '70s–late '80s and then to key moments at the ISP and at UCLA. During my work on artists who reimagine histories of feminism, I've realized that a number of them have been in dialogue with one another as well as with Kelly's model of a project, which embraces a political investment and historical events and takes seriously the feelings that are provoked by them. For example, when I researched *Love Songs*, I realized that members of the LTTR collective had been taught by Kelly at the ISP, and Every Ocean Hughes went on to work with Kelly at UCLA. Hughes described how she is part of the reenactment work *WLM Demo Remix* and is quoted in *Multi-Story House*, discussed in chapter 1, and how her interest in feminist histories was in dialogue with Kelly.[54] Rather than a master-disciple relationship, what appears to have evolved between Kelly and her students is a dialogue that has similarities to her collaborative political and creative work in the late 1960s and early 1970s.

This is borne out in the work of Hayes, who, in her best-known piece, *In the Near Future*, stood with placards from past protests at a historically significant site for an hour, as discussed in chapter 1. She began the project in 2005, the same year Kelly started *Love Songs*. A reciprocal conversation appears to be taking place here between these artists, which can be seen in print as Hayes and Andrea Geyer invite Kelly to take part in a conversation with Tsang in their 2009 exhibition catalog *History Is Ours*. In it Kelly talks about the legacy of anti-essentialist feminism: "Our notion of sexuality was linked to its uncertain status in the unconscious and I think this allowed other things to be thought through in a similar way: ethnicities, race, object choice. I feel this is the legacy all of you continue, but more importantly, I see you transform and advance it in your work."[55] In a longer interview, with Margaretta Jolly, she elaborates on this, describing how her students from queer and trans communities "have really been taking up the legacy of anti-essentialist feminism" and, in relation to the trans movement, says, "This is, I feel, extremely important and not perhaps grasped in all its significance by a lot of the women of my age." She continues to say that this engagement has "stretched things in a way that I don't think is fully understood now. So I think it's not just a matter of legacy but it's about to do another turn and I think come back from them to us to rethink some of our paradigms."[56] Here the Benjaminian notion of a constellation is seen by the way in which her students take up and transform the feminist paradigms that have influenced Kelly. This sense of a to-and-fro between generations is echoed in the online conversation that Kelly instigates as well as in the exhibition catalog *Dialogue*, which includes a transcribed conversation with Kelly and a number of her students who have taken up these feminist legacies in a variety of ways.[57] Himid is also continuing these conversations with younger generations of artists, both through her teaching at the University of Central Lancashire and through her Making Histories Visible archive. This has been the site where a number of artists have developed their response to the British Black Arts Movement, as well as a site where artists, using the archive's affiliated print studios, can produce their work.[58]

In *Dialogue*, Kelly also articulates in more detail what she means by "project-based work," building on her discussion of the discursive site set out earlier in the chapter. She recounts: "Since the 1980s, I have been engaged in discussions with a number of artists about what it means to have *a project*. This began at the Whitney Independent Study Program and continued in a more formal way when I started the Interdisciplinary Studio area in the Art Department at UCLA in 1997."[59] In defining what she means by a project, she reframes Rosalind Krauss's definition of medium-specificity to think instead about a "debate-specific site," which she renames the "discursive site": "Referring to my earlier comments about medium, perhaps, I would say that community is the physical support and within it, the particular discourse you share is where the rules come from, what makes it possible to have a method of investigation."[60] She says: "Resorting to my own work for an example: if the women's movement in its initial and subsequent forms is the support, or discursive site, then the discourse is informed by feminism in general, and the rules are generated by psychoanalysis in particular."[61] For Kelly, the moment of the women's movement is then detailed through her focus on psychoanalysis, which leads her to also look at the way in which unconscious desires inform a project. "'The project' addresses the missed possibility," she says, "not for redemption, but for 'making a new man.'"[62]

I first came across Kelly discussing the notion of "project-based work" while researching Pauline Boudry and Renate Lorenz, whose film *Salomania* is discussed in chapter 3. I read a conversation in which Hayes and Geyer had been invited to take part that was transcribed and published in the exhibition catalog *History Is Now*. (Hayes has been in another of Boudry and Lorenz's works, as has Ginger Brooks Takahashi of LTTR.) I looked at other essays in the catalog and saw that Kelly was featured in another conversation there. In this way, a community is pictured in print, something that became a frequent occurrence in my research. Kelly describes "project-based work" in a number of interviews and articles as she tries to articulate what links her and her students. Importantly, she doesn't want this to end up being a formula but describes a subjective relationship to a historical moment.

This sense of a site or scene is something that continues through the artists included in this book who engage with feminist histories through reenactment, recitation, reimagining. I think that Kelly's notion of the Benjaminian dialectical image and an interactive relationship between generations is key, something that is also found in Himid's work in her evocation of previous Black women artists as well as in her representations of communities of which she is part.[63] Over the different conversations, constellations, and mappings of community found in Kelly's and Himid's work, there is a dedication to keep conversations going as places of transformation and remembrance, as well as conflict. From Himid's painting and textual accompaniments to Kelly's online conversation, both artists can be seen to invest in the ways in which they situate their projects as ongoing within intersectional feminist communities. The question of how to leave materials that are useful for other feminists—in either other places or other times—is unsurprisingly recurrent across feminist literature and art. A cornerstone of nearly every feminist movement has been to situate itself within a history that provides a sense of identity and possibility, sometimes drawn from historical fact and sometimes imagined.

In most of the previous chapters I have focused on artists who have used various formats to find and reimagine feminist histories for the present and the futures that go beyond their own life span. In this chapter, I have focused on two artists whose careers have spanned a number of decades and who continually find ways to represent their own histories and those of their political and artistic communities. Rather than seeing themselves as elders or masters, both Himid and Kelly offer their histories as a way to keep a framework alive in the present. As I researched their works, I found that their communities were often quite separate, with only a few points of convergence. In Kelly's online conversation, Sutapa Biswas is one of the invited participants, and she posts a picture of her work *Housewives with Steak-Knives* (1985) as it was installed in Himid's *Thin Black Line(s)* exhibition at Tate Britain in 2011–12. Griselda Pollock also appears as a frequent point of contact, as she has been one of the key writers on both artists' work and appears in Kelly's online conversation.

What I have written here is an attempt to put these two constellations alongside each other, as both are needed to map out the communities of artists, curators, and archivists explored in this book. Rather than keep them in two separate art historical contexts, the ways in which both contribute to a feminist art history that does not ignore intersectional issues and tensions, particularly around race and sexuality, but also class, geography, and artworld visibility, provide context for the reimagining of feminist histories by artists of younger generations.

What joins Kelly and Himid is an intense exploration of their own positionality, attending to the legacies and connections that their practices as artists, writers, curators, and teachers can bring. There is much more to be explored in the conversations and constellations that they hand over to the viewer/reader, as Himid puts it: "My gift . . . to be spoken in a loud voice."[64]

Conclusion
Rooms of Our Own

In the children's story *Elsie Piddock Skips in Her Sleep*, we follow the epony-mous Elsie as she learns to skip while still a small child, the tutelage of the fairies aiding her already legendary skipping skills. Once she grows up, she puts down her skipping rope, at which point most fairy tales would end. However, moving fifty years into the future, when Elsie's skipping feats are no more than barely remembered tales, the story picks up again. A landowner, a Lord who has made his money from industry, decides to wrest the common land of Mount Caburn, the site of Elsie's skipping with the fairies and now the place where generations of girls have followed her practice of skipping at the new moon. The story be-comes a struggle between the community and the landowner, with his desire to take the common land thwarted only by Elsie's magical skipping skills. As all hope appears to be lost, the aged Elsie appears and suggests to a young girl that a seemingly impossible bargain be struck with the landowner: he should allow "all who have ever skipped there [to] skip there once more by turns," and he can "lay his first brick" only after the "last skipper skips the last skip."[1] The Lord agrees to what seems like a foolish bargain made by the villagers, and at the new moon the skipping commences. Beginning with the littlest girls in the village, moving through the "grown maidens" and "young mothers" to "matrons" and "grandmothers," women skip and stumble as the Lord and his friends laugh at them. The villagers themselves, watching along with the fairies, do not laugh but take the task very seriously. When the last grandmother stumbles, the Lord believes he has won and goes to lay the first brick in the ground. At that point, Elsie Piddock, now 109 years old and shrunken to the size of a small girl, appears with the magical skipping rope given to her by fairies; she had put it down when she outgrew it in girlhood but now takes it up again. She proceeds to skip "as NEVER so," escaping the Lord by skipping the Sly Skip and leading him deep underground as she skips the Strong Skip. The Lord never emerges above ground again, at which turn of events his lawyer shrugs and leaves the land to the people. The book tells us that Elsie Piddock skips out of sight but can still be seen skipping at the new moon.

In this story, from 1937, by the writer Eleanor Farjeon, a lesson is given: what starts off as child's play ends up being a weapon against capital. The proposal to the landowner sounds absurd: he can buy the land only once the skipping, undertaken by all of the women in the community, has stopped. Elsie Piddock, trained in girlhood through her own desire and the help of the fairies, is an image of what Sara Ahmed has called the "willful subject," and her willfulness allows Elsie Piddock to fight back against the erosion of common rights, beginning with the rights of children and, in particular, of girls.[2] When I read the story, by chance, it connected me to Silvia Federici's scholarship on how the dividing of the common land was joined by the regulation and oppression of women's bodies, communities, and time.[3] In this book, I am not going back as far as the transition to capitalism that Federici explores, but I want to pick up on this seemingly impossible image—of an old lady skipping through eternity to hold the common ground. This image speaks of the work of feminism and feminists and the way time has to be bent, reimagined, and replayed. Keeping feminist histories alive requires Elsie Piddock–like skipping over and over and over again.[4]

As Federici has so deftly explored, the ways in which the body was reimagined through machinic imagery to fit in with capitalist work patterns regulated gender, class, and the imagination. She describes her focus on witches as standing in for "the embodiment of a world of female subjects that capitalism had to destroy: the heretic, the healer, the disobedient wife, the woman who dares to live alone, the obeha woman who poisoned the master's food and inspired the slaves to revolt."[5] Alongside this list could be added many of the figures that have been reanimated from feminism's histories across the artworks in this book: Salome, feminist protesters, and lesbian stereotypes, along with the archives and communities that have housed them. In this conclusion, I turn to the ways in which writers have imagined the common ground of women's creativity, primarily through Virginia Woolf's notion of a room of one's own, but also through her proposal for a new, poor college. I turn to writing to end a book about contemporary art because I have needed to find literary strategies in my own account of these artworks. My experience of writing, through engaging with these literary models of creative, critical, and embodied feminist history making, opens out the common land that Elsie Piddock skips over to the contemporary landscape of the university and how feminists are finding (and have found) ways to hold it as a creative, common space.

REIMAGINING *A ROOM OF ONE'S OWN*

Taking up these images of resistant women and feminists, I have across this book explored how feminist histories can provide support for feminism in our contemporary moment and for possible futures. Writing about the artworks here has led me through histories of feminism that I hadn't known about and has led me to reflect on the communities that have sustained my writing and those that allowed previous feminists to put their experiences, ideas, and proposals into the world, whether as text, image, or institution. It might be commonplace to say that one needs a history to identify with, to be able to write from, but it is foundational and an issue brought up by many writers speaking of struggles to represent marginalized identities.[6] This need for feminist history does not mean that feminism is over. As Juliet Mitchell has commented, the feminist revolution has not failed; it is simply ongoing—what she has famously called "The Longest Revolution."[7] Members of the Women's Liberation Movement in the late 1960s and 1970s knew the importance of finding a foundation and dialogue with previous feminist work, and many early second-wave feminist texts and artworks engage in history writing, research, and speculation to ground their contemporary moment.[8] Importantly, this need for history is concurrent with a dismantling of the conventions and traditions of history writing—something with which the artists in this book are engaged through strategies of reenactment, rewriting, and reimagining. This is also a central concern in Woolf's *A Room of One's Own*, and by way of conclusion, I explore how other writers have taken up Woolf's text, reenacting it in a variety of literary forms. The ways in which Woolf creates a time of one's own is continued through these other texts as their repetitions, quotations, and alterations keep the sense of possibility found in *A Room of One's Own* alive. I join this list of writers returning to Woolf to move her ideas into their own contemporary moment with a reflection on the writing of this book and the places in which it has been written, contextualized by the ideas on the university as a place for both experiment and neoliberal containment. Elsie Piddock skipping to keep the common ground will be joined by communities of writers, artists, and academics striving to keep a space and time open for feminist possibilities that do not simply replicate the structures of capitalism and patriarchy.

A Room of One's Own can be found in countless feminist texts—sometimes as a quick reference, an unconscious echo, and at other times as the site of a detailed reworking, contestation, or thinking through. As Tania Modleski has argued, Woolf's book itself performs a necessary, feminist reworking of history: "Woolf's distinctive accomplishment . . . was to have given a name, a desire, and a history to one of the mute females who lived and died in obscurity. In doing so, Woolf deliberately engaged in a 'dynamic movement of the modification' of historical reality, and realized one of the chief performative and utopian ambitions of feminist criticism."[9] Modleski also writes that Woolf's book "has empowered countless numbers of feminists," not only through its content, but also through the performative style in which it is delivered, which, she suggests, should be understood "as a *productive* force."[10] Modleski turns to Woolf in her essay on feminist literary criticism, in which she argues: "In the broadest sense, feminist critical writing is performative insofar as it embodies a promise."[11] This promise is "a commitment to the future," which, along with her articulation of feminist writing as a "*productive* force," is key to the embodied knowledges performed in the artworks here as well as to the essays that have drawn on Woolf's literary experiments to which I now turn.[12]

In her essay "In Search of Our Mothers' Gardens" (1972), Alice Walker takes quotes from Woolf's book and suggests alternatives so she can write a history of African American women's creativity. She quotes Woolf, with her alterations in brackets: "'Yet genius of a sort must have existed among women as it must have existed among the working class. [Change this to 'slaves' and 'the wives and daughters of sharecroppers.'] . . . Indeed, I would venture to guess that Anon, who wrote so many poems without signing them, was often a woman.'"[13] Walker then finds these often unauthored traces of creativity not on the page, but in her mother's garden, describing how her mother planted and tended to flowers wherever they lived: "For her, so hindered and intruded upon in so many ways, being an artist has still been a daily part of her life. The ability to hold on, even in very simple ways, is work black women have done for a very long time."[14] Here creativity is found in the everyday: in a quilt lovingly sewn, in a garden in which flowers are made to sing.

Walker's focus on these everyday acts of creativity joins the interweaving of reading and writing about feminist histories, along with other forms of relationality and community building, that are found in many feminist reflections on Woolf's essay. In her introduction to the Italian feminist group Milan Women's

Bookstore Collective, Teresa de Lauretis discusses how the group was based in thinking through women's relationships with one another, and this was done, in part, through the creation of a "genealogy of women"—like Walker's invocation of generations of African American women.[15] De Lauretis describes this as "a symbolic community" that "is at once discovered, invented, and constructed through feminist practices of reference and address. Those practices ... include the reading or rereading of women's writings; taking other women's words, thoughts, knowledges, and insights as frame of reference for one's analyses, understanding, and self-definition."[16] The Milan Women's Bookstore Collective itself redefines Woolf's concept this way: "The room of one's own must be understood differently, then, as a symbolic placement, a space-time furnished with female gendered references, where one goes for meaningful preparation before work, and confirmation after."[17] De Lauretis also takes up this description and goes on to cite Adrienne Rich's essay on "re-visioning," linking the literary to actual relationships: "Let me anticipate right away that this notion of genealogy is not limited to literary figures but reaches into relationships between women in everyday life."[18] This combination of "women in everyday life" and figures from history chimes with my construction of feminist constellations that feature in a time of one's own. Drawing together feminists in the present moment and those evoked and reenacted from the past, the artists in this book create Benjaminian combinations that revitalize both. Even when the writer is alone in her room, she needs an imagined community, a feminist constellation, in which she can place herself and with whom she can converse.[19] De Lauretis quotes Rich, who explores the "girl or woman who tries to write" and who, although she finds "the image of Woman in books written by men," does not find "that absorbed, drudging, puzzled, sometimes inspired creature, herself, who sits at a desk trying to put words together."[20] I would argue that this is precisely the character that we find in Woolf's *A Room of One's Own*, performed with a deft wit through the conceit of speaking to a group of women about this act of "trying to put words together."

Moving forward in time from the moment of Walker's and Rich's essays and the Milan Women's Bookstore Collective's early feminist experiments, Gloria Anzaldúa opens her famous epistolary letter "Speaking in Tongues: A Letter to Third World Women Writers" by saying, "Dear mujeres de color, companions in writing—/I sit here naked in the sun, typewriter against my knee trying to visualize you."[21] The letter then combines reflections on the difficulties for women of color to become writers and populates her space with friends who encourage and support this particular piece of writing. Writing in a very different time, space, and body from Woolf, Anzaldúa also evokes the need for space, financial security, and a sense of community within which it is possible to write, to be creative. Like Woolf, she is suspicious of institutions such as universities and the potential to be assimilated into the systems she is working against. She says:

> Forget the room of one's own—write in the kitchen, lock yourself up in the bathroom. Write on the bus or the welfare line, on the job or during meals, between sleeping or waking. I write while sitting on the john. No long stretches at the typewriter unless you're wealthy or have a patron— you may not even own a typewriter. While you wash the floor or clothes listen to the words chanting in your body. When you're depressed, angry, hurt, when compassion and love possess you. When you cannot help but write.[22]

The words of Woolf are re-formed into a cry to grab time and space wherever possible: Jane Austen writing at a modest table in the corner of a sitting room becomes Anzaldúa sitting on the john. Here Woolf's ideas are again taken up to be shaken out, remade for the contemporary moment of the writer, for her community—in this case, women of color who are often unable to access the privileged spaces of the white, middle-class writer.[23] In the introduction to *This Bridge Called My Back*, Anzaldúa and Cherríe Moraga explain that the book's origins were in the feeling that both of the editors did not have a community within white feminist groups. They say of the contributors: "Most of the women appearing in this book are first-generation writers. Some of us do not see ourselves as writers, but pull the pen across the page anyway or speak with the power of poets."[24] This is something found many the texts written by feminists across class, nationality, and educational backgrounds. As Mitchell describes her experience: "Being a writer is not for me an identity. It is a struggle. Something I delay as long as possible; it mainly has to do with a need to understand what I cannot grasp."[25] This sense of urgency, of working things out through texts that are addressed to a broader feminist community and project, is something that fuels all the writers quoted here and underpins the need to explore histories of feminism in the artworks in this book. However, the obstacles to this are many, and structural. In Anzaldúa and Moraga's introduction there is a short section titled "Time and Money." In it they say: "*How do you concentrate on a project when you're worried about paying the rent?* We have sorely learned why so few women of color attempt this kind of project—no money to fall back on. In compiling this book we both maintained two or more jobs just to keep the book and ourselves alive."[26] As Woolf discusses in *A Room of One's Own*, it is a private income that finally allows her fictional "I" to write; sixty years later, this financial security is still elusive for many feminists, particularly for women of color, working-class women, and those for whom the security of academic institutions is not an option.[27]

MY OWN ROOM

When I think of a time of one's own, I think of Woolf's text, but also I think of Anzaldúa sitting naked at her typewriter in the heat of New York; Walker writing with a small child playing nearby (as she describes in another iteration of Woolf's work in the essay "One Child of One's Own"); Ursula Le Guin imagining Woolf joined by a small child who speaks to the spirit of imagination that Woolf presents in the opening pages of her book; bell hooks writing about her own ways to find enough time to think and write; and the Milan Women's Bookstore Collective reading together to find one another.[28] I also think of moments when this room becomes precarious in recent writings, as in Julia Bryan-Wilson's response to a questionnaire on "the contemporary" in the journal *October*, which begins with the sentence, "They have cut off the hot water in the building where I teach."[29] Bryan-Wilson's text goes on to describe a now familiar experience of the university as a place under threat and notes how, as she puts it "these destabilizing times are recalibrating my sense of temporality."[30]

My experience of studying and working in universities in London has also informed a sense of temporality as disrupted, looping, and precarious that underpins the theorization of history and time in this book. I started this book out of a long writer's block with another project, and I finished it—having gone through numerous cycles of productivity and nonproductivity but with none of the special research time that I imagined I would need to carve out a time of my own. Instead, a time of my own turned out to be the corners, the edges, the mornings around my everyday. In my present moment, my "now," I write as a university lecturer who is inside the walls of the institution that kept Woolf out, except as an invited speaker or dinner guest. However, the institution from which I write is vastly different from the age-old walls of Oxbridge, nearer to Bryan-Wilson's faltering US Women's Studies Department or the imagined concept of a "poor college, a new college" that Woolf sketches out in *Three Guineas*. I write from an Art Department that does not follow the rules of traditional academia, allowing some measures of freedom. However, it also means that the department feels the sharp end of measures that are cutting university education, particularly in the arts and humanities, as graduates do not conform to models of employability and profit that are fictions driving the UK university today.

The office that I sit in to finish this book is my first permanent university office; it is not a shared or borrowed space. It is in an old halls of residence earmarked for demolition at an undetermined point in time. The office is spacious because it was once a student's bedroom, with the sink covered over by a work top and cables running through casually as it is only a temporary fix for a space that is not seen as lasting. The strange temporality of this office has been my place to allow thought to "let its line down into the stream."[31] It is a luxury to have a room of my own, albeit one that has uncanny echoes of my student accommodations more than twenty years ago. Here, my fantasies and reality meet: since I returned to the university to study for my doctorate, I have aimed to have a place in which to sit and read that I can call my own. This ambition was one I thought might never be achieved, a fantasy available only to those older than me, or more ambitious, or with jobs at older, more financially secure institutions. The course of my career has taught me much about the limits of my ambitions and how I might balance them or compromise them in the search for a life that is not stretched to the breaking point. Across the course of writing this book I have experienced numerous thresholds—births, deaths, illnesses, job changes, and periods of leave—all of which have heightened my experience of disrupted temporality as political and affective. As I sit in my office now, I can still feel the layers of the previous places in which this book has been written: a corner of a bedroom; a grand office in an eighteenth-century building lent during a professor's sabbatical; a shared office with other visiting lecturers. They are joined with all the places I've scribbled down notes or had moments of clarity in the midst of other tasks or felt the crushing sense of not being able to write, whether from other duties or various forms of creative impasse. As Anzaldúa describes, these are not always personal, but often political, structural experiences that can prevent feminist and otherwise marginalized voices from feeling able to be heard. It is through texts such as hers, and the others explored here, that I have found my own way to create times and places to write.

In the book *Depression: A Public Feeling*, Ann Cvetkovich analyzes the experience of working in academia and the experience of depression, bringing them together in a profoundly political and affective conjunction. Her project combines memoir and critical essay in a manner with which Woolf also works. Cvetkovich describes the impasses when working on her first book and the lack of authority that she felt in writing. She asks, "How can we make room for crazy thoughts to become intellectual projects and communities and movements?"[32] In this book, I have explored how artists have taken this question and turned it into communal spaces for learning and feeling about feminist histories. I also take it as a way into my own project, which began with attempts to describe my experience of feminist histories as a form of fandom, a denigrated form of passionate attachment and scholarly attention. In my tracing of feminist approaches to writing here, I found again and again this attention to making room for "crazy thoughts" that could be reworded as feminist impulses, and often queer impulses. Cvetkovich contextualizes this through Eve Kosofsky Sedgwick's thinking on creativity, describing it as "the powerfully non-normative implications of focusing on creative thought that doesn't have an immediate outcome."[33] Here, creativity is necessary not because it can be immediately and clearly instrumentalized. Cvetkovich's exploration of spiritual despair as a way into contemporary discussions of depression also feels useful in terms of thinking about what is needed from feminism's histories at a moment when both the broader political landscape and the smaller landscape of the university and the art world are depressingly constrained.

In *A Room of One's Own*, Woolf describes the two days of research and analysis that propel her narrative as interrupted by incidents that provoke feelings of rage, sadness, contentment, and forgetfulness. This book has equally been marked by strong feelings and incidents that have meant having a room of one's own has only been a start. Sometimes I have sat in my office in pain, or exhaustion, or busyness for months before being able to turn to this project again. There have been periods of depression, writer's block, consuming teaching and lecturing, body pain, and absence from work due to maternity leave and childcare as well as to too much work in too many places when various jobs piled up against one another. Since moving into the office that I inhabit now, I've thought of it as a metaphor for how a time of one's own might be imagined: a room that is here for me to work in but is a crumbling, temporary space that nonetheless provided reprieve after numerous years of temporary contracts and moving among different university departments and courses. As friends have pointed out, to have a room of one's own is still a luxury, however precarious or temporary it is felt to be. This luxury is not always experienced as such, and this is partly why I write about it here. My position as a lecturer in a well-known Art Department is a place of relative security in a landscape in which many artists and writers struggle to find permanent and stable incomes. However, it is precisely this juncture between the secure and still not feeling stable, and the structural problems that face many writers and artists struggling to find the time and space to be creative, to think, and to write, that I want to explore. As I write, I have in mind not only my own experiences, but also those of all of the friends and colleagues who have dropped out of prestigious jobs, who have taken sick leave due to stress or pain, or who work relentlessly long hours to maintain their careers, as well as those deemed unsuitable for permanent teaching positions or those who have put other aspects of their life ahead of career success, only to find that the university will see them as without potential. For those of us teaching in the university, most of our time is spent on maintaining our perceived status, as what is actually taught in the classroom and what we write and research is less important than the metrics and survey feedback.[34]

With these thoughts in mind, I asked a friend, the photographer Lisa Castagner, to photograph my office (figures C.1–C.3). I did this after a particularly strange experience: one day I arrived to find a sign banning me from entering my office, stating that the building was unsafe and about to be torn down. When I called the number listed on the sign, I found that it had been meant for the building next door to mine. But in that brief time that I thought it would be demolished, I experienced a sense of relief. I wrote at the time: "The relief is in part because everything feels like a scene in a theatre. A sense of transitoriness, of fictionality." At the time I was going through an intense period of depression and body pain, brought on by finally having a permanent university post. It seemed that the previous years of precarity, as well as the exhaustion of balancing parenting with work, albeit as a part-time worker, had finally expressed themselves, flooring me for months at a time. While this eventually shifted, the looping temporalities of depression and pain (often experienced as never-ending while paradoxically with the familiar feeling of return) produced a vividness to working on this project that I have come to think of as a counterweight to the hopefulness found in many of the artworks here, driving an insistence on feminism as an unfinished project, tools for living in the present, rather than a historical entity.

THE NEW COLLEGE, THE POOR COLLEGE

Since the late 1960s, many feminists have committed to opening up learning that might traditionally take place in the university and, within the university, have encouraged women to use their skills with confidence and wisdom as well as to find ways for women to earn enough money to create the financial freedom to which Woolf, like many others, have pointed.[35] Audre Lorde puts this powerfully in a conversation with Adrienne Rich. On being asked, "How do you feel writing connected for you with teaching?" she replies, "I know teaching is a survival technique . . . [b]ecause I myself was learning something I needed, to continue living."[36] This sense of teaching and learning being intimately connected, as well as vital feminist work, is explored from a different perspective by Woolf in 1938, in her "sequel" to *A Room of One's Own*: *Three Guineas*.[37] Written during the rise of fascism, Woolf's text interweaves a feminist politics

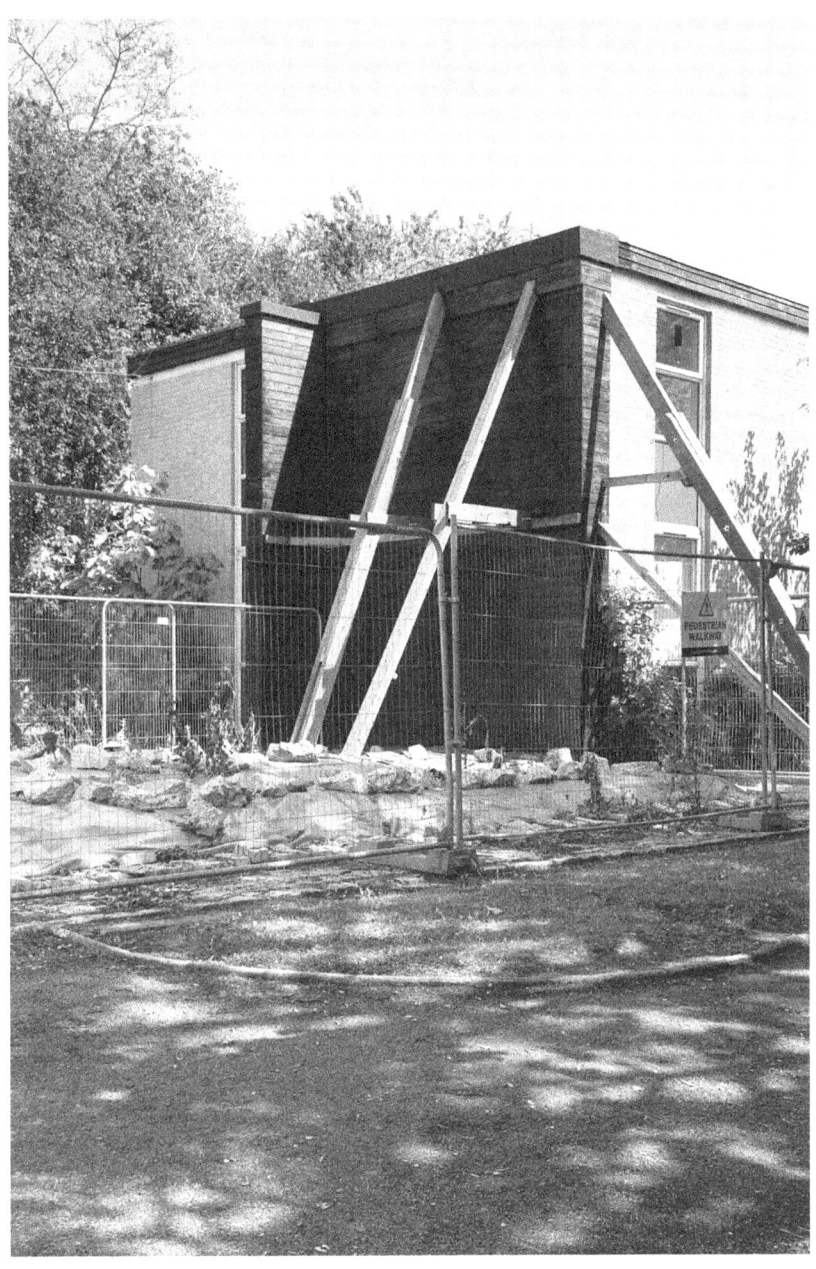

FIGURE C.1. Exterior of the author's office after the adjacent building was demolished, July 2015. Photograph by Lisa Castagner. Courtesy of Lisa Castagner.

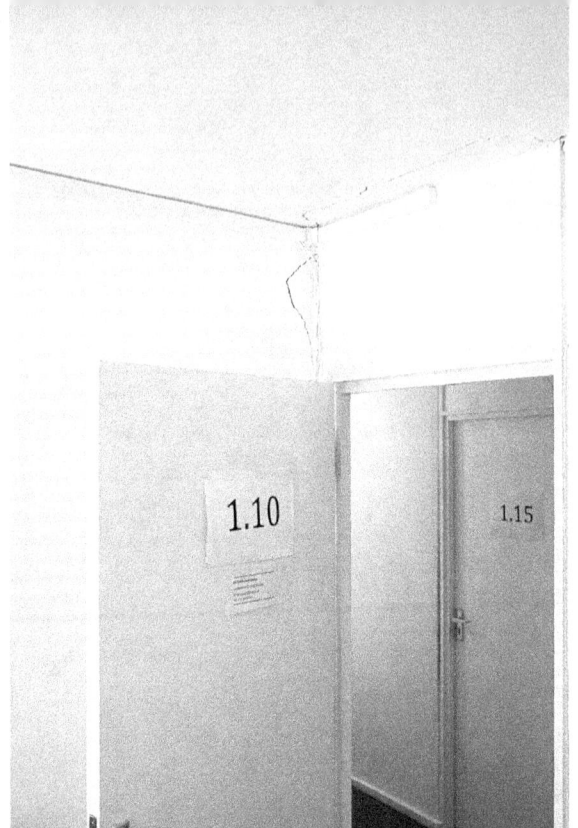

FIGURE C.2. Office door, July 2015. Photograph by Lisa Castagner. Courtesy of Lisa Castagner.

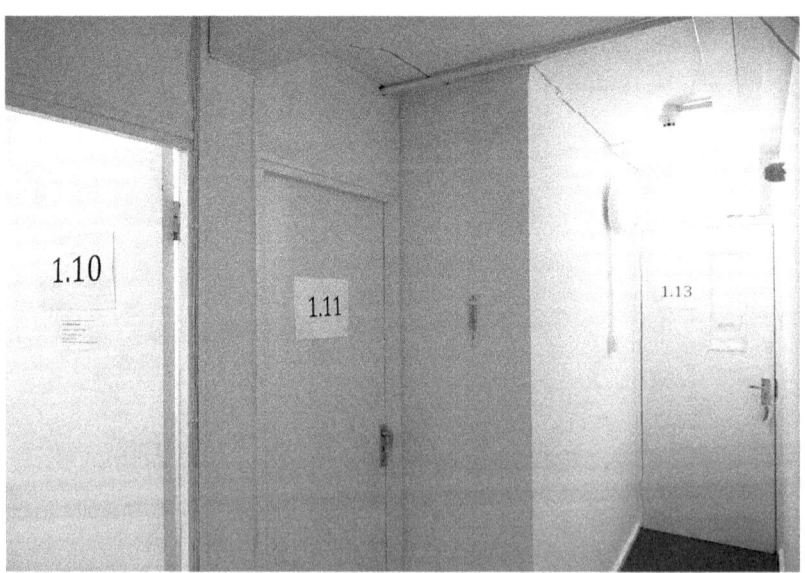

FIGURE C.3. Office corridor, July 2015. Photograph by Lisa Castagner. Courtesy of Lisa Castagner.

with a meditation on how to stop war. This is done in part by exploring what education might look like for women, proposing a "poor," "new" college, in opposition to the traditions of Oxford and Cambridge that were mostly excluding or marginalizing women during the period in which she was writing. What she proposes is very similar to what Fred Moten and Stefano Harney sketched out more recently in their concept of the "undercommons," as well as to Lorde and Rich's writing on feminist pedagogy. Woolf describes her model of a university as opposed to the traditions, privileges, and distinctions that she mocks in the pages of *Three Guineas*, saying: "It would be a place where society was free; not parceled out into the miserable distinctions of rich and poor, of clever and stupid."[38] She describes how it should be "an experimental college, an adventurous college," and asks, "What should be taught in this new college, the poor college? Not the arts of dominating other people; not the arts of ruling, of killing, of acquiring land and capital."[39] She ends her fantasy of this new, poor college with a striking image of destruction:

> No guinea of earned money should go to rebuilding the college on the old plan; just as certainly none could be spent upon building a college upon a new plan; therefore the guinea should be earmarked "Rags. Petrol. Matches." And this note should be attached to it. "Take this guinea and with it burn the college to the ground. Set fire to the old hypocrisies. . . . And let the daughters of educated men dance around the fire and heap armfuls of dead leaves upon the flames. And let their mothers lean from the upper windows and cry "Let it blaze! Let it blaze! For we have done with this 'education'!"[40]

In this scene of daughters and mothers destroying the college founded by their brothers, fathers, and husbands, Woolf provides a counterimage to her lonely exclusion from the university library in *A Room of One's Own*. An anarchic feminist community is imagined, only to be rejected, although the afterimage of this scene is strong. She says that this scene has "something hollow about it" and claims that it is inspired by the words of a former head teacher at Eton, who described women's education as needing to be structured differently from men's.[41] She says that women must be able to earn money so they can influence the situation regarding war as independent people rather than as dependent wives and mothers, so she cannot propose that a women's college reject the structures and hierarchies of the university. Instead, she says that we can pour "mild scorn" on the prizes and degrees of the university and refuse to lecture when invited; otherwise, without the university, even in its imperfect present form, the daughters of educated men will be confined to the private house.[42] She concludes by rejecting her fantasy of destruction and reformation by saying: "We must help to rebuild the college which, imperfect as it may be, is the only alternative to the education of the private house. We must hope that in time that education may be altered."[43]

Woolf's fantasy scene brings up the issue of feminist generations, which is explored in the early chapters of this book, with the model of fandom being used to complicate it. The fact that this scene is a fantasy rather than a reality underscores one of my key arguments: that artists, writers, and curators are turning to feminism's histories not as dutiful or rebellious daughters but as creative fan-scholars, learning from history by anachronizing its scenes and narratives. The image of the mothers cheering the daughters needs to be reimagined as an intergenerational grouping that includes friends, lovers, teachers, students, idols, and fans, as well as mothers and daughters, fathers, and brothers. Where generational relations have been invoked in this book, they are often queered or are an elective kinship that is up for negotiation on both sides, a kinship based in a queer community or a pedagogical scene, or both. Nevertheless, the fantasy of mothers cheering on daughters, when thought of as a feminist artistic community, returns to issues set out in the introduction: what Helen Molesworth calls the "deferred and delayed temporality of the recognition of feminist art," pointing out "how women artists have often forged connections over disjointed periods of space and time."[44] Feminist artists from previous decades are not always visible to younger artists and writers as part of a chronological narrative; instead, they are found at moments that join together the moment of their finding and the moment of the works' production. I have focused on these moments of finding, with my own experiences of becoming a feminist having this quality of looping temporalities. A further project would be to concentrate on the experience of those who are "found," with all of the difficulties inherent in a personal past becoming remade at the hands of someone who hasn't experienced it. As Rosalyn Deutsche describes, "As an older feminist, I think I relate differently to the current feminist events because it's my past that's being written as history, and that's somewhat alarming."[45] However, this is a fairly simple story that Deutsche herself complicates, and one that obscures the conversations that are taking place within and around feminism in the first decades of this century: intergenerational conversations about queer and trans politics, racial exclusions within mainstream feminism, the cost of neoliberal versions of feminist politics, and the overarching need to form intersectional feminist alliances and to tell feminist stories differently. In this book, the figures of Lubaina Himid, Mary Kelly, and Yvonne Rainer represent different responses to this experience of being historicized. Himid and Kelly focus on how their own histories are part of communal projects, understanding the need to set out a detailed history for others to take up, whereas Rainer is happy to play the part of queer father and collaborator while remaining strict on the interpretation of her own artistic past.

In my reading of *Three Guineas*, I want to take from Woolf's image of daughters and mothers dancing around the fire the formation of feminist communities that it activates. Rather than seeing it in opposition to history and tradition, I see it as being part of the interrogation of history, in part through its reenactment to imagine histories differently, that also takes place through the artworks discussed in this book. In her concept of "a poor college, a new college," Woolf is proposing the university as a space of learning that resonates with a time of one's own, as well as with Bertolt Brecht's model of the learning-play and the constellations of feminist histories and figures found in a feminist chorus. For this conclusion, I want to also join Woolf's meditation on the university with Harney and Moten's proposal for the undercommons. They see how "education may be altered" within the traditional structure of the university, proposing forms of community and study found in this book. They say, "We are committed to the idea that study is what you do with other people" and that the university is not necessary for this, but nonetheless it is an "incredible gallery of resources."[46] Their description of the undercommons is romantic and anarchic, refusing to submit to the conditions of the neoliberal university and instead finding moments of community and resistance around its edges. They explore the debt involved in university education, reimagining it for the student who doesn't graduate. They describe how most students graduate, but, they write, "Some still stay, committed to black study in the university's undercommon rooms. They study without an end, plan without a pause, rebel without a policy, conserve without a patrimony."[47] This commitment to "black study," to studying beyond the goal of graduating, chimes with much of the learning that the artists and writers in this book ask us to undertake. Like the figure of the fan, Harney and Moten explore the ways of learning that prioritize a politically motivated but open-ended desire to find out how to live differently. Like the fan, they describe how students beyond the university find one another, a description that has similarities to Anzaldúa's of going beyond a room of one's own: "Here they meet those others who dwell in a different compulsion, in the same debt, a distance, forgetting, remembered again but only after. These other ones carry bags of newspaper clippings, or sit at the end of the bar, or stand at the stove cooking, or sit on a box at the newsstand, or speak through bars, or speak in tongues."[48] The text continues to describe the encounter with these students of the undercommons: "These other ones have a passion to tell you what they have found, and they are surprised you want to listen, even though they've been expecting you."[49] This sense of passion, surprise, and expectation captures my experience of feminism, which has been a patchwork of learning, thinking, conversing, and writing over the course of my adult life. It could also stand in for a description of the figures and histories with which the artworks in this book invite the viewer to reengage. These histories have been waiting for us in the present, and the figures connected to them are still waiting for us to hear what they have to say. From writing in a room of one's own to sharing a creative thought with others to being with others found in books, archives, artworks, anecdotes, this is how a community can be present even when one is alone.

For me, the reimagining of feminist histories in contemporary art, and their queer potential for our present, is part of what Harney and Moten describe as the undercommons. What I want to take from their proposal (which they also describe in terms of a rehearsal) is how it creates space for learning in a group, prioritizing teaching as a communal activity, a conversation, something that is key to the artworks explored in this book and that links to the feminist discussions of a room of one's own.[50] As Arlie Hochschild analyzed in 1973, the university operates as a competitive marketplace designed for academics who can participate in its linear model of successes achieved early and quickly—what she describes as "the clockwork of male careers."[51] Like Woolf and Hochschild, Harney and Moten propose that the elements of competition and distinction that are presented at the forefront of the university should be refused in favor of the conversations that can take place, seeing the teaching that brings academics into the university, but is often trivialized, as the site where their notion of the undercommons can be realized. As in Brecht's concept of the learning-play, what matters in the undercommons is a notion of study as "a new way of being together and thinking together," as many feminists also tried to imagine and enact. As Hochschild writes in her 2003 reflection on her 1973 essay: "American culture incorporated what of feminism fit with capitalism and individualism, but it resisted the rest. It incorporated the idea of equal pay for equal work and diversity but dispensed with any challenges to the priorities of the system women wanted in on. So it looks to me as if the good fight is still ahead."[52]

This good fight, which can be seen in the image of Elsie Piddock skipping into the future as much as in the rewriting of Woolf's analysis of women and creativity through different moments in time and space, is continued by feminists who see the necessity of changing the world we live in and joined by the list of those studying in the undercommons.[53] In relation to the university, the place from which I write and from which a number of the artists in this book sustain themselves, there is still the imperative to find the spaces of learning that it allows. This joins up with broader discussions about creativity in our contemporary moment.[54] The university is no longer the comfortable site of contemplation and detached scholarship, bolstered by money and privilege, as described so devastatingly by Woolf. As women, and feminists, have entered the university, they have reformed it in ways that have centralized the issue of learning as a radical tool.

To learn from the histories of feminism that have been tracked across this book, those histories first had to be collected, narrated, written up, brought to life. The techniques used to do this have been my focus, from fannish practices of rewriting and re-performing to expanded versions of reenactment and rehearsal, the staging of communal experiences of speaking together and to one another, and the visualizing of constellations. The artistic practices explored gather from feminism's histories and set them on a stage for a contemporary feminist audience, insisting on their importance through close reading, listening, writing, performing, and discussing. The recurrence of artworks that foreground reading and writing led to me to reflect on my role as a writer of this recent art history, and to explore feminist writers who have tried to bring a feminist present or future to life through an intense, sometimes fantastical engagement with the past.

As I sit here, surrounded by my collection of books, posters, artworks, and objects—a feminist collection that sustains me as much as my friends to whom I write (both real and imagined, here in the present and in the past)—I want to end with one last willful woman, one last moment in which the power of creating a history, of having a feminist constellation from which to create, is brought into sharp focus. This willfulness is found in a memoir of a writer who knows how to queerly mine history for imagined and potential spaces: Jeanette Winterson. She recalls how reading in the local public library allowed her to imagine a world outside her home, the private house that Woolf describes in constricting detail. In describing her autodidactic forays into the shelves marked "English Literature," she echoes Lorde's famous pronouncement: "Poetry is not a luxury." Winterson says: "So when people say that poetry is a luxury . . . I suspect that the people doing the saying have had things pretty easy. A tough life needs a tough language—and that is what poetry is. That is what literature offers—a language powerful enough to say how it is."[55] I link the urgency felt for these literary histories with the power of the feminist histories reenacted and reread across the course of this book. Winterson contrasts the world found in the library with her family home, and with a traumatic moment when her mother discovers the paperback books that she has been hiding under her mattress, a world under her every night. Winterson recounts her mother throwing the books into the garden and setting them alight. This incident brings into focus the necessity of a room of one's own, however provisional or transitory. After watching her precious books burn, Winterson says, she began to memorize texts so they would stay inside her. She talks about the body as an archive: "There was a time when record-keeping wasn't an act of administration; it was an art form. . . . If you can't write it down how will you pass it on? You remember. You recite."[56] Winterson's memory points to the inadequacy of Woolf's fantasy of the daughters dancing around the fire, the inadequacy that Woolf acknowledges. Instead, Winterson's experience watching the fire burn makes her more determined to hold the histories and the words that she needs, a determination that is felt by feminists at many points across history as they continue with their eyes on the future, like Elsie Piddock. In our current precarity within the world, and within the world of the university, perhaps we can take from this some strength and determination. As Winterson recounts as she watches the bonfire of her books, rather than admit defeat, she decides to fight: "'Fuck it,' I thought, 'I can write my own.'"[57]

1. The cover image is from *Untitled (David Wojnarowicz Project)* (2001–2007), a series by Every Ocean Hughes (then known as Emily Roysdon).

2. The exhibition was "Public Library," part of the first Publish and be Damned zine fair, curated by Emily Pethick and Kit Hammonds, Cubitt Gallery, London, 2004. Publish and be Damned took place annually from 2004 to 2013.

3. For a complex discussion of postfeminism and art, see Jones, "Feminism, Incorporated." The essay is reprinted in the first edition of Jones's *The Feminism and Visual Culture Reader* (2003), but she does not include it in the second edition, published in 2010, as she notes that feminism is again assumed to be culturally important. For a discussion of the *Bad Girls* exhibitions and intergenerational tension, see Buszek, "Conclusion/Commencement"; Butler et al., "Feminist Curating and the 'Return' of Feminist Art." While there was much development in feminist approaches to art history during the 1990s, contemporary artists were often reluctant to identify their work as feminist or to make explicit their feminist legacies. Successful exhibitions such as *Inside the Visible* explored histories of women artists that often engaged with feminist concerns, but through a diffuse and theoretically nuanced notion of difference that included gender as one intersectional concern: see Zegher, *Inside the Visible*.

4. Many artists and curators who engaged with histories of feminism in the 2000s have links to feminist and queer music scenes across the United States, United Kingdom, and Western Europe. For more on the relationship between music and cultural production within queer and feminist communities, see Halberstam, "What's That Smell?"; Kearney, "The Missing Links"; Leonard, *Gender in the Music Industry*.

5. The book ends with shifts in the political landscape in the United Kingdom and North America, with the vote to leave the European Union and the vote for Donald Trump as US president creating a backdrop of increasing populist politics, nationalism, and xenophobia. Across the period of the book, the rise of social movements moved conversations about feminism, racial justice, and queer politics into the mainstream, so that

whereas in the early 2000s it was still possible to question whether feminism was an outmoded politics, by 2017 it had become an essential but also contested site.

6. In her foundational book, Dinshaw explains how she follows "what I call a queer historical impulse, an impulse towards making connections across time": Dinshaw, *Getting Medieval*, 1. Other concepts that have been influential include Elizabeth Freeman's notion of "temporal drag," Ann Cvetkovich's "archive of feelings," and Heather Love's "feeling backward." For an early summary of the field, see Dinshaw et al., "Theorizing Queer Temporalities."

7. Georges Didi-Huberman has proposed that a sense of anachronism is experienced in front of all artworks. His provocative formulation is more general than the sense of anachronizing set out in the artworks here: Didi-Huberman, "Before the Image, before Time." For me, Michael Ann Holly's formulation of art history as a melancholic discipline is closer to understanding desire and temporality when writing about artworks: Holly, "The Melancholy Art."

8. The definitions are from *The Oxford English Dictionary*, 2nd ed. (Oxford: Clarendon, 1986).

9. "Women: The Longest Revolution" is the title of Juliet Mitchell's foundational essay from 1966. In 2016, she confirmed that she still saw feminism as being the longest revolution, rather than a political project that had been attempted and failed, at a seminar celebrating fifty years since the article's publication held at the Institute of Advanced Studies, University College London, held on November 2.

10. Many artists in this book have also been writing about these issues and engaging in dialogue with key theorists: see, e.g., Boudry et al., *Temporal Drag*; Cvetkovich and Mitchell, "A Girl's Journey into the Well of Forbidden Knowledge"; Geyer and Hayes, *History Is Ours*; Lorenz, *Not Now! Now!*; Mitchell, "Deep Lez."

11. See Bradley, "Introduction"; Harney and Moten, *The Undercommons*.

12. I'm thinking here of Ahmed, *Living a Feminist Life*; Halberstam, *Gaga Feminism*; Preciado, *Testo Junkie*, as well as of the intersection with more recognizably academic books and experimental modes of writing: see, e.g., Gumbs, *M Archive*; Muñoz, *Cruising Utopia*.

13. Butler and Mark, *WACK!*

14. B. Ruby Rich, "Feminism and Sexuality in the 1980s," *Feminist Studies* 12, no. 3 (Fall 1986), 529, quoted in Henry, *Not My Mother's Sister*, 2.

15. For detailed discussion of feminist approaches to time, generation, and "waves," see Apter, "'Women's Time' in Theory"; Buszek, *Pin-Up Grrrls*; Pollock, "The Politics of Theory."

16. See Jenkins, *Textual Poachers*, 23.

17. In her influential book *An Archive of Feelings*, Ann Cvetkovich briefly suggests the model of archivist as fan, saying "The archivist of queer culture must proceed like the fan or collector whose attachment to objects is often fetishistic, idiosyncratic, or obsessional" (253).

18. According to Ginger Brooks Takahashi, the editors of *LTTR* knew one another "in various ways," including through a "queer punk scene," and had subsequently attended the prestigious Whitney Independent Study Program (ISP), although only K8 hardy and Ulrike Müller were in the program at the same time: Ginger Brooks Takashi, conversation

with the author, May 8, 2008. Every Ocean Hughes describes the combination that the group inhabited, saying, "While in the ISP, I lived with one foot in the theoretically and politically engaged art world, and . . . I had the other foot in the queer pop punk music scene": quoted in Arakistain and Roysdon, "Art We Still Trespassing?," 228. For an excellent account of the queer punk music scene in the United States see Halberstam, "What's That Smell?" See also Buchloh et al., "The Whitney Independent Study Program at 50."

19. Many of the contributors are now well-known trans, queer, and feminist artists and thinkers. For the embedding of LTTR in recent feminist art histories, see Wagner, "Riot on the Page" and the exhibition *Here We LTTR: 2002–2008*, Tensta Konsthall, Stockholm, May 23–September 27, 2015. LTTR was already being contextualized as a historical precedent in the concluding conversation in the 2017 exhibition catalog: see Burton and Bell, *Trigger*.

20. See, e.g., Lord, "Their Memory Is Playing Tricks on Her," which looks at the interaction of queerness, lesbian identity, and feminism but does not stabilize this relationship under the term "queer feminist." Within the collection *Otherwise: Imagining Queer Feminist Art Histories*, there are different articulations of how "queer" and "feminist" might interact. One of the editors, Amelia Jones, contends that there is a "richness of queer feminist *art practice*, in contrast to the lack of fully articulated queer feminist *art history* or *theory*": Jones and Silver, *Otherwise*, 6. This is in contrast with some of the contributors who continue to underline the necessity of keeping "queer" and "feminist" alongside each other, as in Latimer, "Improper Objects." I would argue that there is a rich body of writing that puts "feminism" and "queerness" in conversation with each other but mostly maintains the tension between these terms and how queerness might interact with lesbian and gay histories. This doesn't often take place within the discipline of art history, although this is changing rapidly. Here I keep the terms "queer" and "feminist" in dialogue, as has been the case for most of the artists featured in this collection. As with any periodization, there are exceptions. For instance, Sasha Roseneil's *Common Women, Uncommon Practices* (2000) is subtitled "The Queer Feminism of Greenham."

21. Every Ocean Hughes (published as Emily Roysdon), "Editorial," *LTTR*, no. 1, 2002, 1, available at lttr.org/journal and in the Women's Art Library, Special Collections, Goldsmiths, University of London.

22. De Lauretis, "The Practice of Sexual Difference and Feminist Thought in Italy," 2.

23. See Ahmed, *Living a Feminist Life*; Anim-Addo et al., "Black British Feminisms." For a US history, see Gumbs, "We Can Learn to Mother Ourselves"; Hogan, *The Feminist Bookstore Movement*.

24. Lorde and Rich, "An Interview with Audre Lorde."

25. Rich, "To Invent What We Desire," 214.

26. Lorde, "Poetry Is Not a Luxury," 37.

27. Lorde, "Poetry Is Not a Luxury," 39.

28. Ahmed, *Living a Feminist Life*. See also Gumbs, "Eternal Summer of the Black Feminist Mind."

29. Ahmed, *Living a Feminist Life*, 12.

30. Gumbs, "We Can Learn to Mother Ourselves." Gumbs explores Rich's letter that follows this resignation in "Communiqué to White Ally Heaven."

31. For an overview, see Pollock, "Screening the Seventies"; Wilson, *Art Labor, Sex Politics*.

32. The only feminist artist who seems to have engaged with theories of the learning-play in the 1970s is Martha Rosler. She says she was influenced by the learning-plays in an interview with Benjamin Buchloh, in Zegher, *Martha Rosler*, 55. I thank Catherine Long for sharing her research on this.

33. Milan Women's Bookstore Collective, *Sexual Difference*, 26. I thank Helena Reckitt for sending me this quotation.

34. An image from the series *In the Near Future* was used on the front of Hesford's book *Feeling Women's Liberation*, without comment by the author on this choice. In this way the dialogue between feminist historian and artist around the histories of the Women's Liberation Movement, as well as around other civil rights campaigns, was staged implicitly.

35. Sharon Hayes, *In My Little Corner of the World, Anyone Would Love You*, 2016, description on artist's website, accessed May 1, 2019, http://shaze.info/work/in-my-little -corner-of-the-world. The Tanya Leighton Gallery provided the full production credits for this work:

Readers: Pangia, Tiny, Mal Cherifi, Sharron Cooks, Kristen Dieffenbacher, TS Hawkins, Jeannine Betu Kayembe, Jennifer Angelina Petro, Swift Shuker, Karl Surkan, Madeline Rafter, Mahogany Rose, Tatyana Yassukovich

Writers: J. H., Ms. R. L., H. R., Arnica, Shirley, Anne, R. M. C., Margaret, Elandria, Tommi, and multiple unnamed editors, writers, and readers from newsletters and small run magazines produced and distributed in the United States and the United Kingdom between 1955 and 1977. Material for the spoken text and the risograph prints was collected from the Hall-Carpenter Archives, London School of Economics; Women's Library, London School of Economics; Gay News Photographic Archive, Bishopsgate Institute; Archive, George Padmore Institute; Lesbian Archive and Information Centre Collection, Glasgow Women's Library; Archives of Sexuality and Gender, Gale Primary Sources; Herstory, microfilm collection, Women's History Library, Berkeley, California; Transgender Oral History Project; Digital Transgender Archive; John J. Wilcox Jr. Archives, William Way LGBT Community Center; and LGBT Community Center National History Archive.

Production: Director of Photography, Michelle Lawler; Assistant Camera, Douglas Lennox; Gaffer, Jih-E Peng; Sound Recorder, M. Asli Dukan; Sound Engineer, Josh Allen; Production Manager, Sarah Kolker; Production Consultation, Phuong Nguyen; Production Assistance, Heather Holmes, Hassen Saker, Lindsay Buchman; Research assistance: Rose Gibbs, Tara Gibbs, Heather Holmes; Installation design in collaboration with Andrea Geyer.

The artist thanks the archives and archivists for their thoughtful care of the vital records from which this piece was made and extends a special thanks to all the editors, writers, and readers of these newsletters and magazines whose radical conversations and communications create pathways forward for all of us.

36. Sharon Hayes, *In My Little Corner of the World, Anyone Would Love You*, press release, 2016, Studio Voltaire, London, accessed June 1, 2016, https://www.studiovoltaire .org/exhibitions/archive/sharon-hayes.

37. However, I was able to identify Elandria V. Henderson's text because of its inclusion in Crow, *Radical Feminism*. Rose Gibbs, one of the London researchers for the project, was kind enough to share details of her archival research into London organizations: see Castagnini and Gibbs, "Restaging the Collective."

38. Hayes, "Temporal Relations."

39. Hayes, "Temporal Relations," 64. See also the comments on Hayes's work in Elizabeth Freeman's preface to Lorenz, *Not Now! Now!*, 11.

40. Elsewhere, Hayes has explained her method of respeaking as a "performative copy, . . . an utterance which does something in its repetition": Hayes and Rainer, "Familiarity, Irony, Ambivalence," 34. Hayes cites Gertrude Stein's work as an example, as well as performance works.

41. Hayes, "Certain Resemblances."

42. Schneider, *Performing Remains*, 2.

43. Freeman, "Packing History, Count(er)ing Generations."

44. Dinshaw, "Temporalities," 107.

45. Dinshaw, "Temporalities," 108.

46. De Lauretis, quoted in Hayes, "Certain Resemblances," 87.

47. Friedrich Nietzsche and Michel Foucault are the other writers most usually referenced.

48. Dinshaw, *Getting Medieval*, 17, summarizing arguments made across a range of writing by Bhabha.

49. Freeman, *Time Binds*, xvi.

50. Dinshaw, *Getting Medieval*, 17–18.

51. Agamben, "What Is the Contemporary?" Agamben does not explicitly say that this essay is a reworking of Benjamin's essay, but it picks up motifs, including the discussion of Nietzsche, fashion, and the constellation.

52. Agamben has contributed significantly to the research and thinking on Benjamin, including recovering lost material: see de la Durantaye, *Giorgio Agamben*, esp. 148–49. See also Agamben, "Threshold or *Tornada*."

53. Agamben, "What Is the Contemporary?," 40.

54. Agamben, "What Is the Contemporary?," 47.

55. Agamben, "What Is the Contemporary?," 47.

56. Walter Benjamin, "Theses on the Philosophy of History" (1940), 263, quoted in Dinshaw, *Getting Medieval*, 17. In the rest of this book I quote from the newer translation of Benjamin's essay, titled "On the Concept of History." Benjamin describes a constellation, writing, "Image is that wherein what has been comes together in a flash with the now to form a constellation": Benjamin, *The Arcades Project*, 262. Agamben, "What Is the Contemporary?," 53. Here Agamben refers to Foucault and Benjamin.

57. Meyer, *What Was Contemporary Art?* Peter Osborne writes in detail about these three historical markers in *Anywhere or Not at All*, 18–22.

58. Aranda et al., *What Is Contemporary Art?*; Blocker, *Becoming Past*; Foster, "A Questionnaire on 'The Contemporary'"; Smith, *What Is Contemporary Art?* See also Smith, "Contemporaneity in the History of Art" and Smith, "Contemporary Art and Contemporaneity," as well as collections such as Dumbadze and Hudson, *Contemporary Art* and Jones, *A Companion to Contemporary Art since 1945*.

59. As Peter Osborne puts it, "The social actuality of 'generational' change no longer just corresponds to human generations, but equally, possibly predominantly, to 'generations' of *technologies*, to which all human generations are subjected, albeit unequally. The fiction of the contemporary is thus becoming, in this respect at least, progressively contracted. The present of the contemporary is becoming shorter and shorter": Osborne, *Anywhere or Not at All*, 24.

60. See Smith, *What Is Contemporary Art?*

61. See Dimitrakaki, "Researching Culture/s and the Omitted Footnote," for a nuanced account of the difficulties of writing from and about different cultural contexts and how this reveals assumptions that underpin definitions of *contemporary art* and feminist practices.

62. Osborne, *Anywhere or Not at All*, 17.

63. For notable exceptions, see Jones, "Performance, Live or Dead"; Knaup and Stammer, *Re.act.feminism*; Reckitt, *Not Quite How I Remember It*; Ross, *The Past Is the Present; It's the Future Too*; Schneider, "Remembering Feminist Remimesis."

64. Much of the literature on contemporary art history crosses over with that looking at definitions of contemporary art. See, e.g., Blocker, *Becoming Past*; Foster, "A Questionnaire on 'The Contemporary'"; Amelia Jones, "Introduction: Writing Contemporary Art into History, a Paradox?," in *A Companion to Contemporary Art since 1945*, 3–16; Ross, *The Past Is the Present; It's the Future Too*; Meyer, *What Was Contemporary Art?*

65. Pollock, *Generations and Geographies in the Visual Arts*.

66. For two important recent reflections on how to write feminist art history that pay attention to the specificity and materiality of encounters with artworks, see Jones, *Seeing Differently*; Pollock, *Encounters in the Virtual Feminist Museum*. The literature on reenactment is discussed in chapter 2, but Jones has also done much work on this, as has Rebecca Schneider. See, esp., Schneider, *Performing Remains*.

67. Bryan-Wilson, "Practicing *Trio A*," 74.

68. Molesworth, "How to Install Art as a Feminist." 507.

69. Molesworth, "How to Install Art as a Feminist," 512. She also quotes from Benjamin, "On the Concept of History."

70. Molesworth, "How to Install Art as a Feminist," 507. In "Mediating Generation," Lisa Tickner begins with two images: Virginia Woolf, photographed looking uncomfortable in her mother's dress, and a self-portrait by her sister Vanessa Bell, posing herself as her mother, as photographed by their aunt Julia Margaret Cameron. Molesworth is also referring to Mignon Nixon, "Child Drawing," in *Eva Hesse Drawing*, ed. Catherine de Zegher (New York: Drawing Center, 2006), 27–56.

71. Hemmings, *Why Stories Matter*.

72. Here I am quoting from what Sam McBean calls "feminism's queer temporalities": McBean, *Feminism's Queer Temporalities*.

CHAPTER ONE. FANS OF FEMINISM

This chapter is an updated version of "Fans of Feminism: Re-writing Histories of Second-Wave Feminism in Contemporary Art," *Oxford Art Journal* 34, no. 2 (June 2011): 265–86, doi:10.1093/oxartj/kcr021.

1. See, e.g., Armstrong, "'Global Feminisms' and 'WACK!'"; the special issue of *Frieze*, no. 105 (March 2007); the special section in *Art in America*, vol. 95, no. 6 (June–July 2007).

2. See Butler and Jones, "History Makers." Amelia Jones discusses both the problems of *Sexual Politics* and the different approach by Connie Butler in *WACK!*.

3. For more details, see the interview by Bryan-Wilson and Hayes, "'We Have a Future.'" Hayes's series is also discussed briefly by Rosalyn Deutsche in the Deutsche et al., "Feminist Time."

4. The project description is from Hayes's website, accessed April 2, 2010, http://www.shaze.info/#. For a detailed account of the project, see Freeman, *Time Binds*, 59–62.

5. While these two examples are American, my analysis could be extended to examples from Europe, with projects such as Oriana Fox's *Once More with Feeling* (accessed April 10, 2010, http://www.orianafox.com/performance/Once_More_With_Feeling.html), an event at the Tate Modern London, in 2009 that drew on histories of feminist performance art encountered in the archives at the Women's Art Library, London, or *Re.act. feminism: Performance Art of the 1960s and 70s Today* (accessed April 10, 2010, http://www.adk.de/reactfeminism/index.htm.), curated by Bettina Knaup and Beatrice E. Stammer and hosted by the Akademie der Künste, Berlin.

6. See, e.g., Hills, *Fan Cultures*; Jenkins, *Textual Poachers*.

7. The first issue of the magazine came out in 1983. For more on the Women's Art Library, see Greenan, "How Images Are the Making of the Women's Art Library/Make."

8. A longer discussion of Fox's work is in Grant, "Reaching for the Moon." The video is available at www.orianafox.com.

9. Jenkins, *Textual Poachers*, 18.

10. Fiske, "The Cultural Economy of Fandom," 46.

11. Jenkins, *Textual Poachers*, 23.

12. The views of Jenkins and Fiske, which privilege resistance and rebellion in their conceptualization of the fan, have been contested by a number of writers. While their models do focus on a particular type of fandom, their thinking provides a conceptual model that is useful to my argument, which is using fandom as a metaphor rather than an empirical study of the range of fan practices: see. e.g., Hills, *Fan Cultures*, 3–19.

13. For an in-depth discussion of various fan stereotypes, see Jenkins, *Textual Poachers*.

14. Jenkins, *Textual Poachers*, 12.

15. Jensen, "Fandom as Pathology," 9.

16. See Bryan-Wilson, "Repetition and Difference," for an account of some of LTTR's events. A web archive of *LTTR* nos. 1–5 is available at lttr.org/journal.

17. For an introduction to different kinds of zine production and their histories, see Duncombe, *Notes from Underground*.

18. For a discussion of women and zines, see Piepmeier, *Girl Zines*.

19. Ginger Brooks Takahashi, interview with the author, Brooklyn, NY, May 8, 2008.

20. B. Ruby Rich, "Feminism and Sexuality in the 1980s," *Feminist Studies* 12, no. 3 (Fall 1986), 529, quoted in Henry, *Not My Mother's Sister*, 2.

21. Rosalyn Deutsche, in Deutsche et al., "Feminist Time," 56. The section "Generations" is a nuanced discussion of the potential and pitfalls of the idea of feminist generations.

22. Freeman, "Packing History, Count(er)ing Generations," 729.

23. Rhani Lee Remedes, "The SCUB Manifesto," *LTTR*, no. 1, 2002, 12.

24. "COMMUNICATION: What happens when two boxes try to talk? Nothing, right? Time to cut up the boxes. NOW": Remedes, "The SCUB Manifesto," 12.

25. Barry Blinderman, quoting David Wojnarowicz, "Biographical Dateline," in *David Wojnarowicz: Tongues of Flame*, ed. Barry Blinderman (Normal: University Galleries, Illinois State University, 1990), 118, quoted in Anderson, "Monks of the Dead River."

26. *Little Caesar*, no. 5, April 1978. *Little Caesar* was edited by Dennis Cooper, who is now well known as a cult writer of queer fiction and art criticism. In the special issue on Rimbaud, photographs of James Dean and the artist Chris Burden (just after having been shot) were captioned "Rimbaud, 1955" and "Rimbaud, 1973," respectively. In this framing of Rimbaud as an object of queer fandom, temporal drag is enacted: see Cooper and Lafreniere, "Dennis Cooper on Zine Days (They Were Good) and Transgressive Blogs (There Is Such a Thing)." For selected pages of Cooper's zine, see his website, accessed April 1, 2010, http://www.dennis-cooper.net/littlecaesar.htm.

27. An analysis of the relationship among gay male, lesbian, and feminist histories in *LTTR* is beyond the scope of this chapter. However, the importance of (gay) masculinity in the construction of lesbian and transgender identities is a theme that is particularly strong in the first issue of *LTTR*.

28. Ridykeulous, "Who Do You Think You LTTR?," *LTTR*, no. 4, September 2005, 5.

29. A. K. Burns, "Art Face On," *LTTR*, no. 4, September 2005, 7.

30. Burns, "Art Face On," 7.

31. Ginger Takahashi, K8 Hardy, Ulrike Müller, Emily Roysdon, and Lanka Tattersall, "Pants Down at Noon," *LTTR*, no. 4, September 2005, 1.

32. Ulrike Müller, "*LTTR* 5 Bulletin," *LTTR*, no. 5, October 2006, 46.

33. Kelly and White, "The Body Politic," 135.

34. For a discussion of *Love Songs* in relation to Alain Badiou's concept of "event," see Deutsche, "Not-Forgetting." Susan Richmond discusses the project in relation to Luce Irigaray's concept of the maternal gift in "From Stone to Cloud."

35. *Multi-Story House* was coauthored by the artist Ray Barrie.

36. Kelly and White, "The Body Politic," 133.

37. Kelly elaborated on this link between Freud and the notion of the political primal scene, saying, "I felt it was that kind of curiosity about origins, . . . that you might look at these more archaic structures and how they are generationally passed on. I thought even if I'm not trying to prove that in a clinical sense, that I'm looking at it more metaphorically, . . . filling in these pieces of the past, these kinds of explanations, what's going on there? What do people feel is actually missing? And I say 'missing' simply because it is to do with absences in Freud, it is what you don't know, what you don't hear that you try to fill in": Mary Kelly, interview with the author, September 2008.

38. In relation to this notion, I fit exactly within Kelly's parameters, as I was born in 1975 and can remember identifying with Kelly's son, rather than with Kelly, when first shown her work *Post-partum Document* (1973–79).

39. "There was something [about] the humor and the pleasure, it's the most upbeat work I ever [made]": Kelly interview.

40. Kelly, "(P)age 49," 163.

41. Plath, *The Collected Poems*, 147.

42. Kelly and White, "The Body Politic," 134.

43. See Ehrenreich et al., "Beatlemania," 90. Thanks to Kate Random Love for pointing this out. Random Love explores these links in the chapter "Romance and Repetition: Fandom in the Work of Elizabeth Peyton," in "The Possibility of an Island."

44. Although the Nineteenth Amendment gave all women the right to vote, for Black women and men, there were decades of further struggle as states practiced voter discrimination, until the 1965 Voting Rights Act. Rosalyn Deutsche describes the relationship between the two moments as a haunting. "The 1970 demonstration, mounted by a second wave of feminists, was haunted by earlier street performances—late-nineteenth- and early-twentieth-century suffragist parades. The archival photo, then, also depicts a restaging. Literally and figuratively, Kelly's work is a visual remix: a recording produced by bringing together ingredients in a new formation that modifies their identities": Deutsche, "Not-Forgetting," 33.

45. Hayes's project *Revolutionary Love: I Am Your Worst Fear, I Am Your Best Fantasy* (2008) took the reenactment of protest into the political arena. "On the occasions of the 2008 Democratic and Republican national conventions, she travelled to Denver and St. Paul for her two-part large-scale performance . . . in which she recruited large groups of queer people to read a scripted love letter in unison near the convention sites": Bryan-Wilson and Hayes, "We Have a Future," 80.

46. Kelly and White, "The Body Politic," 134. In discussing the piece, Kelly comments, "What was so remarkable was the women of the present, they . . . had the same clothes more or less, and some looked uncannily the same": Kelly, interview.

47. See, e.g., Bacon-Smith, *Enterprising Women*; Jenkins, *Textual Poachers*.

48. Kelly interview. The statements on the house's interior are drawn mainly from Kelly's friends. Kelly says that she used remembered comments from Sally Alexander, Rosalind Delmar, Maxine Molyneaux, Jean McCrindle, Ray Barrie, Francette Pacteau, Page Dubois, Martha Rosler, Suzanne Lacy, Sherry Milner, and herself.

49. These dialogues between peers and students in Kelly's work are explored further in chapter 5.

50. The film was shown as part of a screening inspired by Mulvey's text at the Whitechapel Art Gallery, London, June 2007.

51. Laura Mulvey, interview with the author, January 2010. Mulvey discusses this in more detail in the introduction to the second edition of *Visual and Other Pleasures*, ix–xxvi.

52. Emma Hedditch, interview with the author, February 2010.

53. I explore these links in "Returning to *Riddles*."

54. In the context of contemporary art, this can also be seen as part of a broader interest in histories of political activism and avant-garde practice, as explored in Foster, "An Archival Impulse."

55. The exhibition was *Snatches of Lesbian Activism 1970–2005*, on display in September 2008. Emma Hedditch is the coordinator of the Cinenova collection of women's film in London (www.cinenova.org). On the archival impulse in Hayes's work, Julia Bryan-

Wilson says, "Recovering a photograph from a dusty box is thus an act of desire. Collecting is rooted in a possessive urge, and whole archives are generated out of and depend on this desire. So much history gets disseminated, circulated, and uncovered because photos or letters produce a pleasure that exceeds their function as factual records": Bryan-Wilson and Hayes, "We Have a Future," 80.

56. Takahashi interview.

57. For a discussion of the Lesbian Herstory Archives and artistic engagement with it, see Cvetkovich, *An Archive of Feelings*, 239–71.

58. The event took place at Issue Project Room at the Old American Can Factory, Brooklyn, NY, May 6, 2009, accessed April 2, 2010, http://issueprojectroom.org/2009 /04/15/grey-room. For the extension of the project, see Müller and Fitzpatrick, "Putting the Invent in Inventory." These links are also found between Mulvey and Kelly, who were both involved in the protest over the Miss World Contest that Kelly uses as the basis for part of *Love Songs*, with the intergenerational, transnational feminist networks that underpin these artistic projects explored in more detail in chapter 5.

59. "*Ecstatic Resistance* is a project, practice, partial philosophy, set of strategies, and group exhibition" that "asserts the impossible as a model for the political": Every Ocean Hughes (Emily Roysdon), *Ecstatic Resistance*, accessed June 9, 2021, http://everyocean hughes.com/work/ecstatic-resistance. The exhibitions took place at Grand Arts in Kansas City, MO, November 13–January 16, 2009, and at X Initiative, New York City, November 21, 2009–February 6, 2010.

60. See, e.g., *Ms Understood*, an exhibition of ephemera related to the Women's Liberation Movement in London, at the Women's Library, London, October 8, 2009–March 31, 2010, and *Out of the Archives*, an exhibition of contemporary artists' engagement with material from the Women's Library's collection, held at the Women's Library, London, May–September 2010. Similarly, the Lesbian Herstory Archives hosted a number of "At the Archives" events in 2009, which included putting contemporary artists into conversation with lesbian artists, writers, and activists known for their work in the 1970s.

61. Kelly, "Mary Kelly in Conversation with Matilde Digmann."

62. Exhibition held at Cubitt Gallery, London, January 30–February 1, 2004, accessed June 8, 2021, https://www.cubittartists.org.uk/Event/a-political-feeling-i-hope-so.

63. Andrea Geyer and Sharon Hayes, "Notes on Cambio de Lugar Change of Place Ortswechsel," *LTTR*, no. 1, September 2002, 23–29.

CHAPTER TWO. *KILLJOY'S KASTLE* IN LONDON

A shorter version of this chapter appeared as "The Graveyards of Community Gathering: Archiving Lesbian and Feminist Life in London," in *Inside Killjoy's Kastle: Dykey Ghosts, Feminist Monsters, and Other Lesbian Hauntings*, ed. Allyson Mitchell and Cait McKinney (Vancouver: University of British Columbia Press, 2019), 176–93.

1. The term *feminist killjoy* was coined by Sara Ahmed as a way to think through the willfulness needed and disruption caused by going against the social order and the effects of such action: see Ahmed, "Feminist Killjoys (and Other Willful Subjects)."

2. *Killjoy's Kastle* was first shown in Toronto in 2013 and at the ONE Archive in Los Angeles in 2015.

3. An important conversation between Ego Ahaiwe Sowinski and Nazmia Jamal is published as Ahaiwe Sowinsky and Jamal, "Love and Affection."

4. To make the gravestones, Jamal collaborated with Blake Baron Ray, Ros Murray, Ochi Reyes, Arvind Thandi, and Sita Balani.

5. The gravestones in the original version of *Killjoy's Kastle* listed an international selection of lesbian organizations.

6. Ochi Reyes, email to the author, March 29, 2014.

7. Comments in this section are from an Nazmia Jamal, interview with the author, August 22, 2014. The interview also forms the basis of much of the information about the installation in the rest of the chapter, unless noted otherwise.

8. The exception was the inclusion of "SCUM 1968–∞," which was carved by her friend and neighbor Blake Baron Ray, who also helped Jamal carve up the sheets of polystyrene.

9. Mason-John and Khambatta, *Making Black Waves*.

10. For an excellent introduction to the historical use of the term *Black* and the range of alternatives in the context of British art, see Boyce and Price, "Dearly Beloved or Unrequited?" For a discussion of the problems of this term, see "Black: Whose Term Is It Anyway?," in Mason-John and Khambatta, *Making Black Waves*, 32–37.

11. Nazmia Jamal, email to the author, November 19, 2014.

12. See Helena Reckitt's essay on the collaborations in Mitchell and McKinney, *Inside Killjoy's Kastle*.

13. "Theatre for Learning" is the title of a posthumously published essay by Brecht.

14. Brecht, "The German Drama," 79.

15. See Steinweg, "Two Chapters from 'Learning Play and Epic Theatre.'"

16. Brecht, "The German Drama," 78.

17. Brecht, "The German Drama," 80.

18. Allyson Mitchell, email to the author, March 7, 2016.

19. See the account of Claes Oldenburg erasing all trace of his collaborations with his former girlfriend Hannah Wilke in Kraus, *I Love Dick*, 195–202.

20. Mitchell, "Deep Lez," 182. See also Love and Smith, *Deirdre Logue and Allyson Mitchell*.

21. Mitchell, "Deep Lez," 182–83.

22. See the blog set up during the campaign to save LWP from eviction: SaveLambethWomensProject, accessed January 15, 2016, https://savelambethwomensproject.wordpress.com.

23. Ahaiwe Sowinski, "Lambeth Women's Project."

24. Burin and Ahaiwe Sowinski, "Sister to Sister."

25. Burin and Ahaiwe Sowinski, "Sister to Sister," 113.

26. Burin and Ahaiwe Sowinski, "Sister to Sister," 116. This essay is part of a wider interest in bringing Black women's archives to the fore. See also the essays in Zanish-Belcher and Voss, *Perspectives in Women's Archives*. I thank Allyson Mitchell and Cait McKinney for directing me to this important collection.

27. Ahaiwe Sowinski, "Lambeth Women's Project."

28. X Marks the Spot et al., *Human Endeavour*. The members of X Marks the Spot are Ego Ahaiwe Sowinski, Lauren Craig, Mystique Holloway, Zhi Holloway, and Gina Nembhard.

29. She also said that the sign had been made by women, possibly by the Lambeth Women's Woodwork Shop: Ego Ahaiwe Sowinski, email to the author, June 27, 2017.

30. Ego Ahaiwe Sowinski in conversation with Suzy Mackie, See Red Women's Workshop, Don't Break Down, Break Out Symposium, London, May 20, 2017, www.ravenrow .org/media/67/. This is something that Jamal is also very engaged with, having created an archive of her own in the Lesbian Archive, Glasgow Women's Library. This is a way of holding the different identities and activities that Jamal has been involved in, something she discussed as part of the panel "Asian Futures" at the I/mages of Tomorrow conference, Goldsmiths, London, June 2, 2017.

31. Diamond, *Unmaking Mimesis*, 49.

32. In "Sister to Sister," Burin and Ahaiwe Sowinski describe how "a black British perspective continues to be absent from mainstream feminist rhetoric" (115). Their use of the term *mainstream* echoes the discussion of "white, mainstream feminist theory" in Amos and Parmar, "Challenging Imperial Feminism," 4. By using the term *mainstream feminism* rather than *white feminism*, they indicate that the story is more complicated than simply "white" or "Black" feminism. Many of the organizations included in the gravestones barely register within Black feminist writing for various reasons: their lesbian-feminist context, their fleeting nature, their activism, or their Britishness.

33. Burin and Ahaiwe Sowinski, "Sister to Sister," 118.

34. The concept of archival therapy builds on the literature about keeping archives alive, particularly archives about women's lives and, especially, Black women's lives. See also Gumbs, "Eternal Summer of the Black Feminist Mind"; Zanish-Belcher and Voss, *Perspectives on Women's Archives*. These texts are often written from the perspective of archivists themselves and provide an important addition to more famous texts on archiving in queer and feminist contexts, such as Cvetkovich, *An Archive of Feelings*; Eichhorn, *The Archival Turn in Feminism*.

35. Mirza and Gunaratnam, "The Branch on Which I Sit," 128. This idea of Black feminism as a lifeline is taken from Ahmed, "Black Feminism as Life-Line," Feministkilljoys, August 27, 2013. https://feministkilljoys.com/2013/08/27/black-feminism-as-life-line.

36. Brecht, "The German Drama," 80.

37. See Ann Cvetkovich on this project: Cvetkovich and Mitchell, "A Girl's Journey into the Well of Forbidden Knowledge."

38. I write about my own experience in chapter 3. See also Ahmed, *Living a Feminist Life*.

39. See wojtek, "A Book Bloc's Genealogy," *Libcom.org* (blog), posted November 21, 2012, http://libcom.org/library/book-bloc's-genealogy; Grindon, "Book Bloc."

40. Arts Against Cuts, "Book Bloc Comes to London," *Arts Against Cuts* (blog), December 9, 2010, https://artsagainstcuts.wordpress.com/2010/12/09/book-bloc -comes-to-london-2.

41. Luther, interviewed in Grindon, "Book Bloc."

42. "Book Bloc Shield," instruction sheet produced for the exhibition *Disobedient Objects*, Victoria and Albert Museum, London, July 26, 2014–February 1, 2015, published in Grindon, "Book Bloc."

43. Brecht, "Theatre for Learning," 24.

44. Brecht, "Theatre for Learning," 25.

45. *English Oxford Living Dictionary*, s.v. "FAFF," accessed July 17, 2017, https://en.oxforddictionaries.com/definition/faff.

46. Nazmia Jamal, email to the author, April 7, 2014.

47. Jamal interview.

48. This commemoration and activation also relates to Elizabeth Freeman's well-known concept of temporal drag and the relationship between different moments in feminism, discussed in chapter 1: see Freeman, *Time Binds*, 59–94.

49. Mason-John and Khambatta, *Making Black Waves*, 13.

50. Mason-John and Khambatta, *Making Black Waves*, 9. The Black Gay and Lesbian Centre no longer exists; the Lesbian Archive has now become part of the Glasgow Women's Library; and, as is explored later, the Feminist Library secured new premises at the Sojourner Truth Centre in Peckham, London, in 2019.

51. This sense of urgency is something that can be found throughout the literature on Black feminist and lesbian histories. In the British context, there has not been the explosion of writing and filmmaking charting queer and feminist histories that there has been in the United States, but exceptions include publications such as the *Sisterhood and After* project, which includes oral histories with a range of British feminists, extracts of which can be found at the British Library online. See also Cohen, "Researching Difference and Diversity within Women's Movements." At the time of writing, a documentary titled *Rebel Dykes* was in the last stages of production. The film charts the post-punk, anarchist, sex-positive dyke scene in London in the 1980s, including organizations and events documented on the gravestones, such as the Lesbian Strength March and "Chain Reactions," the first lesbian fetish night: see Kate Lloyd, "Meet the Lesbian Punks Who've Been Written out of London's History," *Time Out London*, April 25, 2017, and Harri Shanahan and Siân Williams, dirs., *Rebel Dykes*, 2021.

52. Mason-John and Khambatta, *Making Black Waves*, 59.

53. Mason-John and Khambatta, *Making Black Waves*, 14.

54. Mason-John and Khambatta, *Making Black Waves*, 14–15, 57.

55. The poster, "The Haunted House, Votes for Women: 20th Century," is by David Wilson and is in the collection of the Museum of London, which describes it this way: "This poster first appeared as a cartoon in the 'Daily Chronicle' in April 1907. It represents the growth of the campaign for female suffrage by showing the dominant silhouette of a woman haunting the Houses of Parliament." See http://www.museumoflondonprints.com/image/68551/david-wilson-the-haunted-house-votes-for-women-20th-century.

56. Some context can be found in Amos et al., "Many Voices, One Chant." However, in collections about Black British feminism, the organizations in *Making Black Waves* do not feature, though other Black British feminist organizations such as OWAAD and Southall Black Sisters have been written about extensively: see, e.g., Mirza, *Black British Feminism*.

57. This is something Jamal discussed as part of our interview about her role as curator at the BFI Flare installation.

CHAPTER THREE. A TIME OF ONE'S OWN

This chapter is a significantly revised version of "A Time of One's Own," *Oxford Art Journal* 39, no. 3 (December 1, 2016): 357–76, doi:10.1093/oxartj/kcw025.

1. Some of these authors are associated with trans-exclusionary feminism. This is not a position that I agree with, but I keep the names here as they were authors who were influential in my early feminist thinking. Often it would be through arguing in relation to what was written that my own position as a feminist became clear, particularly with the work of Sheila Jeffries, but also with the heterosexual focus of books such as Germaine Greer's *The Female Eunuch*.

2. *A Political Feeling, I Hope So*, Cubitt Gallery, London, January 30–February 1, 2004. The quote is from the accompanying publication. It continues, "a homemade fantasy of fake differentiation—made from duvet covers": Hedditch, *A Political Feeling, I Hope So*, back cover text.

3. Emma Hedditch, *A Political Feeling, I Hope So*, 2004, accessed June 11, 2021, https://www.cubittartists.org.uk/event/a-political-feeling-i-hope-so.

4. See Weeks, *The Problem with Work*.

5. Schneider, *Performing Remains*, 2.

6. Deutsche, in Deutsche et al., "Feminist Time," 56.

7. See, e.g., Apter, "'Women's Time' in Theory."

8. Kristeva, "Women's Time," 33.

9. Carolyn Dinshaw discussing her book *Getting Medieval*, in Dinshaw et al., "Theorizing Queer Temporalities," 178.

10. For a discussion of Benjamin's theorization of temporality in relation to Brecht's idea of the learning-play, see Ridout, *Passionate Amateurs*, esp. chap. 3. See also Freeman, *Time Binds*, which has an extensive discussion of challenges to what she calls "chrononormativity."

11. Schneider, *Performing Remains*, 2. Other key discussions of reenactment in contemporary art include Jones, "Performance, Live or Dead"; Jones and Heathfield, *Perform, Repeat, Record*; Knaup and Stammer, *Re.act.feminism*; Lütticken, *Life, Once More*; Reckitt, *Not Quite How I Remember It*.

12. See Löwy, "The Opening-Up of History," 115. I take this reference to Löwy's work from Ridout's exploration of theatrical disruptions to the productive time of capital: see Ridout, *Passionate Amateurs*, esp. introduction, chap. 3.

13. Schneider, *Performing Remains*, 7. The Stein reference comes from "Plays," in *Gertrude Stein: Writings and Lectures 1909–1945*, ed. Patricia Meyerowitz (Baltimore: Penguin, 1967), 60–61.

14. Diamond, *Unmaking Mimesis*, 104.

15. See Freeman, *Time Binds*.

16. On the significance of Brecht for feminist theory and art practice in the UK context, see Wilson, *Art Labor, Sex Politics*. See also Pollock, "Screening the Seventies."

17. Mueller, "Learning for a New Society."

18. Brecht, "The German Drama," 80. In this essay, Brecht also highlights the importance of technology, including film, in realizing this new kind of theater.

19. See Brecht, "The German Drama"; Mueller, "Learning for a New Society."

20. The learning-play is "essentially dynamic; its task is to show the world as it changes (and also how it may be changed)": Brecht, "The German Drama," 79.

21. Mueller, "Learning for a New Society," 83.

22. Fore, "*Gestus Facit Saltus*," 168. His quote is taken from Bertolt Brecht, *Gesammelte Werke*, ed. Elisabeth Hauptmann (Frankfurt am Main, Germany: Werkausgabe Edition Suhrkamp, 1968), 22.1, 126, translation by Fore. Sharon Hayes picks up on Brecht's model of "demonstration" in "The Not-Event."

23. Pauline Boudry and Renate Lorenz, email to the author, May 13, 2013.

24. Pauline Boudry and Renate Lorenz, "Salomania," accessed May 20, 2013, http://www.boudry-lorenz.de/texts.

25. Rainer's "NO Manifesto" is in Rainer, "Some Retrospective Notes on a Dance for 10 People and 12 Mattresses Called *Parts of Some Sextets*," 51.

26. Lorenz, in Boudry et al., "Stages," 1999.

27. Burgers, "The Spectral Salome."

28. Matt Hills has posited the figure of the fan scholar as being a fan who employs techniques drawn from academia in their fan production, in distinction to the scholar fan or aca-fan: see Hills, "Street Smarts . . . and the Great British Amateur."

29. Boudry and Lorenz, email to the author.

30. Boudry, "Stages," 2001.

31. Boudry and Lorenz, email to the author.

32. Boudry and Lorenz, email to the author.

33. Pauline Boudry, "In the film *Salomania*, we have two or even three different beginnings," in Boudry, "Stages," 2000.

34. "Wu Tsang rejects the straightforward FTM [female-to-male] identity tagline in favour of being called 'trans feminine but also sometimes . . . a "trans guy" because I am also that. Or a MUCH more straightforward ID would be: butch queen in heels'": Rich, *New Queer Cinema*, 284n23. The quote is from Chris Vargas, "Interview: Wu Tsang," *Original Plumbing*, February 20, 2011, http://www.originalplumbing.com/2011/02/20/chrisblog-interview-wu-tsang.

35. Bryan-Wilson, "Practicing *Trio A*," 60. Bryan-Wilson is quoting from Rainer, "Working round the L-Word."

36. Woolf tells us the text is "based on two papers read to the Arts Society at Newnham and the Odtaa at Girton in October 1928": Woolf, *A Room of One's Own*, 5.

37. Woolf, *A Room of One's Own*, 7.

38. Woolf, *A Room of One's Own*, 112.

39. See Sørensen, "Judith Shakespeare—Undead or Alive?"

40. Thanks to Ian Hunt for suggesting that there is a relationship between the learning-play and consciousness-raising.

41. Ridout, *Passionate Amateurs*. "Image is that wherein what has been comes together in a flash with the now to form a constellation": Benjamin, *The Arcades Project*, 62.

42. Benjamin, "On the Concept of History," 391.

43. Boudry and Lorenz, "Letter to Yvonne Rainer," n.p. They are referring to B. Ruby Rich, "Yvonne Rainer: An Introduction," in Rainer et al., *The Films of Yvonne Rainer* (Bloomington: Indiana University Press, 1989), 4.

44. Boudry and Lorenz, "Letter to Yvonne Rainer."

45. This artwork was originally written up as a score, published in 2014 as part of the exhibition *Poetry Will Be Made by All!*, LUMA Foundation and the 89+ Project, Zurich. A PDF and print-on-demand book can be accessed at http://poetrywillbemadebyall.com /book/discourage. The live performances of the piece were presented in Newcastle and London in 2013 and in Glasgow in 2014, with the filmed version being made in collaboration with the filmmaker Erin Buelow. The film was not intended to take precedence over the live performances but forms the basis for my discussion as I have not seen the live piece.

46. Unless otherwise stated, all quotes are from the film.

47. Faye Green, interview with the author, July 15, 2015.

48. "Transmitter" is the name given to a small group of people who have learned *Trio A* from Rainer and who have been authorized by her to train others to perform the dance: see Catterson, "I Promised Myself I Would Never Let It Leave My Body's Memory"; Giersdorf, "'Trio A' Canonical"; Rainer, "Trio A."

49. Green interview. Green continues, "I don't know what she would think of the work, but I kind of hope she would quite like it, just because I passionately love the dance, and I also wouldn't have been drawn to it if she didn't have a specific way of learning it."

50. Green interview. Phelan describes Anna O's symptoms as "performances in which her body finds time, and more particularly, finds its past": Phelan, "Dance and the History of Hysteria," 97.

51. Diamond, *Unmaking Mimesis*, 49–50.

52. Rainer discusses the paradox of trying to "preserve" *Trio A* in "Trio A." She has also performed the exasperated teacher in Charles Atlas's video portrait *Rainer Variations* (2002), a collaboration between Rainer and Atlas that features a series of reenactments, including a sequence in which Rainer attempts to teach *Trio A* to the Martha Graham impersonator Richard Move in a camp confusion of temporalities and influences.

53. See Jones, in Butler and Jones, "History Makers." See also Buszek, "Conclusion/ Commencement."

54. Bryan-Wilson, "Practicing *Trio A*."

55. Bryan-Wilson, "Practicing *Trio A*," 70.

56. Eichhorn, *The Archival Turn in Feminism*, 9.

CHAPTER FOUR. A FEMINIST CHORUS

1. Hemmings, *Why Stories Matter*.

2. Hemmings, "Citation Tactics," 180. Hemmings's footnote to this definition says that it is drawn from "Word Reference Tools," 239.

3. Hemmings, "Citation Tactics," 181.

4. Hemmings, "Citation Tactics," 181.

5. Hemmings's work has been taken up extensively in art and art history. For example, the first time I was introduced to her work was at a panel organized by Joanne Heath and Alexandra Kokoli on feminist art and curating where nearly every speaker "recited" from Hemmings's book. This was the panel "Recollecting Forward: Feminist Futures in Art Practice, Theory and History," Association of Art Historians Annual Conference, April 10–12, 2014, Royal College of Art, London. See also Horne and Tobin, "An Unfinished Revolution in Art Historiography"; Knaup, "Telling Stories Differently."

6. Victoria Horne explores the modes of "re-visioning" and "reciting" in "Kate Davis." Horne's approach to these modes is slightly different from mine, although there is useful crossover.

7. This event was a Subjectivity and Feminisms Performance Dinner held on February 28, 2014, at Chelsea College of Art, London.

8. Lucy Reynolds, email to the author, November 23, 2017. Reynolds also says that she did not want a professionalized choir, "So the idea of the (female) chorus that you write about, I was consciously trying to work against in a way."

9. Lucy Reynolds, interview with the author, October 20, 2017.

10. Reynolds, *A Feminist Chorus*. See also "A Feminist Chorus: Index," MAP Magazine, accessed February 26, 2018, https://mapmagazine.co.uk/index/a-feminist-chorus, which includes sound and video recordings of the 2014 Glasgow version of *A Feminist Chorus*.

11. The scores for the second and third parts of *A Feminist Chorus* were also recorded separately and installed as sound pieces in the Hen Run at the Glasgow School of Art and at 5 Blythswood Square in Glasgow. The recording of the Hen Run piece can be accessed at "'A Feminist Chorus' Voices at the Glasgow School of Art," MAP Magazine, September 11, 2014, https://mapmagazine.co.uk/lucy-reynolds-feminist-chorus-hen-run.

12. Reynolds, *A Feminist Chorus*, n.p. In the catalog, this section of the project is titled "The Score, Part 1," followed by facsimile pages from the texts chosen to be read aloud.

13. Other versions of *A Feminist Chorus* have taken place as part of "Mackintosh Architecture," Royal Institute of British Architects, London, February 2015; at the Wysing Arts Centre, Cambridge, September 2015; as part of the event "Now You Can Go," Showroom, London, December 2015; as a European Chorus as part of the event "No Fun without EU," Vyner Street, London, 2016; as "Un Refrain Féministe/A Feminist Chorus," at the Grand Action Cinema, Paris, April 2018; and as "A Feminist Chorus: A Tender Map," in the exhibition *A Simultaneity of Stories-so-Far*, Grand Union Gallery and Studios, Birmingham, UK, May–July 2021. Reynolds noted that this is a project that costs very little to perform, which has led to invitations to present it in various contexts: Reynolds interview.

14. This work was the result of a commission from the Women's Art Library to support an artist to work within the collection. This is supported by *Feminist Review* and has been taking place annually since 2009. The vocalists were Barbara Alden, Amy Cunningham, Robin Dann, Huw Hallam, Becky Hardwick, Lara Karady, Toby O'Connor, and Portia Winters.

15. From notes for the press release in the Clare Gasson file, Women's Art Library, special collections, Goldsmiths, London.

16. From "Notes for the River 5 November 2011," Clare Gasson file, Women's Art Library, special collections, Goldsmiths, London.

17. Clare Gasson, email to the author, April 22, 2018.

18. Clare Gasson, interview with the author, July 20, 2017.

19. The various dictionary definitions point to how the chorus can be both the song and the group singing. "The simultaneous utterance of song by a number of people; anything sung by many at once"; "The simultaneous utterance of any vocal sounds, as speech, laughter, etc., by a number of persons; the sounds so uttered": *Oxford English Dictionary*, 2nd ed. (Oxford: Oxford University Press, 1989).

20. Kitto, "The Greek Chorus."

21. See Haigh, "The Chorus," 312–13.

22. See also Judith Butler's thinking about how these gatherings can be political in Butler, "Bodies in Alliance and the Politics of the Street."

23. Arnott, "The Audience and the Chorus," 27.

24. Brecht, "Theatre for Learning," 26.

25. Brecht, "The German Drama," 78.

26. Brecht, "Explanations [about *The Flight of the Lindberghs*]," 38, 40.

27. Reiner Steinweg, *Das Lehrstück: Brechts Theorie einer ästhetischen Erziehung* (PhD diss, Stuttgart, Germany: Metzler, 1969), 23–24, quoted in Mueller, "Learning for a New Society," 86. See the rest of Mueller's essay for a detailed discussion of Brecht's use of radio in the early learning-plays. See also Wirth, "The Lehrstück as Performance."

28. Ridout, *Theatre and Ethics*, 48.

29. "Choral performance, along with athletics and military training . . . , was thus felt to be integral both to 'good bodily formation/melodies' and to 'good order/discipline/law' (eutaxia/eukosmial/euexia/eunomia)": Griffith, "Telling the Tale," 18. See also Zarifi, "Chorus and Dance in the Ancient World."

30. Bodek, *Proletarian Performance in Weimar Berlin*.

31. Bodek, *Proletarian Performance in Weimar Berlin*, 80–136.

32. Bodek, "*Proletarian Performance in Weimar Berlin*, 137–57.

33. Brecht, "Theatre for Learning," 27. Bodek explores lecture series set up by the Communist Party of Germany that educated agitprop troupe performers (as part of a move to educate the party membership in general), with courses on economics, politics, science, history, and literature from a communist perspective. When the permit to hold these lectures in school buildings was rescinded, many artists and authors opened their homes, including Brecht. Bodek proposes, "One of these classes may have inspired Brecht to consider the political implications of agitprop for epic theatre": Bodek, *Proletarian Performance in Weimar Berlin*, 83.

34. Brecht, "Theatre for Learning," 27. This is part of Brecht's contention that theater does not have to hold learning and entertainment as separate, an argument he advances in a number of places in relation to his concept of the learning-play.

35. Mueller, "Learning for a New Society," 88.

36. Mueller, "Learning for a New Society," 90, emphasis added. The quote within the quote is from Steinweg, *Das Lehrstück*, 21.

37. Hemmings, "Citation Tactics," 181.

38. For details of this ongoing project, which has instructions for how to carry out a reading of the text, see the I Want a President website, accessed March 15, 2016, https://iwantapresident.wordpress.com/about. In the other iterations of this project, the text has been translated into the language of the country where it is being read out.

39. Guy, "I Want a Dyke for President." I took part in the initial discussion about this translation but was not part of the final performance.

40. Guy, "I Want a Dyke for President," 43.

41. For the history of this piece and Leonard's thoughts on its re-performance, see Guy, "I Want a Dyke for President." There are links here to the group LTTR, discussed in chapter 1, as it was through the publication of Leonard's text as a postcard in the fifth issue of LTTR that led to the Swedish artists seeing it.

42. See the full text in Guy, "I Want a Dyke for President," 53.

43. Guy explores the content and syntax of Leonard's text in detail in "I Want a Dyke for President."

44. Mitchell, "Concepts of Women's Liberation," 61.

45. This isn't the only precedent for the feminist consciousness-raising group. Other commentators point to various traditions of small group meetings in political movements and, in particular, the influence of the Civil Rights Movement in the United States. See the assessment of the consciousness-raising group in Hesford, *Feeling Women's Liberation*, 179–81. See also the detailed history and analysis in Richardson, "Refusing the Unconscious?"

46. Mitchell, "Concepts of Women's Liberation," 62.

47. This was circulated in numerous formats and was published in Firestone and Koedt, *Notes from the Second Year*. See also the compilation of texts that expand on the practice of consciousness-raising from a range of perspectives, published in Redstockings, *Feminist Revolution*. For a version of instructions aimed at women artists, see West-East Coast Bag (WEB), "Consciousness-Raising Rules."

48. She continues, "We talked and talked for years and in this time we also lived, acted and changed": Rowbotham, *The Past Is before Us*, 297.

49. Rowbotham, *The Past Is before Us*, 298.

50. For suggestions for possible actions coming out of consciousness-raising, see Sarachild, "A Program for Feminist 'Consciousness Raising.'"

51. See, e.g., Gilmore, *Feminist Coalitions*; Hesford, *Feeling Women's Liberation*; Hogan, *The Feminist Bookstore Movement*.

52. See Reynolds, "A Collective Response," and Tobin, "Moving Pictures," as well as other essays in this special issue of *MIRAJ / Moving Image Review and Art Journal*. See also Tobin, "I'll Show You Mine, If You Show Me Yours"; Robinson, "The Early Work of Griselda Pollock." For a contemporary perspective, see Gogarty and Feiss, "Capitalist Life."

53. One of the first prompts for me to start thinking about collaboration was at the invitation of Irene Revell and Clare Louise Stanton when they were planning the event series *Someone Else Can Clean Up This Mess* at Flat Time House, London, March 2014.

54. From "Feminist Duration Reading Group: Hydrofeminism," December 5, 2017, information given as part of the Facebook event post, https://www.facebook.com

/events/532618703757883. There is also a brief mission statement and history: "The Feminist Duration Reading group is dedicated to exploring under-known and under-recognised feminisms from beyond the dominant Anglo-American axis. Started at Goldsmiths, University of London in 2015, since 2016 it has been generously hosted by SPACE in Hackney." Reckitt has published an essay on a project that is linked to this group: see Reckitt, "Generating Feminisms."

55. For more on the letter form, see Grant, "A Letter Sent, Waiting to Be Received."

56. "Historical Documents," in Morgan, *Sisterhood Is Powerful*, 512–56.

57. "Feminist Duration Reading Group."

58. A history of the WOCI is in X Marks the Spot et al., *Human Endeavour*. See also the blog posts on the Rita Keegan Archive project website, including Althea Greenan, "Dr. Althea Greenan on Rita in the Bishop's Library," *Rita Keegan Archive Project* (blog), October 20, 2020, https://ritakeeganarchiveproject.com/2020/10/20/rita-in-the-bishops-library.

59. Since 2020, the WOCI Reading Group has been run by Samia Malik with Alaa Kassim.

60. "Spotlight: Women of Colour Index Reading Group," *Interwoven Histories* (blog), September 7, 2017, https://www.interwovenhistories.co.uk/post/166607968691/woci.

61. Comment from a participant in the WOCI Reading Group, March 1, 2018, Women's Art Library, Goldsmiths, about the previous reading group text. Key quotes from the texts are also reproduced online, which continues their circulation outside the archive and the reading group.

62. Rehana Zaman, telephone interview with the author, January 23, 2018.

63. Michelle Williams Gamaker, email to the author, January 28, 2018.

64. Samia Malik, "WOCI and WOCI Reading Group," unpublished text sent to the author, January 31, 2018.

65. They are also barely present in university teaching. Sara Ahmed discusses her experience of teaching courses that focus on race, including scholarship by Black feminists and feminists of color, in *Living a Feminist Life*, 111–12. The founders of the WOCI Reading Group are taking part in an ongoing conversation to have the group as part of art curricula.

66. Brooklyn Museum, *We Wanted a Revolution: Black Radical Women 1965–85*, April 21–September 17, 2017, https://www.brooklynmuseum.org/exhibitions/we_wanted_a _revolution. This was part of "Year of Yes: Reimagining Feminism" at the Brooklyn Museum to celebrate ten years of the Elizabeth A. Sackler Center for Feminist Art. The Year of Feminism in 2007 was named after the opening of the center and the major touring exhibition *WACK! Art and the Feminist Revolution*: see Jones, "1970/2007."

67. For a contextualization of the UK situation at this time, see Eddo-Lodge, *Why I'm No Longer Talking to White People about Race*; Gilroy, "Conclusion"; Nixon, "Death Work in Venice."

68. *Soul of a Nation: Art in the Age of Black Power*, Tate Modern, London, July 12–October 22, 2017. See also Smith, "Abundant Evidence."

69. *The Place Is Here* was on show at the Van Abbemuseum, Eindhoven, Netherlands, in 2016; an expanded version was at the Nottingham Contemporary Gallery in 2017 before moving to the South London Gallery. "Black Arts Movement" is a contested term, as

it homogenizes a set of practices and debates. For more, see Bailey et al., *Shades of Black*, esp. introduction; Hall, "Assembling the 1980s."

70. See Mills, "Dialectics of Belonging and Strategies of Space." This work was initially titled, "Moments and Connections."

71. For information on the US version of the project, see Leonard, *I Want a President*.

CHAPTER FIVE. CONVERSATIONS AND CONSTELLATIONS

1. See Dorothy Price's excellent essay "Dreaming Has a Share in History," which explores Himid's recent visibility in the art world within the context of a Benjaminian and Blochian analysis of nonsynchronous time. I am indebted to Price's scholarship on Himid and her generosity in sharing her expertise.

2. As in previous chapters, I use the terms *women of color* and *Black women* at different moments. This reflects the shift in language between the 1980s–90s and 2010s. Since the 1980s, particularly in the United Kingdom, *Black* has referred to a political sense of Blackness, including people of African and Asian descent as well as those from other colonized regions. (The term is often capitalized to make this political identity clear.) In recent years, the term *people of color* has come to the fore to describe Black and minority ethnic identities. Hannah Black touches on the histories of both terms in "Lubaina Himid," 14–15. See also Boyce and Price, "Dearly Beloved or Unrequited?"; Mills, "Dialectics of Belonging and Strategies of Space."

3. Lubaina Himid, in Beckett and Himid, "Diasporic Unwrappings," 217.

4. Kelly spent increasing amounts of time in the United States during the 1980s, teaching at the ISP as a visiting artist, until she took on the post of director of studies at the ISP from 1989–96.

5. Parker and Pollock, *Framing Feminism*.

6. I thank Althea Greenan for pointing me toward this conversation and for discussing its soundscape. See Himid and Pollock, *Framing Feminism*.

7. Ahmed, *Living a Feminist Life*, 2.

8. Two of Griselda Pollock's essays feature this image, as does Price, "Retrieving, Remapping, and Rewriting Histories of British Art." See Pollock, "How the Political World Crashes In on My Personal Everyday"; Pollock, "*Revenge*."

9. Himid, artist's statement, in Sulter, "Without Tides, No Maps," 32.

10. Dorothy Price (published under the name Dorothy Rowe) points out this biographical information in her rich and detailed essay on this series: "In *Between the Two My Heart Is Balanced*, the 'ankledeep' women, *dramatis personae* inhabited by Sulter and Himid": Rowe, "Retrieving, Remapping, and Rewriting Histories of British Art," 18. The footnote follows up, "In Maud Sulter's *Jeanne Duval: A Melodrama*, National Gallery of Scotland, Edinburgh, 2003, p. 14, Sulter claims herself as inhabiting both *Between the Two* and *Five*, a point which Himid also confirms in email correspondence, 20 March 2008": Rowe, "Retrieving, Remapping, and Rewriting Histories of British Art," 289–314n83. However, in an oral history conducted for the British Library's National Life Stories series two years earlier, Himid said, "The paintings of the women were not of Maud and I but were certainly of that celebration and kind of exasperation of what happens when two

black women attempt to embark upon a relationship and attempt to change the world. And I suppose a couple of those were more successful than others but they became, there were four, I think four paintings in the end with two black women in them, but they became, I became known as somebody who painted paintings with two black women in them and actually I've only ever painted four in the whole of my life, but that's sort of what's happened": Himid and Dyke, *Lubaina Himid*, track 16.

11. Jane Beckett, Deborah Cherry, and Griselda Pollock have championed Himid's work in their writings since the late 1980s and early 1990s. Pollock bought the painting *Five* and put it on long-term loan to the Leeds Art Gallery. For more details, see Pollock, "How the Political World Crashes In on My Personal Everyday."

12. Himid, artist's statement, in Sulter, "Without Tides, No Maps," 32.

13. Himid, artist's statement, in Sulter, "Without Tides, No Maps," 32.

14. Rowe, "Retrieving, Remapping, and Rewriting Histories of British Art," 295.

15. The American artist Sondra Perry also returned to Turner's painting with her immersive installation *Typhoon Coming On* (2018).

16. Sharpe, "The Wake."

17. Lubaina Himid, quoted in Rowe, "Retrieving, Remapping, and Rewriting Histories of British Art," 304.

18. Lubaina Himid, in Himid and Smith, "Lubaina Himid Study Day."

19. Sulter was more vocal about the importance of their relationship, honoring Himid's excellence as an artist and supportive partner in many texts. As referenced by Dorothy Price, Sulter wrote about her depiction in two of the *Revenge* paintings. In the essay, she celebrates her relationship with Himid and discusses what it means to be someone's muse, making an implicit comparison between Duval and her lover Charles Baudelaire and herself and Himid: see Sulter, "Maud Sulter on Negotiating the Muse."

20. Rowbotham, *The Past Is before Us*, 298. For a longer discussion of consciousness-raising and Rowbotham's analysis of the process, see chapter 4 in this volume.

21. Himid, in Beckett and Himid, "Diasporic Unwrappings," 213.

22. These phrases are from the key for *Thin Black Line(s)*. The map is referred to as *Moments and Connections* in the exhibition catalog.

23. Himid, "Letters to Susan," 25. I explore this epistolary essay in "A Letter Sent, Waiting to Be Received."

24. Mills's work picks up on the centrality of conversations in Himid's practice and formulates an approach to the artist interview through it that is explored in her forthcoming book *Black Women Artists: Voices of Belonging and Strategies of Resistance*. She explores *Thin Black Line(s)* in a great detail in "Dialectics of Belonging and Strategies of Space" and has been very generous in sharing her research with me.

25. Himid, "Mapping"; Himid and Sulter, "Issue Editorial."

26. Cherry, "Suitcase Aesthetics," 800.

27. Himid, in Cherry, "Suitcase Aesthetics," 800. Himid's quote is cited as having come from an email to Cherry in July 2016.

28. Mills, "Dialectics of Belonging and Strategies of Space," 24. Mills is drawing on the discussion of a "shared history of art and ideas" in Mercer, "Introduction," *Cosmopolitan Modernisms* (London: inIVA; Massachusetts: MIT Press, 2005), 6–23.

29. Himid discusses "collaborating" on *We Will Be* with her housemates Marlowe Russell and Sylvia, saying, "They'd come back with drawing pins from the newsagent and they'd stick 'em in this thing and it took, actually the three of us, our first collaborative piece actually, the three of us made that piece": Himid and Dyke, *Lubaina Himid*, 155–56.

30. Kristeva, "Women's Time."

31. Himid, "Mapping," 63.

32. Seeing this work and reading about its initial exhibition brought to mind the queer women who founded Black Lives Matter. See the Winter 2018 issue of *Sinister Wisdom*, "Black Lesbians—We Are the Revolution!," and the work of Alexis Pauline Gumbs.

33. Himid describes this exhibition in detail, alongside *The Thin Black Line* and *5 Black Women*: Himid, "Letters to Susan."

34. An expanded version of *The Place Is Here* that included *A Fashionable Marriage* was on view at the Nottingham Contemporary Gallery in 2017.

35. Thick/er Black Lines was initiated by Rianna Jade Parker, Aurella Yussuf, Hudda Khaireh, and Kariima Ali. Parts of the map are online: Thick/er Black Lines website, accessed November 8, 2020, https://thickerblacklines.com/projects.

36. A project that is outside the time frame covered by this book was the Reading Room for the Turner Prize in 2018, Tate Britain, London, which produced an important contextualization of the artworks on show and was part of the move to actively decolonize museums, galleries, and universities.

37. For a discussion of the colonial histories of mapmaking, see Anderson, "Census, Map, Museum." I thank Lara Perry for talking to me about the difference between maps and constellations and for pointing me toward key references.

38. Benjamin, "N [On the Theory of Knowledge, Theory of Progress]," 462. Agamben explores this section of text in detail in "Threshold or *Tornada*."

39. Agamben, "What Is the Contemporary?," 46.

40. See Himid, "Inside the Invisible." Himid's phrase "Inside the Invisible" plays with the title of Catherine de Zegher's important feminist exhibition *Inside the Visible* (1996). Agamben reframes this notion of (in)visibility in a discussion of the unforgettable that remains within what has been forgotten. He sees Benjaminian now-time as these unforgettable but forgotten moments finding their time in the present: see Agamben, *The Time That Remains*, esp. 39–40.

41. O'Keefe, "Chosen," 224.

42. Hayes, "Footnotes on Genealogy."

43. Hayes, "Footnotes on Genealogy."

44. Kelly, "On Fidelity," 1.

45. Benjamin, "On the Concept of History," 390. Agamben also picks up on this phrase in a section on citation, writing, "Just as through citation, a secret meeting takes place between past generations and ours, so too between the writing of the past and the present a similar kind of meeting transpires; citations function as go-betweens in this encounter": Agamben, "Threshold or *Tornada*," 139. He goes on to link this with Benjamin's writing on how gesture must be citable in Brecthian epic theater.

46. Kelly, "The Dialogic Imagination," 11.

47. This online discussion has recently been given its own webpage with the title taken

from the Walter Benjamin quote: Kelly, "A Secret Agreement." I thank Flora Dunster for pointing out this email conversation to me.

48. Kelly, "On the Passage of a Few People through a Rather Brief Period of Time." The event that this text was published in relation to took place on May 22, 2015, at the Tate Modern, London. She says that the title of the work "refer[s] to the film made by Guy Debord in 1959, and in particular, to the notion that what is directly lived in the past reappears in the present as an image frozen in the distance." What Kelly doesn't mention is that it was also used as the title of an exhibition about the Situationists International curated by Peter Wollen, at the ICA, London, in 1989. Wollen and Kelly knew each other, and Kelly is featured in *Riddles of the Sphinx*, the film Wollen and Laura Mulvey made in 1977.

49. Kelly has been particularly active in archiving her own history through various exhibition catalogs. See, e.g., Carson and Kelly, "Excavating *Post-partum Document*." For an excellent overview of feminist and artistic communities in London in the 1970s and Kelly's work, see Wilson, *Art Labor, Sex Politics*. Kelly has also been interviewed as part of the British Library's Sisterhood and After: The Women's Liberation Oral History Project (C1420/58, 2012). This longer interview gives details regarding elements of her history that are less discussed but inform her feminist politics, including her experience living in Beirut in the late 1960s. She also discusses this in the online conversation.

50. Kelly invited Meleko Mokgosi, Ryan Kelly and Brennan Gerard, Sharon Hayes, Alexandro Segade, Michelle Dizon, and Wu Tsang to contribute to the conversation about the 2000s. For more on the Whitney ISP, including a short reflection by Kelly, see Buchloh et al., "The Whitney Independent Study Program at 50."

51. This is discussed in Kelly, "The Dialogic Imagination." See also Kelly, "Mary Kelly."

52. Wu Tsang, in Kelly, "A Secret Agreement."

53. Kelly, "A Secret Agreement." She continues, "Although, the project's aim is neither inclusiveness, nor objectivity, I would like to gather a representative archive of statements that, perhaps, could be read symptomatically as well as historically or theoretically. What has become most legible in the response to *Circa 1968*, so far, calls attention to this possibility. As Walter Benjamin suggested, 'There is a secret agreement between past generations and the present one.' And it is this implication of historical memory that I would like to explore in the online discussion": Kelly, "A Secret Agreement."

54. Every Ocean Hughes (formerly known as Emily Roysdon), email to the author, April 27, 2008. As mentioned in chapter 1, Hughes's *Ecstatic Resistance* project (2009), which began with a pair of "sister" exhibitions, articulates Kelly's interest in political communities through contemporary queer networks.

55. Mary Kelly, in Geyer et al., "In Conversation with Mary Kelly and Wu Ingrid Tsang," 67.

56. Kelly and Jolly, *Mary Kelly Interviewed by Margaretta Jolly*, 61.

57. Kelly et al., "The Dialogic Imagination."

58. See, e.g., Collective Creativity, *Redefining Legacy: Navigating "Emerging" Practice as Artists of Colour*, 2015, video, https://vimeo.com/123412348. For details of the archive, see the Making Histories Visible website, accessed June 9, 2020, http://makinghistories visible.com/about.

59. Kelly, "The Dialogic Imagination," 10.

60. Kelly, in Geyer et al., "In Conversation with Mary Kelly and Wu Ingrid Tsang," 68.

61. Kelly, "The Dialogic Imagination," 10–11.

62. Kelly, "The Dialogic Imagination," 11.

63. Himid has also engaged explicitly with Walter Benjamin's theories of history in a series of kanga paintings made in 2016. For more on these see Price, "Dreaming Has a Share in History."

64. Himid, "Letters to Susan," 25.

CONCLUSION

1. Farjeon, *Elsie Piddock Skips in Her Sleep*. All quotes in the following paragraph are from this edition, which is not paginated.

2. Ahmed, *Willful Subjects*. Ahmed relates her discussion of willful subjects, mostly women and girls, to her famous figure of the "feminist killjoy." She says, "To be identified as willful is to become a problem": Ahmed, *Willful Subjects*, 3. She also describes her book as a willfulness archive that queers the will and thinks about the relationship between willfulness and unhappiness, as well as necessity. She ends her introduction with a quote from Gloria Anzaldúa, who features later in this conclusion. Willful women—both friends and famous feminists read about in books—have sustained me throughout my life. As Ahmed explores, willfulness is often accompanied by the pain or unpredictability of the willful act, which accounts for some of the rawness of feminist politics and conversation.

3. See Federici, *Caliban and the Witch*; Federici, "Feminism and the Politics of the Common in an Era of Primitive Accumulation."

4. In this story, the Fairy Skipping-Master, Andy-Spandy, teaches Piddock fairy skips after learning about her legendary skills. He gives her a magic rope that she has to put away when she gets too tall to use it, but she brings it out again for her never-ending feat of skipping to hold the common ground. Here fairies, girls, and old women join to make a powerful community.

5. Federici, *Caliban and the Witch*, 11.

6. This need for a tradition or history is explored in Woolf, *A Room of One's Own*. It is powerfully theorized more broadly in Warner, *Publics and Counterpublics*. I thank James Boaden and Gaby Moser for reminding me of this.

7. Mitchell, "Women."

8. See, e.g., Shulamith Firestone's famous rendering of the history of American feminism, as well as overarching history of the relationship between men and women. She coined the phrase "fifty-year ridicule" to describe the period between the fight for suffrage in the late nineteenth and early twentieth centuries and the beginning of the Women's Liberation Movement in the late 1960s: see Firestone, *The Dialectic of Sex*, 24. She describes this period as including "a blackout of feminist history to keep women hysterically circling through a mass of false solutions": Firestone, *The Dialectic of Sex*, 28.

9. Modleski, "Some Functions of Feminist Criticism," quoting Shoshana Felman, *The Literary Speech Act: Don Juan with J. L. Austin, or Seduction in Two Languages*, translated by Catherine Porter (Ithaca, NY: Cornell University Press, 1983), 77.

10. Modleski, "Some Functions of Feminist Criticism," 20–21.

11. Modleski, "Some Functions of Feminist Criticism," 14.

12. Modleski, "Some Functions of Feminist Criticism," 14.

13. Woolf, *A Room of One's Own*, quoted, with alterations, in Walker, "In Search of Our Mothers' Gardens," 407.

14. Walker, "In Search of Our Mothers' Gardens," 408.

15. De Lauretis, "The Practice of Sexual Difference and Feminist Thought in Italy," 2. I thank Helena Reckitt for introducing me to this book through the Feminist Duration Reading Group (discussed in chapter 4), which engaged with the Milan Women's Bookstore Collective in detail.

16. De Lauretis, "The Practice of Sexual Difference and Feminist Thought in Italy," 2.

17. Milan Women's Bookstore Collective, *Sexual Difference*, 26. I thank Helena Reckitt for sending me this quotation.

18. De Lauretis, "The Practice of Sexual Difference and Feminist Thought in Italy," 2.

19. Benedict Anderson's notion of the imagined community does not completely capture how a feminist community has to be imagined across time and space as well as within an actual community of people: Anderson, *Imagined Communities*.

20. Rich, "When We Dead Awaken," 21. Rich also discusses Woolf's *A Room of One's Own* in this essay and her own position in relation to it.

21. Anzaldúa, "Speaking in Tongues," 165.

22. Anzaldúa, "Speaking in Tongues," 170.

23. There is an echo of Anzaldúa's exhortation in *Three Guineas*, where Woolf says, "The daughters of educated men have always done their thinking from hand to mouth; not under green lamps at study tables in the cloisters of secluded colleges. They have thought while they stirred the pot, while they rocked the cradle." She continues, "It falls to us now to go on thinking": Woolf, *Three Guineas*, 243.

24. Moraga and Anzaldúa, "Introduction," xxiv.

25. Mitchell, "*Women*, xviii.

26. Moraga and Anzaldúa, "Introduction," xxv.

27. Woolf writes about the importance of financial security and the odd jobs available to middle-class women in the early twentieth century: Woolf, *A Room of One's Own*, 39. I discuss this at more length in Grant, "Learning and Playing." For a recent analysis of how Woolf's thoughts can be brought to bear on queer studies and its position within the university, see Brim, *Poor Queer Studies*.

28. hooks, "Women Artists"; Le Guin, "The Fisherwoman's Daughter"; Milan Women's Bookstore Collective, *Sexual Difference*; Walker, "One Child of One's Own."

29. Julia Bryan-Wilson, response in Foster, "A Questionnaire on 'The Contemporary,'" 4.

30. Bryan-Wilson, response in Foster, "A Questionnaire on 'The Contemporary,'" 4.

31. Woolf, *A Room of One's Own*, 7.

32. Cvetkovich, *Depression*, 20.

33. Cvetkovich, *Depression*, 22. Cvetkovich is referencing Sedgwick, *Tendencies*, 3–19.

34. For an influential analysis of this situation, see Fisher, *Capitalist Realism*.

35. Woolf repeats the phrase "the new college, the poor college" a number of times:

Woolf, *Three Guineas*, 199. Juliet Mitchell describes the commitment to sharing education within the Women's Liberation Movement, writing, "One tenet of the movement was that women who had had their educational potential realized should offer services to women who hadn't. . . . Ann Oakley and I made it a founding strategy of the three collections of essays we edited on women": Mitchell and Shin, "Juliet Mitchell." See also Rich, "Claiming an Education." For details of Lorde's teaching career and how essential it was to her both politically and creatively, see Lorde and Rich, "An Interview with Audre Lorde."

36. Lorde, in Lorde and Rich, "An Interview with Audre Lorde," 719.

37. In her diary entry for Tuesday, January 20, 1931, Woolf says, "I have this moment, while having my bath, conceived an entire new book—a sequel to *A Room of One's Own*": Woolf, *A Writer's Diary*, 166.

38. Woolf, *Three Guineas*, 201.

39. Woolf, *Three Guineas*, 199.

40. Woolf, *Three Guineas*, 202–3.

41. Woolf provides a footnote citing the source of this. However, it does not contain the flammable image that Woolf evokes when imagining a different kind of feminist education.

42. Woolf, *Three Guineas*, 204. It was Mignon Nixon who first brought this section to my attention in her inaugural professorial lecture.

43. Woolf, *Three Guineas*, 208.

44. Molesworth, "How to Install Art as a Feminist," 507, 512.

45. In the same conversation with Deutsche (who asks that generations be seen as relations rather than entities), Miwon Kwon, Ulrike Müller, and Mignon Nixon put the issue of feminist generations within the context of pedagogical relations and colonial narratives: Deutsche et al., "Feminist Time," 56.

46. Moten, in Harney and Moten, "The General Antagonism," 110; Harney, in Harney and Moten, "The General Antagonism," 112.

47. Harney and Moten, "Debt and Study," 67.

48. Harney and Moten, "Debt and Study," 68.

49. Harney and Moten, "Debt and Study," 68.

50. For their use of the term *rehearsal*, see Harney and Moten, "The General Antagonism," esp. 107, 110. There are striking similarities with Brecht's discussion of the learning-play.

51. Hochschild, "Inside the Clockwork of Male Careers."

52. Hochschild, "Inside the Clockwork of Male Careers," 254.

53. Harney and Moten give numerous lists of those who populate the undercommons. One of them figures the university as "Maroon communities of composition teachers, mentorless graduate students, adjunct Marxist historians, out or queer management professors, state college ethnic studies departments, closed-down film programs, visa-expired Yemeni student newspaper editors, historically black college sociologists, and feminist engineers. And what will the university say of them? It will say they are unprofessional": Harney and Moten, *The Undercommons*, 30.

54. See Harney and Moten, *The Undercommons*; Weeks, *The Problem with Work*. My former colleague, the late Mark Fisher, circulated a text entitled "SPACE TO THINK"

(sent via email on October 2, 2013) that echoes much of what I recount here. It was also written in the creative collapse that followed his permanent appointment at Goldsmiths, which coincidentally occurred at the same time as mine. He was an articulate spokesperson for much of these personally experienced but nonetheless structural issues around creativity and the university. I mourn his absence both personally and intellectually.

55. Winterson, *Why Be Happy When You Could Be Normal?*, 40.

56. Winterson, *Why Be Happy When You Could Be Normal?*, 42.

57. Winterson, *Why Be Happy When You Could Be Normal?*, 43.

Adkins, Lisa, and Maryanne Dever. "Feminism Re-engaged." *Australian Feminist Studies* 30, no. 83 (2015): 1–2. doi:10.1080/08164649.2015.1011486.

Agamben, Giorgio. "Threshold or *Tornada*." In *The Time That Remains: A Commentary on the Letter to the Romans*, 138–45. Stanford, CA: Stanford University Press, 2005.

Agamben, Giorgio. "What Is the Contemporary?" In *What Is an Apparatus? and Other Essays*, edited by Stefan Pedatella, translated by David Kishik and Stefan Pedatella, 39–54. Stanford, CA: Stanford University Press, 2009. (Originally published in Italian in 2008 as "Che cos'è il contemporaneo.")

Ahaiwe Sowinski, Ego. "Lambeth Women's Project." Paper presented at "Don't Break Down, Break Out: A Symposium," Raven Row, London, 2017. http://www.ravenrow.org/media/67.

Ahaiwe Sowinski, Ego. "Rebuilding Momentum during Global Pandemic Times: Rita Keegan Archive Project (RKAP)." *Rita Keegan Archive Project*, July 13, 2020. https://ritakeeganarchiveproject.com/2020/07/13/rebuilding-momentum-during-a-global-pandemic-times-rita-keegan-archive-project-rkap.

Ahaiwe Sowinski, Ego, and Nazmia Jamal. "Love and Affection: The Radical Possibilities of Friendship between Women of Colour." In *To Exist Is to Resist: Black Feminism in Europe*, edited by Akwugo Emejulu and Francesca Sobande, 129–40. London: Pluto, 2019.

Ahmed, Sara. "Feminist Killjoys (and Other Willful Subjects)." *Scholar and Feminist Online* 3, no. 8 (Summer 2010). http://sfonline.barnard.edu/polyphonic/print_ahmed.htm.

Ahmed, Sara. *Living a Feminist Life*. Durham, NC: Duke University Press, 2017.

Ahmed, Sara. *Willful Subjects*. Durham, NC: Duke University Press, 2014.

Allen, Felicity, ed. *Education*. Documents of Contemporary Art Series. Cambridge, MA: MIT Press, 2011.

Amos, Valerie, Gail Lewis, Amihna Mama, and Pratibha Parmar, eds. "Many Voices, One Chant: Black Feminist Perspectives." Special issue, *Feminist Review* 17, no. 1 (November 1984). https://journals-sagepub-com.gold.idm.oclc.org/toc/fer/17/1.

Amos, Valerie, and Pratibha Parmar. "Challenging Imperial Feminism." *Feminist Review* 17, no. 1 (November 1, 1984): 3–19. doi:10.1057/fr.1984.18.

Anderson, Benedict. "Census, Map, Museum." In *Imagined Communities: Reflections on the Origin and Spread of Nationalism*, rev. ed., 163–85. London: Verso, 1983.

Anderson, Benedict. *Imagined Communities: Reflections on the Origin and Spread of Nationalism*, rev. ed. London: Verso, 1983.

Anderson, Fiona. "'Monks of the Dead River': David Wojnarowicz's *Rimbaud in New York* (1978–79)," research seminar, Kings College, London, 2009.

Anderson, Joel. *Theatre and Photography*. London: Palgrave Macmillan, 2015.

Anim-Addo, Joan, Yasmin Gunaratnam, and Suzanne Scafe, eds. "Black British Feminisms." Special issue, *Feminist Review* 108 (2014). https://journals-sagepub-com.gold .idm.oclc.org/toc/fer/108/1.

Anzaldúa, Gloria. "Speaking in Tongues: A Letter to 3rd World Women Writers" (1980). In *This Bridge Called My Back: Writings by Radical Women of Color*, 2nd ed., edited by Cherríe Moraga and Gloria Anzaldúa, 165–74. New York: Kitchen Table: Women of Color Press, 1983.

Applin, Jo. "Generational Objects: Ida Applebroog's History of Feminism." *Oxford Art Journal* 40, no. 1 (2017): 133–51. doi:10.1093/oxartj/kcx001.

Apter, Emily. "'Women's Time' in Theory." *differences* 21, no. 1 (January 1, 2010): 1–18. doi:10.1215/10407391-2009-013.

Arakistain, Xavier, and Emily Roysdon. "Art We Still Trespassing? A Trans-Atlantic Conversation between Emily Roysdon and Xavier Arakistain." In *Otherwise: Imagining Queer Feminist Art Histories*, edited by Amelia Jones and Erin Silver, 226–35. Manchester, UK: Manchester University Press, 2016.

Aranda, Julieta, Brian Kuan Wood, and Anton Vidokle, eds. *What Is Contemporary Art?* Berlin: Sternberg, 2010.

Armstrong, Carol. "'Global Feminisms' and 'WACK!'" *Artforum International* 45, no. 9 (2007): 360–62.

Arnott, Peter D. "The Audience and the Chorus." In *Public and Performance in the Greek Theatre*, 5–43. London: Routledge, 1989.

Arnott, Peter D. *Public and Performance in the Greek Theatre*. London: Routledge, 1989.

Arns, Inke, and Gabriele Horn. *History Will Repeat Itself: Strategies of Re-enactment in Contemporary (Media) Art and Performance*. Frankfurt am Main: Revolver, 2007. Exhibition catalog.

Arondekar, Anjali, Ann Cvetkovich, Christina B. Hanhardt, Regina Kunzel, Tavia Nyong'o, Juana María Rodríguez, Susan Stryker, Daniel Marshall, Kevin P. Murphy, and Zeb Tortorici. "Queering Archives: A Roundtable Discussion." *Radical History Review* 2015, no. 122 (2015): 211–31. doi:10.1215/01636545-2849630.

Bacon-Smith, Camille. *Enterprising Women: Television Fandom and the Creation of Popular Myth*. Philadelphia: University of Pennsylvania Press, 1992.

Bail, Kathy, ed. *DIY Feminism*. St. Leonards, Australia: Allen and Unwin, 1996.

Bailey, David A., Ian Baucom, and Sonia Boyce, eds. *Shades of Black: Assembling Black Arts in 1980s Britain*. Durham, NC: Duke University Press, 2005.

Baldry, H. C. *The Greek Tragic Theatre*. London: Chatto and Windus, 1974.

Barr, Marleen S. *Feminist Fabulation: Space/Postmodern Fiction*. Iowa City: University of Iowa Press, 1992.

Barrie, Pauline, and Katy Deepwell. "Founding Feminism: Women's Workshop, Artists Union and Women Artists Slide Library." *n.paradoxa* 38 (July 2016): 56–65.

Batalion, Judith. "Mad Mothers, Fast Friends, and Twisted Sisters: Women's Collaborations in the Visual Arts, 1970–2000." PhD diss., Courtauld Institute of Art, 2007.

Beckett, Jane. "Lubaina Himid's *Plan B*: Close up Magic and Tricky Allusions." In *Difference and Excess in Contemporary Art: The Visibility of Women's Practice*, edited by Gillian Perry, 156–77. Oxford: Blackwell, 2004.

Beckett, Jane, and Lubaina Himid. "Diasporic Unwrappings—Lubaina Himid in Conversation with Jane Beckett." In *Women, the Arts and Globalization Eccentric Experience*, edited by Marsha Meskimmon and Dorothy Rowe, 190–221. Manchester: Manchester University Press, 2015.

Benjamin, Andrew E., ed. *Walter Benjamin and History*. Walter Benjamin Studies Series. London: Continuum, 2005.

Benjamin, Walter. *The Arcades Project*. Edited by Rolf Tiedemann. Translated by Howard Eiland and Kevin McLaughlin. Cambridge, MA: Harvard University Press, 1999.

Benjamin, Walter. *Illuminations*. London: Pimlico, 1999.

Benjamin, Walter. "N [On the Theory of Knowledge, Theory of Progress]." In *The Arcades Project*, edited by Rolf Tiedemann, translated by Howard Eiland and Kevin McLaughlin, 456–88. Cambridge, MA: Harvard University Press, 1999.

Benjamin, Walter. "On the Concept of History" (1940). In *Selected Writings, 4: 1938–1940*, edited by Michael William Jennings and Howard Eiland, 389–400. Cambridge, MA: Harvard University Press, 1996.

Berardini, Andrew. "Wack! Art and the Feminist Revolution." *Art Review*, no. 11 (May 2007): 124–25.

Berlant, Lauren. *Cruel Optimism*. Durham, NC: Duke University Press, 2011.

Bhabha, Homi K. *The Location of Culture*. London: Routledge, 1994.

Bishop, Claire. *Artificial Hells: Participatory Art and the Politics of Spectatorship*. Brooklyn: Verso Books, 2012.

Black, Hannah. "Lubaina Himid: Revision." *Afterall* 43 (March 2017): 6–17. doi:10.1086/692549.

Blocker, Jane. *Becoming Past: History in Contemporary Art*. Minneapolis: University of Minnesota Press, 2016.

Bly, Lyz, and Kelly Wooten, eds. *Make Your Own History: Documenting Feminist and Queer Activism in the 21st Century*. Los Angeles: Litwin, 2012.

Bodek, Richard. *Proletarian Performance in Weimar Berlin: Agitprop, Chorus, and Brecht*. Columbia, SC: Camden House, 1997.

Bordowitz, Gregg. "Repetition and Change: The Film Installations of Pauline Boudry and Renate Lorenz." *Afterall* 31 (September 2012): 12–25. doi:10.1086/668919.

Boudry, Pauline, Anja Casser, and Renate Lorenz, eds. *Aftershow*. Berlin: Sternberg, 2014. Exhibition catalog.

Boudry, Pauline, Jessica Dorrance, Elizabeth Freeman, Renate Lorenz, and Andrea Thal. "Stages: A Conversation between Andrea Thal, Pauline Boudry and Renate Lo-

renz, Berlin, September 2010." In *Temporal Drag: Pauline Boudry and Renate Lorenz,
1998–2003*. Ostfildern, Germany: Hatje Cantz, 2011.

Boudry, Pauline, Jessica Dorrance, Elizabeth Freeman, Renate Lorenz, and Andrea Thal.
Temporal Drag: Pauline Boudry and Renate Lorenz. Ostfildern, Germany: Hatje Cantz,
2011.

Boudry, Pauline, and Renate Lorenz. "Letter to Yvonne Rainer." In *Aftershow*, edited by
Pauline Boudry, Anja Casser, and Renate Lorenz, np. Berlin: Sternberg, 2014. Exhibition catalog.

Boudry, Pauline, and Renate Lorenz. *Salomania/Toxic Play in Two Acts*. London: South
London Gallery and Electra, 2012.

Boyce, Sonia, and Dorothy Price. "Dearly Beloved or Unrequited? To Be 'Black' in Art's
Histories." Special issue, *Art History* 44, no. 3 (June 2021): 462-480.

Bradley, Rizvana. "Introduction: Other Sensualities." *Women and Performance* 24, nos.
2–3 (September 2, 2014): 129–33. doi:10.1080/0740770X.2014.976494.

Brecht, Bertolt. *Bertolt Brecht on Film and Radio*. Edited and translated by Marc Silberman. London: Methuen, 2000.

Brecht, Bertolt. *Brecht on Theatre: The Development of an Aesthetic*, 2nd ed. Edited by
John Willet. Translated by John Willett. London: Methuen Drama, 1964.

Brecht, Bertolt. *Brecht Sourcebook*. Edited by Carol Martin and Henry Bial. London:
Routledge, 2000.

Brecht, Bertolt. "Explanations [about *The Flight of the Lindberghs*]" (1929). In *Bertolt
Brecht on Film and Radio*, edited and translated by Marc Silberman, 38–40. London:
Methuen, 2000.

Brecht, Bertolt. "The German Drama: Pre-Hitler." In *Brecht on Theatre: The Development
of an Aesthetic*, 2nd ed., edited and translated by John Willet, 77–81. London: Methuen
Drama, 1964. (Originally published in the *New York Times*, November 24, 1935.)

Brecht, Bertolt. *The Measures Taken and Other Lehrstücke*. Edited by John Willett. Translated by Ralph Manheim, Carl Mueller, and Wolfgang Sauerlander. New York: Arcade,
2001.

Brecht, Bertolt. "Theatre for Learning" (1961). In *Brecht Sourcebook*, edited by Carol Martin and Henry Bial, translated by Edith Anderson, 21–28. London: Routledge, 2000.

Brim, Matt. *Poor Queer Studies: Confronting Elitism in the University*. Durham, NC:
Duke University Press, 2020.

Brodsky, Judith K., and Ferris Olin. "Stepping out of the Beaten Path: Reassessing the
Feminist Art Movement." *Signs* 33, no. 2 (January 1, 2008): 329–42. doi:10.1086/518276.

Brooke, Alice, Giulia Smith, and Rózsa Farkas, eds. *Re-materialising Feminism*. London:
Arcadia Missa, 2014.

Broude, Norma, and Mary D. Garrard, eds. *The Power of Feminist Art: The American
Movement of the 1970s, History and Impact*. London: Thames and Hudson, 1994.

Brown, Wendy. *Politics out of History*. Princeton, NJ: Princeton University Press, 2001.

Bryan-Wilson, Julia. "Openings: Sharon Hayes." *Artforum International* 44, no. 9 (May
2006). https://www.artforum.com/print/200605/openings-sharon-hayes-10867.

Bryan-Wilson, Julia. "Practicing *Trio A*." *October* 140 (May 2012): 54–74. doi:10.1162
/OCTO_a_00089.

Bryan-Wilson, Julia. "Repetition and Difference: LTTR." *Artforum* 44, no. 10 (2006): 109–10.

Bryan-Wilson, Julia. "Sharon Hayes Sounds Off." *Afterall* 38 (Spring 2015): 16–27. doi:10 .1086/681283.

Bryan-Wilson, Julia, and Sharon Hayes. "We Have a Future: An Interview with Sharon Hayes." *Grey Room*, no. 37 (Fall 2009): 78–93. doi: 10.1162/grey.2009.1.37.78.

Buchloh, Benjamin, Hal Foster, Mary Kelly, and Gregg Bordowitz et al. "The Whitney Independent Study Program at 50." *October* 168 (Spring 2019). https://www.mitpress journals.org/toc/octo/168.

Burgers, Johannes Hendrikus. "The Spectral Salome: Salomania and Fin-de-Siècle Sexology and Racial Theory." In *Decadence, Degeneration, and the End: Studies in the European Fin de Siècle*, edited by Marja Härmänmaa and Christopher Nissen, 165–82. New York: Palgrave Macmillan, 2014.

Burin, Yula, and Ego Ahaiwe Sowinski. "Sister to Sister: Developing a Black British Feminist Archival Consciousness." *Feminist Review* 108, no. 1 (November 1, 2014): 112–19. doi:10.1057/fr.2014.24.

Burton, Johanna, and Natalie Bell, eds. *Trigger: Gender as a Tool and a Weapon*. New York: New Museum, 2017. Exhibition catalog.

Buszek, Maria Elena. "Conclusion/Commencement." In *Pin-Up Grrrls: Feminism, Sexuality, Popular Culture*, 355–64. Durham, NC: Duke University Press, 2006.

Buszek, Maria Elena. *Pin-Up Grrrls: Feminism, Sexuality, Popular Culture*. Durham, NC: Duke University Press, 2006.

Butler, Connie, and Amelia Jones. "'History Makers': Amelia Jones in Conversation with Connie Butler, Curator of *WACK!*" *Frieze*, no. 105 (March 2007): 134–39.

Butler, Connie, Amelia Jones, and Maura Reilly. "Feminist Curating and the 'Return' of Feminist Art." In *The Feminism and Visual Culture Reader*, edited by Amelia Jones, 31–44. London: Routledge, 2003.

Butler, Cornelia H., and Lisa Gabrielle Mark, eds. *WACK! Art and the Feminist Revolution*. Los Angeles: Museum of Contemporary Art, 2007. Exhibition catalog.

Butler, Judith. "Bodies in Alliance and the Politics of the Street." In *Notes toward a Performative Theory of Assembly*, 66–98. Mary Flexner Lectures. Cambridge, MA: Harvard University Press, 2015.

Carson, Juli, and Mary Kelly. "Excavating *Post-Partum Document*." In *Rereading Post-Partum Document. Mary Kelly*, edited by Mary Kelly and Sabine Breitwieser, 183–234. Vienna: Generali Foundation, 1999.

Castagnini, Laura, and Rose Gibbs. "Restaging the Collective: A Conversational Review of Sharon Hayes' *In My Little Corner of the World, Anyone Would Love You* and Alex Martinis Roe's *Our Future Network*." *Un Magazine*, 2016. http://unprojects.org.au /magazine/issues/issue-10-2/restaging-the-collective.

Castro, J. G. "'Global Feminisms': The Elizabeth A. Sackler Center for Feminist Art, Brooklyn." *Sculpture* 26, no. 10 (December 2007): 72–73.

Catterson, Pat. "I Promised Myself I Would Never Let It Leave My Body's Memory." *Dance Research Journal* 41, no. 2 (Winter 2009): 3–11.

Chakrabarty, Dipesh. *Provincializing Europe: Postcolonial Thought and Historical Difference*, new ed. Princeton, NJ: Princeton University Press, 2008.

Chan, Audrey, Alexandra Grant, and Elana Mann. "Rupture and Continuity in Feminist Re-performance." *Afterall* 33 (June 2013): 38–45. doi:10.1086/672018.

Cherry, Deborah. "Suitcase Aesthetics: The Making of Memory in Diaspora Art in Britain in the Later 1980s." *Art History* 40, no. 4 (2017): 784–807. doi:10.1111/1467-8365.12338.

Cohen, Rachel Beth. "Researching Difference and Diversity within Women's Movements: Sisterhood and After." *Women's Studies International Forum* 35 (May 2012): 138–40. doi:10.1016/j.wsif.2012.03.010.

Cook, Roger. "Speech Acts." *Frieze*, January 3, 2010 "Speech Acts: An Interview with American Artist Sharon Hayes." *Frieze* 129, March 1, 2010. https://frieze.com/article/speech-acts.

Cooper, Dennis, and Steve Lafreniere. "Dennis Cooper on Zine Days (They Were Good) and Transgressive Blogs (There Is Such a Thing)." *Vice*, January 2008. https://www.vice.com/en/article/vdzdb9/dennis-cooper-v14n12.

Coote, Anna, and Beatrix Campbell. *Sweet Freedom: The Struggle for Women's Liberation*. Oxford: Basil Blackwell, 1987.

Craig, Lauren. "Busy Vitrine: Collective // Condensed \\ Curation." *Rita Keegan Archive Project* (blog), July 27, 2020. https://ritakeeganarchiveproject.com/2020/07/27/busy-vitrine-collective-condensed-curation.

Crone, Bridget, ed. *The Sensible Stage: Staging and the Moving Image*. Bristol, UK: Picture This, 2012.

Crow, Barbara A., ed. *Radical Feminism: A Documentary Reader*. New York: New York University Press, 2000.

Cuir, Raphael. "Wack! Art and the Feminist Revolution." Translated by L.-S. Torgoff. *Art Press*, no. 336 (August 2007): 76–78.

Cvetkovich, Ann. *An Archive of Feelings: Trauma, Sexuality, and Lesbian Public Cultures*. Durham, NC: Duke University Press, 2003.

Cvetkovich, Ann. *Depression: A Public Feeling*. Durham, NC: Duke University Press, 2012.

Cvetkovich, Ann, and Allyson Mitchell. "A Girl's Journey into the Well of Forbidden Knowledge." *GLQ* 17, no. 4 (2011): 603–18. doi:10.1215/10642684-1302388.

Danbolt, Mathias, Jane Rowley, and Louise Wolthers, eds. *Lost and Found: Queerying the Archive*. Copenhagen: Museum Tusculanum Press, 2010.

Deepwell, Katy, ed. *New Feminist Art Criticism: Critical Strategies*. Manchester, UK: Manchester University Press, 1995.

de la Durantaye, Leland. *Giorgio Agamben: A Critical Introduction*. Stanford, CA: Stanford University Press, 2009.

de Lauretis, Teresa. "The Practice of Sexual Difference and Feminist Thought in Italy: An Introductory Essay." In *Sexual Difference: A Theory of Social-Symbolic Practice*, by Milan Women's Bookstore Collective, translated by Teresa de Lauretis and Patricia Cicogne, 1–25. Bloomington: Indiana University Press, 1990.

Derrida, Jacques. *Archive Fever: A Freudian Impression*. Chicago: University of Chicago Press, 1996.

Derrida, Jacques. *Specters of Marx: The State of the Debt, the Work of Mourning, and the New International*. New York: Routledge, 2006.

Deutsche, Rosalyn. "Not-Forgetting: Mary Kelly's Love Songs." *Grey Room*, no. 24 (Summer 2006): 26–37. doi:10.1162/grey.2006.1.24.26.

Deutsche, Rosalyn, Aruna D'Souza, Miwon Kwon, and Ulrike Müller, Mignon Nixon, and Senam Okudzeto. "Feminist Time: A Conversation." *Grey Room* 31 (2008): 32–67. doi:10.1162/grey.2008.1.31.32.

Diamond, Elin. "Brechtian Theory/Feminist Theory: Toward a Gestic Feminist Criticism." *TDR/The Drama Review* 32, no. 1 (1988): 82–94. doi:10.2307/1145871.

Diamond, Elin. *Unmaking Mimesis: Essays on Feminism and Theater*. London: Routledge, 1997.

Dick, Leslie, Sharon Hayes, Mary Kelly and Kerry Tribe. "Something Like a Bridge: A Conversation on the Occasion of 'Gloria: Another Look at Feminist Art in the 1970s.'" *X-TRA* 5, no. 3 (Spring 2003): 10–15. https://www.x-traonline.org/article/something-like-a-bridge.

Didi-Huberman, Georges. "Before the Image, before Time: The Sovereignty of Anachronism." In *Compelling Visuality: The Work of Art in and out of History*, edited by Claire J. Farago and Robert Zwijnenberg, 31–44. Minneapolis: University of Minnesota Press, 2003.

Didi-Huberman, Georges. *Confronting Images: Questioning the Ends of a Certain History of Art*. University Park: Pennsylvania State University Press, 2005.

Dimitrakaki, Angela. "Researching Culture/s and the Omitted Footnote: Questions on the Practice of Feminist Art History" (2004). In *The Feminism and Visual Culture Reader*, 2nd ed., edited by Amelia Jones, 360–68. London: Routledge, 2010.

Dimitrakaki, Angela. "The 2008 Effect." *Third Text* 27, no. 4 (July 1, 2013): 579–88. doi:10.1080/09528822.2013.810890.

Dinshaw, Carolyn. *Getting Medieval: Sexualities and Communities, Pre- and Postmodern*. Durham, NC: Duke University Press, 1999.

Dinshaw, Carolyn. *How Soon Is Now? Medieval Texts, Amateur Readers, and the Queerness of Time*. Durham, NC: Duke University Press, 2012.

Dinshaw, Carolyn. "Temporalities." In *Middle English*, edited by Paul Strohm, 107–23. Oxford Twenty-First Century Approaches to Literature. Oxford: Oxford University Press, 2007.

Dinshaw, Carolyn, Lee Edelman, Roderick A. Ferguson, Carla Freccero, Elizabeth Freeman, Judith Halberstam, Annamarie Jagose, Christopher Nealon, and Nguyen Tan Hoang. "Theorizing Queer Temporalities: A Roundtable Discussion." *GLQ* 13, nos. 2–3 (2007): 177–95. doi:10.1215/10642684-2006-030.

Dumbadze, Alexander Blair, and Suzanne Hudson, eds. *Contemporary Art: 1989 to the Present*. Chichester, UK: John Wiley and Sons, 2013.

Duncombe, Stephen. *Notes from Underground: Zines and the Politics of Alternative Culture*. Haymarket Series. London: Verso, 1997.

Eagleton, Terry. "Brecht and Rhetoric." In *Against the Grain: Essays 1975–1985*, 167–72. London: Verso, 1986.

Eddo-Lodge, Reni. *Why I'm No Longer Talking to White People about Race*. London: Bloomsbury, 2017.

Ehrenreich, Barbara, Elizabeth Hess, and Gloria Jacobs. "Beatlemania: Girls Just Want to Have Fun." In *The Adoring Audience: Fan Culture and Popular Media*, edited by Lisa A. Lewis, 84–106. London: Routledge, 1992.

Eichhorn, Kate. *The Archival Turn in Feminism: Outrage in Order*. Philadelphia: Temple University Press, 2013.

Eichhorn, Kate. "The Archive Function." *Australian Feminist Studies* 30, no. 83 (2015): 37–49. doi:10.1080/08164649.2014.998452.

Farjeon, Eleanor. *Elsie Piddock Skips in Her Sleep* (1937). London: Walker, 2001.

Federici, Silvia. *Caliban and the Witch: Women, the Body and Primitive Accumulation*. Brooklyn: Autonomedia, 2004.

Federici, Silvia. "Feminism and the Politics of the Common in an Era of Primitive Accumulation" (2010). In *Revolution at Point Zero: Housework, Reproduction, and Feminist Struggle*, 138–48. Oakland, CA: PM, 2012.

Federici, Silvia. *Revolution at Point Zero: Housework, Reproduction, and Feminist Struggle*. Oakland, CA: PM, 2012.

Ferguson, Roderick A. "Of Sensual Matters: On Audre Lorde's 'Poetry Is Not a Luxury' and 'Uses of the Erotic.'" *WSQ: Women's Studies Quarterly* 40 (January 2013): 295–300. doi:10.1353/wsq.2013.0017.

Firestone, Shulamith. *The Dialectic of Sex: The Case for Feminist Revolution*. 1970; repr., London: Verso, 2015.

Firestone, Shulamith, and Anne Koedt, eds. *Notes from the Second Year: Women's Liberation; Major Writings of the Radical Feminists*. New York: Radical Feminism, 1970. https://library.duke.edu/digitalcollections/wlmpc_wlmms01039.

Fisher, Mark. *Capitalist Realism: Is There No Alternative?* Ropley, UK: O Books, 2009.

Fiske, John. "The Cultural Economy of Fandom." In *The Adoring Audience: Fan Culture and Popular Media*, edited by Lisa A. Lewis, 30–49. London: Routledge, 1992.

Fletcher, Annie. "On Feminism (Through a Survey of Several Recent Exhibitions)." *Afterall* 17 (Spring 2008): 109–13.

Fore, Devin. "*Gestus Facit Saltus*: Bertolt Brecht's Fear and Misery of the Third Reich." In *Realism after Modernism: The Rehumanization of Art and Literature*, 133–85. October Book. Cambridge, MA: MIT Press, 2012.

Foster, Hal, "An Archival Impulse." *October* 110 (October 2004): 3–22. doi:10.1162/0162287042379847.

Foster, Hal, ed. "A Questionnaire on 'The Contemporary.'" *October* 130 (Fall 2009). doi:10.1162/octo.2009.130.1.3.

Foucault, Michel. "Nietzsche, Genealogy, History" (1971). In *Language, Counter-Memory, Practice: Selected Essays and Interviews*, edited by Donald F. Bouchard, translated by Donald F. Bouchard and Sherry Simon. Ithaca, NY: Cornell University Press, 1977.

Fox, Oriana. "Once More with Feeling: An Abbreviated History of Feminist Performance Art." *Feminist Review* 96, no. 1 (October 2010): 107–21. doi:10.1057/fr.2010.11.

Fox, Oriana, ed. *The Moon: Women Watch Themselves Being Looked At*. Forest Hill, UK: CT, 2009.

Fraden, Rena. *Imagining Medea: Rhodessa Jones and Theater for Incarcerated Women*. Chapel Hill: University of North Carolina Press, 2001.

Freeman, Elizabeth. "Packing History, Count(er)ing Generations." *New Literary History* 31, no. 4 (January 2000): 727–44. doi:10.1353/nlh.2000.0046.

Freeman, Elizabeth. *Time Binds: Queer Temporalities, Queer Histories*. Durham, NC: Duke University Press, 2011.

Gallop, Jane. *Anecdotal Theory*. Durham, NC: Duke University Press, 2002.

Getsy, David, ed. *Queer*. Documents of Contemporary Art Series. London: Whitechapel Gallery, 2016.

Geyer, Andrea, and Sharon Hayes. *History Is Ours*. Edited by Cynthia Chris. Heidelberg, Germany: Kunstmuseum St. Gallen, 2009. Exhibition catalog.

Geyer, Andrea, Sharon Haytes, Mary Kelly, and Wu Tsang. "In Conversation with Mary Kelly and Wu Ingrid Tsang." In *History Is Ours*, edited by Cynthia Chris, 66–73. Heidelberg, Germany: Kunstmuseum St. Gallen, 2009. Exhibition catalog.

Giersdorf, Jens Richard. "'Trio A' Canonical." *Dance Research Journal* 41, no. 2 (Winter 2009): 19–24.

Gilmore, Stephanie, ed. *Feminist Coalitions: Historical Perspectives on Second-Wave Feminism in the United States*. Urbana: University of Illinois Press, 2008.

Gilroy, Paul. "Conclusion." In *Parallel Perspectives: Transnational Curation in London 2015–16*, 55–63. London: Kings College London, 2017.

Gogarty, Larne Abse, and Ellen Feiss. "Capitalist Life." In *Re-materialising Feminism*, edited by Alice Brooke, Giulia Smith, and Rózsa Farkas, xxxix–xlvi. London: Arcadia Missa, 2014.

Gordon, Avery. *Ghostly Matters: Haunting and the Sociological Imagination*. Minneapolis: University of Minnesota Press, 2011.

Gouma-Peterson, Thalia, and Patricia Mathews. "The Feminist Critique of Art History." *Art Bulletin* 69, no. 3 (September 1987): 326–57. doi:10.1080/00043079.1987.10788437.

Grant, Catherine. "A Letter Sent, Waiting to Be Received: Queer Correspondence, Feminism and Black British Art." *Women: A Cultural Review* 30, no. 3 (2019): 297–318. doi:10.1080/09574042.2019.1658510.

Grant, Catherine. "Learning and Playing: Re-enacting Feminist Histories." In *Feminism and Art History Now: Radical Critiques of Theory and Practice*, edited by Victoria Horne and Lara Perry, 260–81. London: I. B. Tauris, 2019.

Grant, Catherine. "Reaching for the Moon: Replaying Feminist Art and Activism." In *The Moon: Women Watch Themselves Being Looked At*, edited by Oriana Fox, 16–17. Forest Hill, UK: CT, 2009.

Grant, Catherine. "Returning to *Riddles*." In *Women Artists, Feminism and the Moving Image*, edited by Lucy Reynolds, 57–72. London: Bloomsbury Academic, 2019.

Greaney, Patrick. *Quotational Practices: Repeating the Future in Contemporary Art*. Minneapolis: University of Minnesota Press, 2014.

Green, Faye. *NOT TO DISCOU[RAGE] YOU*. Zurich: LUMA Foundation, 2014. http://poetrywillbemadebyall.com/book/discourage.

Greenan, Althea. "How Images Are the Making of the Women's Art Library/Make." *Art Libraries Journal* 32, no. 1 (January 2007): 4–9. doi:10.1017/S0307472200014796.

Griffith, Mark. "'Telling the Tale': A Performing Tradition from Homer to Pantomime." In *The Cambridge Companion to Greek and Roman Theatre*, edited by Marianne Macdonald and J. Michael Walton, 13–35. Cambridge: Cambridge University Press, 2007.

Grindon, Gavin. "Book Bloc: A Collective Development." *The Occupied Times* (blog), August 8, 2014. https://theoccupiedtimes.org/?p=13145.

Gronlund, Melissa. "Global Feminisms: New Directions in Contemporary Art." *Art Review*, no. 13 (August 2007): 139.

Groom, Amelia, ed. *Time*. Documents of Contemporary Art. London: Whitechapel Gallery, 2013.

Gumbs, Alexis Pauline. "Communiqué to White Ally Heaven." In "Tribute to Adrienne Rich," special issue, *Sinister Wisdom* 87 (Fall 2012): 85–99.

Gumbs, Alexis Pauline. "Eternal Summer of the Black Feminist Mind." In *Make Your Own History: Documenting Feminist and Queer Activism in the 21st Century*, edited by Lyz Bly and Kelly Wooten, 59–68. Los Angeles: Litwin, 2012.

Gumbs, Alexis Pauline. *M Archive: After the End of the World*. Durham, NC: Duke University Press, 2018.

Gumbs, Alexis Pauline. "We Can Learn to Mother Ourselves: The Queer Survival of Black Feminism 1968–1996." PhD diss., Duke University, Durham, NC, 2010. https://dukespace.lib.duke.edu/dspace/bitstream/handle/10161/2398/D_Gumbs_Alexis_a_201005.pdf?sequence=1.

Guy, Laura. "I Want a Dyke for President: Sounding out Zoe Leonard's Manifesto for Art History's Feminist Futures." In *Feminism and Art History Now: Radical Critiques of Theory and Practice*, edited by Victoria Horne and Lara Perry, 41–62. London: I. B. Tauris, 2019.

Haigh, Arthur E. "The Chorus." In *The Attic Theatre: A Description of the Stage and Theatre of the Athenians, and of the Dramatic Performances at Athens, with Facsimiles and Illustrations*, 3rd ed., revised and in part rewritten by A. W. Picard-Cambridge, 285–322. Oxford: Clarendon, 1907.

Halberstam, Jack. *Gaga Feminism: Sex, Gender and the End of Normal*. Queer Action/Queer Ideas. Boston: Beacon, 2012.

Halberstam, Jack. *In a Queer Time and Place: Transgender Bodies, Subcultural Lives*. New York: New York University Press, 2005.

Halberstam, Jack. "What's That Smell? Queer Temporalities and Subcultural Lives." In *In a Queer Time and Place: Transgender Bodies, Subcultural Lives*, 265–319. New York: New York University Press, 2005.

Hall, Stuart. "Assembling the 1980s: The Deluge—and After." In *Shades of Black : Assembling Black Arts in 1980s Britain*, edited by David A Bailey, Ian Baucom, and Sonia Boyce, 1–20. Durham: Duke University Press, 2005.

Hall, Stuart. "Constituting an Archive." *Third Text* 15, no. 54 (2001): 89–92. doi:10.1080/09528820108576903.

Haraway, Donna J. "Reading Buchi Emecheta: Contests for 'Women's Experience' in Women's Studies." In *Simians, Cyborgs, and Women: The Reinvention of Nature*, 107–24. New York: Routledge, 1991.

Haraway, Donna J. *SF: Speculative Fabulation and String Figures/SF: Spekulative Fabulation und String-Figuren*. Ostfildern, Germany: Hatje Cantz, 2011.

Haraway, Donna J. "Situated Knowledges: The Science Question in Feminism and the Privilege of Partial Perspective." In *Simians, Cyborgs, and Women: The Reinvention of Nature*, 575–99. New York: Routledge, 1991.

Harding, Alex. "Whoever Heard of a Black Artist? Britain's Hidden Art History." BBC, July 30, 2018. https://learningonscreen.ac.uk/ondemand/index.php/prog/11C2175A?bcast=127196371.

Harney, Stefano, and Fred Moten. "Debt and Study." In *The Undercommons: Fugitive Planning and Black Study*, 58–68. Wivenhoe, UK: Minor Compositions, 2013.

Harney, Stefano, and Fred Moten. "The General Antagonism: An Interview with Stevphen Shukaitis." In *The Undercommons: Fugitive Planning and Black Study*, 100–59. Wivenhoe, UK: Minor Compositions, 2013.

Harney, Stefano, and Fred Moten. *The Undercommons: Fugitive Planning and Black Study*. Wivenhoe, UK: Minor Compositions, 2013.

Harvey, Sylvia. "Whose Brecht? Memories for the Eighties." *Screen* 23, no. 1 (1982): 45–59. doi:10.1093/screen/23.1.45.

Hayden, Malin Hedlin, and Jessica Sjöholm, eds. *Feminisms Is Still Our Name: Seven Essays on Historiography and Curatorial Practices*. Newcastle, UK: Cambridge Scholars, 2010.

Hayes, Sharon. "Certain Resemblances: Notes on Performance, Event, and Political Images." In *On Horizons: A Critical Reader in Contemporary Art*, edited by Maria Hlavajova, Simon Sheikh, and Jill Winder, 84–99. Utrecht: Basis voor Actuele Kunst, 2011.

Hayes, Sharon. "Footnotes on Genealogy." In *Trigger: Gender as a Tool and a Weapon*, edited by Johanna Burton and Natalie Bell, n.p. New York: New Museum, 2017.

Hayes, Sharon. "The Not-Event." *Art Journal* 70, no. 3 (Fall 2011): 45–46.

Hayes, Sharon. "Temporal Relations." In *Not Now! Now! Chronopolitics, Art and Research*, edited by Renate Lorenz, 56–71. Berlin: Sternberg, 2014.

Hayes, Sharon, and Yvonne Rainer. "Familiarity, Irony, Ambivalence: An Email Conversation between Sharon Hayes and Yvonne Rainer." In *Work the Room: A Handbook of Performance Strategies*, edited by Ulrike Müller, 31–48. Berlin: B_books, 2006.

Heartney, Eleanor. "Global Feminisms: New Directions in Contemporary Art: Brooklyn Museum." *Art Press*, no. 336 (August 2007): 78–79.

Heartney, Eleanor. "Worldwide Women." *Art in America* 95, no. 6 (June–July 2007): 154–65.

Heath, Stephen. "Lessons from Brecht." *Screen* 15, no. 2 (1974): 103–28. doi:10.1093 /screen/15.2.103.

Hebron, Micol. "Wack! Art and the Feminist Revolution." *Flash Art* 40, no. 254 (June 2007): 91–92.

Hedditch, Emma. "Now That We Are Persons." *Mute* (Winter–Spring 2004). http:// www.metamute.org/editorial/articles/now-we-are-persons.

Hedditch, Emma. *A Political Feeling, I Hope So*. London: Cubitt Gallery, 2004. Exhibition catalog.

Hemmings, Clare. "Citation Tactics." In *Why Stories Matter: The Political Grammar of Feminist Theory*, 161–90. Durham, NC: Duke University Press, 2011.

Hemmings, Clare. "Telling Feminist Stories." *Feminist Theory* 6, no. 2 (August 2005): 115–39. doi:10.1177/1464700105053690.

Hemmings, Clare. *Why Stories Matter: The Political Grammar of Feminist Theory*. Durham, NC: Duke University Press, 2011.

Henry, Astrid. *Not My Mother's Sister: Generational Conflict and Third-Wave Feminism*. Bloomington: Indiana University Press, 2004.

Herb Alpert Award in the Arts. "Interview with Sharon Hayes for the Herb Alpert Award in the Arts." 2013. https://herbalpertawards.org/artist/early-formations.

Hesford, Victoria. *Feeling Women's Liberation*. Durham, NC: Duke University Press, 2013.

Hills, Matt. *Fan Cultures*. London: Routledge, 2002.

Hills, Matt. "Street Smarts . . . and the Great British Amateur: The Fan-Scholar." In *Fan Cultures*, 16–20. London: Routledge, 2002.

Himid, Lubaina. "Fragments." *FAN/Feminist Arts News* 2, no. 8 (1988): 8–9.

Himid, Lubaina. "Inside the Invisible: For/Getting Strategy." In *Shades of Black: Assembling Black Arts in 1980s Britain*, edited by David A. Bailey, Ian Baucom, and Sonia Boyce, 41–47. Durham, NC: Duke University Press, 2005.

Himid, Lubaina. "In the Woodpile." *FAN/Feminist Art News* 3, no. 4 (1990): 2–3.

Himid, Lubaina. "Letters to Susan." In *Thin Black Line(s)*, edited by Lubaina Himid, 7–26. Preston, UK: Making Histories Visible Project, Centre for Contemporary Art, University of Central Lancashire, 2011. Exhibition catalog.

Himid, Lubaina. "Mapping: A Decade of Black Women Artists 1980–1990." In *Passion: Discourses on Blackwomen's Creativity*, edited by Maud Sulter, 63–72. Hebden Bridge, UK: Urban Fox, 1990.

Himid, Lubaina, ed. *The Thin Black Line*. London: Institute of Contemporary Art, 1985.

Himid, Lubaina, ed. *Thin Black Line(s)*. Preston, UK: Making Histories Visible Project, Centre for Contemporary Art, University of Central Lancashire, 2011. Exhibition catalog.

Himid, Lubaina, and Anna Dyke. *Lubaina Himid*. Sound. National Life Stories: Artists' Lives, 2006. British Library Sound Archive, C466/249. https://sounds.bl.uk/Oral-history/Art/021M-C0466X0249XX-0001V0.

Himid, Lubaina, and Griselda Pollock. *Framing Feminism: ICA Talk*. Sound. Institute of Contemporary Arts, London, 1988. British Library Sound Archive, C95/330. https://sounds.bl.uk/Arts-literature-and-performance/ICA-talks/024M-C0095X0330XX-0100V0.

Himid, Lubaina, and Marlene Smith. "Lubaina Himid Study Day." Video posted by Black Artists and Modernism and Iniva, London, June 20, 2016. https://vimeo.com/191454808.

Himid, Lubaina, and Maud Sulter, eds. "Issue Editorial." *FAN/Feminist Arts News* 2, no. 8 (Autumn 1988): 3.

Himid, Lubaina, and Maud Sulter, eds. "Passion—Blackwomen's Creativity of the African Diaspora." Special issue, *FAN/Feminist Arts News* 2, no. 8 (Autumn 1988).

Himid, Lubaina, Maud Sulter, and Jill Morgan. *Lubaina Himid: Revenge*. Rochdale, UK: Rochdale Art Gallery, 1992. Exhibition catalog.

Hinrichs, Heide, Jo-ey Tang, and Elizabeth Haines, eds. *Shelf Documents: Art Library as Practice*. Berlin: B_books, 2021.

Hochschild, Arlie Russell. "Inside the Clockwork of Male Careers" (1973). In *The Commercialization of Intimate Life: Notes from Home and Work*, 227–54. Berkeley: University of California Press, 2003.

Hoetger, Megan. "Re-performance: History as an Experience to Be Had." *X-TRA* 15, no. 1 (Fall 2012). http://x-traonline.org/article/re-performance-history-as-an-experience-to-be-had.

Hogan, Kristen. *The Feminist Bookstore Movement: Lesbian Antiracism and Feminist Accountability*. Durham, NC: Duke University Press, 2016.

Holly, Michael Ann. "The Melancholy Art." *Art Bulletin* 89, no. 1 (March 2007): 7–17. doi:10.1080/00043079.2007.10786323.

hooks, bell. *Teaching to Transgress: Education as the Practice of Freedom*. New York: Routledge, 1994.

hooks, bell. "Women Artists: The Creative Process." In *Art on My Mind: Visual Politics*, 125–32. New York: New Press, 1995.

Horne, Victoria. "Kate Davis: Re-visioning Art History after Modernism and Postmodernism." *Feminist Review* 110, no. 1 (May 2015): 34–54. doi:10.1057/fr.2015.12.

Horne, Victoria, and Lara Perry, eds. *Feminism and Art History Now: Radical Critiques of Theory and Practice*. London: I. B. Tauris, 2019.

Horne, Victoria, and Amy Tobin. "An Unfinished Revolution in Art Historiography, or How to Write a Feminist Art History." *Feminist Review* 107, no. 1 (July 2014): 75–83. doi:10.1057/fr.2014.7.

Howard, J. P., and Amber Atiya, eds. "Black Lesbians—We Are the Revolution!" *Sinister Wisdom* 107 (Winter 2018).

Iles, Chrissie, ed. *Sharon Hayes*. New Haven, CT: Yale University Press, 2012. Exhibition catalog.

Jenkins, Henry. *Textual Poachers: Television Fans and Participatory Culture*. London: Routledge, 1992.

Jenkins, Henry, Shoshanna Green, and Cynthia Jenkins. "Normal Female Interest in Men Bonking: Selections from the Terra Nostra Underground and Strange Bedfellows." In *Fans, Bloggers, and Gamers: Exploring Participatory Culture*, 9–38. New York: New York University Press, 2006.

Jensen, Joli. "Fandom as Pathology: The Consequences of Characterization." In *The Adoring Audience: Fan Culture and Popular Media*, edited by Lisa A. Lewis, 9–29. London: Routledge, 1992.

Johnston, Claire, and Paul Willemen. "Brecht in Britain: The Independent Political Film (On 'The Nightcleaners')." *Screen* 16 (1975). doi:10.1093/screen/16.4.101.

Jones, Amelia, "'The Artist Is Present': Artistic Re-enactments and the Impossibility of Presence." *TDR/The Drama Review* 55, no. 1 (2011): 16–45. doi:10.1162/DRAM_a_00046.

Jones, Amelia, ed. *A Companion to Contemporary Art since 1945*. Malden, MA: Blackwell, 2006.

Jones, Amelia, ed. *The Feminism and Visual Culture Reader*, 2nd ed. London: Routledge, 2010.

Jones, Amelia. "Feminism, Incorporated: Reading 'Postfeminism' in an Anti-Feminist Age." In *The Feminism and Visual Culture Reader*, edited by Amelia Jones, 314–28. London: Routledge, 2003. (Originally published in *Afterimage* 20, no. 5 [December 1992]: 10–15.)

Jones, Amelia. "1970/2007: The Return of Feminist Art." *X-TRA* 10, no. 4 (Summer 2008). http://x-traonline.org/article/19702007-the-return-of-feminist-art.

Jones, Amelia, ed. "Performance, Live or Dead." *Art Journal* 70, no. 3 (Fall 2011): 32–63.

Jones, Amelia. "'Presence' in Absentia: Experiencing Performance as Documentation." *Art Journal* 56, no. 4 (1997): 11–18. doi:10.1080/00043249.1997.10791844.

Jones, Amelia. *Seeing Differently: A History and Theory of Identification and the Visual Arts*. London: Routledge, 2012.

Jones, Amelia, ed. *Sexual Politics: Judy Chicago's Dinner Party in Feminist Art History*. Los Angeles: Armand Hammer Museum of Art and Cultural Center, 1996.

Jones, Amelia, and Adrian Heathfield. *Perform, Repeat, Record: Live Art in History*. Bristol, UK: Intellect, 2012.

Jones, Amelia, and Erin Silver, eds. *Otherwise: Imagining Queer Feminist Art Histories*. Manchester, UK: Manchester University Press, 2016.

Joreen. "Trashing: The Dark Side of Sisterhood." 1976. https://www.jofreeman.com /joreen/trashing.htm.

Kearney, Mary Celeste. "The Missing Links: Riot Grrrl—Feminism—Lesbian Culture." In *Sexing the Groove: Popular Music and Gender*, edited by Sheila Whiteley, 207–29. London: Routledge, 1997.

Keating, AnaLouise, ed. *Entre Mundos/Among Worlds: New Perspectives on Gloria E. Anzaldúa*. New York: Palgrave Macmillan, 2008.

Kelly, Mary. "Concentric Pedagogy: Toward an Ethics of the Observer." *October* 168 (May 2019): 43–46. doi:10.1162/octo_a_00345.

Kelly, Mary. "The Dialogic Imagination: An Introduction." In *Dialogue*, edited by Mary Kelly and Cecilia Widenheim, 10–13. Stockholm: Iaspis, 2011.

Kelly, Mary. *Imaging Desire*. Cambridge, MA: MIT Press, 1996.

Kelly, Mary, ed. *Interim*. New York: New Museum of Contemporary Art, 1990.

Kelly, Mary. "Mary Kelly in Conversation with Matilde Digmann." *NY Arts Magazine*, February 2008. http://www.nyartsmagazine.com/index.php?Itemid=714&id=66807 &option=com_content&task=view.

Kelly, Mary. "Mary Kelly: Projects: 1973–2010." Video posted by Stony Brook University, October 25, 2014. https://vimeo.com/95007951.

Kelly, Mary. "On Fidelity: Art, Politics, Passion and Event." In *Feminisms Is Still Our Name: Seven Essays on Historiography and Curatorial Practices*, edited by Malin Hedlin Hayden and Jessica Sjöholm, 1–10. Newcastle, UK: Cambridge Scholars, 2010.

Kelly, Mary. "On the Passage of a Few People through a Rather Brief Period of Time." Tate Modern, 2015. http://www.tate.org.uk/whats-on/tate-modern/talks -and-lectures/mary-kelly-conversation-hans-ulrich-obrist/on-passage-few.

Kelly, Mary. "(P)age 49: On the Subject of History." In *New Feminist Art Criticism: Critical Strategies*, edited by Katy Deepwell, 147–52. Manchester, UK: Manchester University Press, 1995.

Kelly, Mary, ed. "A Secret Agreement: An Era Defined by the Events of 1968." Tate Modern, 2015. http://www.tate.org.uk/whats-on/tate-modern/talks-and-lectures /mary-kelly-conversation-hans-ulrich-obrist/secret-agreement.

Kelly, Mary, and Sabine Breitwieser, eds. *Rereading Post-Partum Document: Mary Kelly*. Vienna: Generali Foundation, 1999.

Kelly, Mary, Sharon Hayes, Jane Jin Kaisen, Andrea Geyer, and Dont Rhine. "The Dialogic Imagination." In *Dialogue*, edited by Mary Kelly and Cecilia Widenheim, 14–31. Stockholm: Iaspis, 2011.

Kelly, Mary, and Margaretta Jolly. *Mary Kelly Interviewed by Margaretta Jolly*. Sisterhood and After: The Women's Liberation Oral History Project. London, 2012. British Library Sound Archive, C1420/58.

Kelly, Mary, and Ian White. "The Body Politic." *Frieze*, no. 107 (May 2007): 131–35. https://frieze.com/article/body-politic.

Kelly, Mary, and Cecilia Widenheim, eds. *Dialogue*. Stockholm: Iaspis, 2011.

Kitto, H. D. F. "The Greek Chorus." *Educational Theatre Journal* 8, no. 1 (1956): 1–8. doi:10.2307/3203909.

Knaup, Bettina. "Telling Stories Differently: Strategies of Appropriating and Disseminating Stories of Feminist and Queer Performance." In *Re.act.feminism: A Performing Archive*, edited by Bettina Knaup and Beatrice Stammer, 71–81. Nuremberg: Verlag für Moderne Kunst, 2014.

Knaup, Bettina, and Beatrice Stammer, eds. *Re.act.feminism: A Performing Archive*. Nuremberg: Verlag für Moderne Kunst, 2014. Exhibition catalog.

Kolbowski, Silvia, Mignon Nixon, Mary Kelly, Hal Foster, Liz Kotz, Simon Leung and Ayisha Abraham. "A Conversation on Recent Feminist Art Practices." *October* 71 (Winter 1995): 49–69. https://www.jstor.org/stable/778741.

Kraus, Chris. *I Love Dick*. London: Serpent's Tail, 2016.

Kristeva, Julia. "Women's Time." Translated by Alice Jardine and Harry Blake. *Signs* 7, no. 1 (1981): 13–35. https://www.jstor.org/stable/3173503.

Lambert, Carrie. "Moving Still: Mediating—Yvonne Rainer's *Trio A*." *October* 89 (1999): 87–112.

Lambert-Beatty, Carrie. "Make-Believe: Parafiction and Plausibility." *October* 129 (August 2009): 51–84. doi:10.1162/octo.2009.129.1.51.

Latimer, Tirza True, ed. "Conversations on Queer Affect and Queer Archives." *Art Journal* 72, no. 2 (2013): 34–105. doi:10.1080/00043249.2013.10791029.

Latimer, Tirza True. "Improper Objects: Performing Queer/Feminist Art/History." In *Otherwise: Imagining Queer Feminist Art Histories*, edited by Amelia Jones and Erin Silver, 93–109. Manchester, UK: Manchester University Press, 2016.

Lee, Hermione. *Virginia Woolf*. London: Vintage, 1997.

Le Guin, Ursula K. "The Fisherwoman's Daughter" (1988). In *Dancing at the Edge of the World: Thoughts on Words, Women, Places*, 212–37. New York: Grove, 1989.

Leonard, Marion. *Gender in the Music Industry: Rock, Discourse, and Girl Power*. Aldershot, UK: Ashgate, 2007.

Leonard, Zoe, ed. *I Want a President: Transcript of a Rally*. New York: Art Resources Transfer, 2016. http://www.artresourcestransfer.org/#art/book/33.

Lewis, Lisa A., ed. *The Adoring Audience: Fan Culture and Popular Media*. London: Routledge, 1992.

Ley, Graham. *The Theatricality of Greek Tragedy: Playing Space and Chorus*. Chicago: University of Chicago Press, 2007.

Lippard, Lucy. "Issues and Commentary: No Regrets." *Art in America* (July 2007): 75–79.

London Women's Liberation Workshop. *Shrew*. London: Women's Liberation Workshop, Shrew Collective, 1969.

Lord, Catherine. "Their Memory Is Playing Tricks on Her: Notes toward a Calligraphy of Rage." In *WACK! Art and the Feminist Revolution*, edited by Cornelia H. Butler and Lisa Gabrielle Mark, 440–57. Los Angeles: Museum of Contemporary Art, 2007.

Lord, Catherine, and Richard Meyer. *Art and Queer Culture*. London: Phaidon, 2013.

Lorde, Audre. "Poetry Is Not a Luxury" (1977). In *Sister Outsider: Essays and Speeches*, 36–39. 1984; repr., Berkeley: Crossing, 2007.

Lorde, Audre. *Sister Outsider: Essays and Speeches*. 1984; repr., Berkeley: Crossing, 2007.

Lorde, Audre, and Adrienne Rich. "An Interview with Audre Lorde." *Signs* 6, no. 4 (July 1981): 713–36. doi:10.1086/493842.

Lorenz, Renate, ed. *Not Now! Now! Chronopolitics, Art and Research*. Schriften der Akademie der Bildenden Künste Wien, vol. 15. Berlin: Sternberg, 2014.

Love, Heather. *Feeling Backward: Loss and the Politics of Queer History*. Cambridge, MA: Harvard University Press, 2009.

Love, Heather, and Sarah E. K. Smith. *Deirdre Logue and Allyson Mitchell: I'm Not Myself at All*. Kingston, ON: Agnes Etherington Art Centre, 2015. Exhibition catalog.

Lovelace, Carey. "Feminist Group Shows: Girls, Girls, Girls." *Art in America* (July 2007): 89–93.

Löwy, Michael. *Fire Alarm: Reading Walter Benjamin's "On the Concept of History."* Translated by Chris Turner. New York: Verso, 2005.

Löwy, Michael. "The Opening-Up of History." In *Fire Alarm: Reading Walter Benjamin's "On the Concept of History,"* translated by Chris Turner, 107–16. New York: Verso, 2005.

Lütticken, Sven, ed. *Life, Once More: Forms of Reenactment in Contemporary Art*. Rotterdam: Witte de With, Center for Contemporary Art, 2005.

Lütticken, Sven. "Planet of the Remakes." *New Left Review* 25 (2004): 103–20.

Macdonald, Marianne, and J. Michael Walton, eds. *The Cambridge Companion to Greek and Roman Theatre*. Cambridge: Cambridge University Press, 2007.

Malik, Samia, and Elizabeth Haines. "Reading as Activism: The WOCI Reading Group." In *Shelf Documents: Art Library as Practice*, edited by Heide Hinrichs, Jo-ey Tang, and Elizabeth Haines, 172–94. Berlin: B_books, 2021.

Mason-John, Valerie, and Ann Khambatta. *Making Black Waves: Lesbians Talk*. London: Scarlet, 1993.

Mastai, Judith, ed. *Social Process, Collaborative Action: Mary Kelly: 1970–75*. Vancouver: Charles H. Scott Gallery, Emily Carr Institute of Art and Design, 1997. Exhibition catalog.

McBean, Sam. *Feminism's Queer Temporalities*. Abingdon, UK: Routledge, 2015.

McBean, Sam. "The Queer Network Novel." *Contemporary Literature* 60, no. 3 (2019): 427–52. doi:10.3368/cl.60.3.427.

McBean, Sam. "Queer Temporalities." *Feminist Theory* 14, no. 1 (April 1, 2013): 123–28. doi:10.1177/1464700112468575.

McCallum, E. L., and Mikko Tuhkanen, eds. *Queer Times, Queer Becomings*. Albany: State University of New York Press, 2011.

McFadden, Jane. "Wack! Art and the Feminist Revolution." *Modern Painters* 19, no. 5 (June 2007): 112.

McFarland, James. *Constellation: Friedrich Nietzsche and Walter Benjamin in the Now-Time of History*. New York: Fordham University Press, 2013.

Méndez, Lourdes. "Exclusionary Genealogies." *n.paradoxa* (2016): 91–96.

Meskimmon, Marsha, and Dorothy Rowe, eds. *Women, the Arts and Globalization Eccentric Experience*. Manchester, UK: Manchester University Press, 2015.

Meyer, Richard. "Feminism Uncovered." *Artforum International* (Summer 2007): 211–12, 538.

Meyer, Richard. *What Was Contemporary Art?* Cambridge, MA: MIT Press, 2013.

Milan Women's Bookstore Collective. *Sexual Difference: A Theory of Social-Symbolic Practice*. Translated by Patricia Cicogne and Teresa de Lauretis. Bloomington: Indiana University Press, 1990.

Miller, Leigh Anne. "The Year in Feminist Art." *Art in America* 95, no. 3 (March 2007): 37.

Millner-Larsen, Nadja, and Gavin Butt. "Introduction: The Queer Commons." *GLQ* 24, no. 4 (2018): 399–419. doi:10.1215/10642684-6957744.

Mills, Ella S. "Dialectics of Belonging and Strategies of Space: Cultural Memory, B/black Women's Creativity, and the Folds of British Art History 1985–2011." PhD diss., University of Leeds, 2016.

Mirza, Heidi Safia. *Black British Feminism: A Reader*. London: Routledge, 1997.

Mirza, Heidi Safia, and Yasmin Gunaratnam. "'The Branch on Which I Sit': Reflections on Black British Feminism." *Feminist Review* 108, no. 1 (November 2014): 125–33. doi:10.1057/fr.2014.13.

Mitchell, Allyson. "Deep Lez" (2009, rev. 2015). In *Queer*, edited by David Getsy, 181–83. Documents of Contemporary Art Series. London: Whitechapel, 2016.

Mitchell, Allyson, and Cait McKinney, eds. *Inside Killjoy's Kastle: Dykey Ghosts, Feminist Monsters, and Other Lesbian Hauntings*. Vancouver, BC: University of British Columbia Press, 2019.

Mitchell, Juliet. "Concepts of Women's Liberation, (I) Consciousness-Raising." In *Woman's Estate*, 60–63. New York: Pantheon, 1972.

Mitchell, Juliet. *Woman's Estate*. New York: Pantheon, 1972.

Mitchell, Juliet. "Women: The Longest Revolution" (1966). In *Women, the Longest Revolution: Essays on Feminism, Literature, and Psychoanalysis*, 17–54. London: Virago, 1984.

Mitchell, Juliet. *Women, the Longest Revolution: Essays on Feminism, Literature, and Psychoanalysis*. London: Virago, 1984.

Mitchell, Juliet, Wendy Hollway, and Julie Walsh. "Interview with Juliet Mitchell—Psychoanalysis and Feminism: Then and Now." *Psychoanalysis, Culture and Society* 20 (June 2015): 112–30. doi:10.1057/pcs.2015.3.

Mitchell, Juliet, and Sarah Shin. "Juliet Mitchell: Looking Back at *Woman's Estate*." *Versobooks.com* (blog), February 3, 2015. http://www.versobooks.com/blogs/1836-juliet -mitchell-looking-back-at-woman-s-estate.

Modleski, Tania. *Loving with a Vengeance: Mass-Produced Fantasies for Women*. New York: Routledge, 1988.

Modleski, Tania. "Some Functions of Feminist Criticism, or The Scandal of the Mute Body." *October* 49 (1989): 3–24. doi:10.2307/778730.

Molesworth, Helen. "How to Install Art as a Feminist." In *Modern Women: Women Artists at the Museum of Modern Art*, edited by Cornelia H. Butler and Alexandra Schwartz, 499–513. New York: Museum of Modern Art, 2010. Exhibition catalog.

Molesworth, Helen. "Worlds Apart." *Artforum International* 45, no. 9 (2007): 101–2.

Moore, Darnell L. "Structurelessness, Structure, and Queer Movements." *Women's Studies Quarterly* 41, nos. 3–4 (2013): 257–60. https://www.jstor.org/stable/23611522.

Moraga, Cherríe, and Gloria Anzaldúa. "Introduction." In *This Bridge Called My Back: Writings by Radical Women of Color*, 2nd ed., edited by Cherríe Moraga and Gloria Anzaldúa, xxiii–xxvi. New York: Kitchen Table: Women of Color Press, 1983.

Moraga, Cherríe, and Gloria Anzaldúa, eds. *This Bridge Called My Back: Writings by Radical Women of Color*, 2nd ed. New York: Kitchen Table: Women of Color Press, 1983.

Morgan, Robin, ed. *Sisterhood Is Powerful: An Anthology of Writings from the Women's Liberation Movement*. New York: Vintage, 1970.

Mueller, Roswitha. "Learning for a New Society: The *Lehrstück*." In *The Cambridge Companion to Brecht*, edited by Peter Thomson and Glendyr Sacks, 79–95. Cambridge Companions to Literature. Cambridge: Cambridge University Press, 1994.

Müller, Ulrike, ed. *Work the Room: A Handbook of Performance Strategies*. Berlin: B_books, 2006.

Müller, Ulrike, and Connie Fitzpatrick. "Putting the Invent in Inventory." Edited by Tirza True Latimer. *Art Journal* 72, no. 2 (2013): 64–69. doi:10.1080/00043249.2013.10791029.

Mulvey, Laura. *Visual and Other Pleasures*, 2nd ed. Language, Discourse, Society. Houndmills, UK: Palgrave Macmillan, 2009.

Muñoz, José Esteban. *The Brown Commons*. Seventh Annual Feminist Theory Workshop, Duke University, March 22, 2013. YouTube, May 8, 2013. https://www.youtube.com/watch?v=huGN866GnZE.

Muñoz, José Esteban. *Cruising Utopia: The Then and There of Queer Futurity*. New York: New York University Press, 2009.

Muñoz, José Esteban. "Ephemera as Evidence: Introductory Notes to Queer Acts." *Women and Performance* 8, no. 2 (1996): 5–16. doi:10.1080/07407709608571228.

Murray, Alex. *Giorgio Agamben*. London: Routledge, 2010.

Myles, Eileen. "My Most Recent Acceptance (2016): Eileen Myles on Zoe Leonard's *I Want a President*." Artforum.com, November 12, 2016. https://www.artforum.com/slant/id=64677.

Nealon, Christopher. *Foundlings: Lesbian and Gay Historical Emotion before Stonewall*. Durham, NC: Duke University Press, 2001.

Neely, Sarah. "Voicing the Silences." *MAP Magazine*, February 2015. http://mapmagazine.co.uk/9793/feminist-chorus-voicing-silences.

Nietzsche, Friedrich Wilhelm. *The Nietzsche Reader*. Edited by Keith Ansell-Pearson and Duncan Large. Malden, MA: Blackwell, 2006.

Nietzsche, Friedrich. *On the Advantage and Disadvantage of History for Life*. Indianapolis: Hackett, 1999.

Nietzsche, Friedrich. *Untimely Meditations*. Cambridge Texts in the History of Philosophy. Cambridge: Cambridge University Press, 1997.

Nixon, Mignon. "Death Work in Venice: *In Memoriam Khadija Saye*." *October* 161 (August 2017): 3–10. doi:10.1162/OCTO_a_00300.

Nixon, Mignon. "'Why Freud?' Asked the Shrew: Psychoanalysis and Feminism, Post-Partum Document, and the History Group." *Psychoanalysis, Culture and Society* 20, no. 2 (June 2015): 131–40. doi:10.1057/pcs.2015.2.

Nochlin, Linda. *Representing Women*. London: Thames and Hudson, 1999.

O'Keefe, Sara. "Chosen: Constellations of Influence." In *Trigger: Gender as a Tool and a Weapon*, edited by Johanna Burton and Natalie Bell, 224. New York: New Museum, 2017.

Osborne, Peter. *Anywhere or Not at All: Philosophy of Contemporary Art*. London: Verso, 2013.

Parker, Rozsika, and Griselda Pollock, eds. *Framing Feminism: Art and the Women's Movement 1970–85*. London: Pandora, 1987.

Pester, Holly. "Archive Fanfiction: Experimental Archive Research Methodologies and Feminist Epistemological Tactics." *Feminist Review* 115, no. 1 (2017): 114–29. doi:10.1057/s41305-017-0042-2.

Pester, Holly. *Go to Reception and Ask for Sara in Red Felt Tip*. London: Book Works, 2015.

Phelan, Peggy. "Dance and the History of Hysteria." In *Corporealities: Dancing, Knowledge, Culture, and Power*, edited by Susan Leigh Foster, 92–108. London: Routledge, 1996.

Phelan, Peggy. "Reciting the Citation of Others; or, A Second Introduction." In *Acting Out: Feminist Performances*, 13–31. Ann Arbor: University of Michigan Press, 1993.

Phelan, Peggy, and Jill Lane, eds. *The Ends of Performance*. New York: New York University Press, 1998.

Piepmeier, Alison. *Girl Zines: Making Media, Doing Feminism*. New York: New York University Press, 2009.

Plate, Liedeke. "Remembering the Future; or, Whatever Happened to Re-vision?" *Signs* 33, no. 2 (January 1, 2008): 389–411. doi:10.1086/518276.

Plath, Sylvia. *The Collected Poems*. Edited by Ted Hughes. New York: Harper and Row, 1981.

Pollock, Griselda. *Differencing the Canon: Feminist Desire and the Writing of Art's Histories*. London: Routledge, 1999.

Pollock, Griselda. *Encounters in the Virtual Feminist Museum: Time, Space and the Archive*. New York: Routledge, 2007.

Pollock, Griselda. "Feminist Pedagogies." *n.paradoxa* 26 (July 2010): 20–28. https://www.ktpress.co.uk/nparadoxa-volume-details.asp?volumeid=26.

Pollock, Griselda, ed. *Generations and Geographies in the Visual Arts: Feminist Readings*. London: Routledge, 1996.

Pollock, Griselda. "'How the Political World Crashes In on My Personal Everyday': Lubaina Himid's Conversations and Voices: Towards an Essay About Cotton.Com." *Afterall* 43 (March 2017): 18–29. doi:10.1086/692550.

Pollock, Griselda. "Is Feminism a Trauma, a Bad Memory, or a Virtual Future?" *Differences* 27, no. 2 (September 2016): 27–61. doi:10.1215/10407391-3621697.

Pollock, Griselda. "The Politics of Theory: Generations and Geographies in Feminist Theory and the Histories of Art Histories." In *Generations and Geographies in the Visual Arts: Feminist Readings*, edited by Griselda Pollock, 3–24. London: Routledge, 1996.

Pollock, Griselda. "*Revenge*: Lubaina Himid and the Making of New Narratives for New Histories." In *Differencing the Canon: Feminist Desire and the Writing of Art's Histories*, 168–96. London: Routledge, 1999. doi:10.4324/9780203397190.

Pollock, Griselda. "Screening the Seventies: Sexuality and Representation in Feminist Practice—A Brechtian Perspective." In *Vision and Difference: Femininity, Feminism and Histories of Art*, 155–99. London: Routledge, 1988.

Pollock, Griselda. *Vision and Difference: Femininity, Feminism and Histories of Art*. London: Routledge, 1988.

Preciado, Paul B. *Testo Junkie: Sex, Drugs, and Biopolitics in the Pharmacopornographic Era*. New York: The Feminist Press, 2013.

Price, Dorothy. "'Dreaming Has a Share in History': Biding Time in the Work of Lubaina Himid." *Art History* 44, no. 3 (June 2021): 650–75.

Princenthal, Nancy. "Feminism Unbound." *Art in America*, no. 6 (2007): 142–53.

Radway, Janice A. *Reading the Romance: Women, Patriarchy, and Popular Literature*. Chapel Hill: University of North Carolina Press, 2006.

Rainer, Yvonne. *Feelings Are Facts: A Life*. Cambridge, MA: MIT Press, 2006.

Rainer, Yvonne. "Some Retrospective Notes on a Dance for 10 People and 12 Mattresses Called *Parts of Some Sextets*, Performed at the Wadsworth Atheneum, Hartford, Connecticut, and Judson Memorial Church, New York, in March, 1965." In *Work, 1961–73*, 45–51. Halifax: Press of the Nova Scotia College of Art and Design, 1974. (Originally published in *Tulane Drama Review* 10, no. 2 [Winter 1965]: 168–78.)

Rainer, Yvonne. "Trio A: Genealogy, Documentation, Notation." *Dance Research Journal* 41, no. 2 (2009): 12–18. doi:10.1017/S0149767700000619.

Rainer, Yvonne. *Work, 1961–73*. Halifax: Press of the Nova Scotia College of Art and Design, 1974.

Rainer, Yvonne. "Working round the L-Word." In *Queer Looks: Perspectives on Lesbian and Gay Film and Video*, edited by Martha Gever, Pratibha Parmar, and John Greyson, 12–20. London: Routledge, 1993.

Rancière, Jacques. *The Names of History: On the Poetics of Knowledge*. Translated by Hassan Melehy. Minneapolis: University of Minnesota Press, 1994.

Random Love, Kate. "The Possibility of an Island: The Adolescent Condition in Contemporary Art in New York." PhD diss., Courtauld Institute of Art, London, 2010.

Reckitt, Helena. "Generating Feminisms: Italian Feminisms and the 'Now You Can Go' Program." *Art Journal* 76, no. 3–4 (2017): 101–11. doi:10.1080/00043249.2017.1418495.

Reckitt, Helena, ed. *Not Quite How I Remember It*. Toronto: Power Plant, 2008. Exhibition catalog.

Reckitt, Helena. "Unusual Suspects: Global Feminisms and WACK! Art and the Feminist Revolution." *n.paradoxa* 18 (2006): 34–42.

Reckitt, Helena, and Gabrielle Moser. "Feminist Tactics of Citation, Annotation, and Translation: Curatorial Reflections on the Now You Can Go Programme." *On Curating*, no. 29 (May 2016). http://www.on-curating.org/issue-29-reader/feminist-tactics-of-citation-annotation-and-translation-curatorial-reflections-on-the-now-you-can-go-programme.html#.XKIH5qZ7mi4.

Redstockings, ed. *Feminist Revolution*. New York: Random House, 1978.

Reilly, Maura, and Linda Nochlin, eds. *Global Feminisms: New Directions in Contemporary Art*. London: Merrell, 2007.

Reynolds, Lucy. "A Collective Response: Feminism, Film, Performance and Greenham Common." *MIRAJ/Moving Image Review and Art Journal* 4, no. 1 (December 2015): 90–101. doi:10.1386/miraj.4.1-2.90_1.

Reynolds, Lucy. *A Feminist Chorus: A Score in Three Parts*. Glasgow: MAP Magazine, 2015.

Rich, Adrienne. "Claiming an Education" (1977). In *On Lies, Secrets, and Silence: Selected Prose, 1966–1978*, 231–35. New York: W. W. Norton, 1995.

Rich, Adrienne. *The Fact of a Doorframe: Poems Selected and New: 1950–1984*. New York: W. W. Norton, 1985.

Rich, Adrienne. "To Invent What We Desire." In *What Is Found There: Notebooks on Poetry and Politics*, 214–16. New York: W. W. Norton, 1993.

Rich, Adrienne. *On Lies, Secrets, and Silence: Selected Prose, 1966–1978*. New York: W. W. Norton, 1995.

Rich, Adrienne. *What Is Found There: Notebooks on Poetry and Politics*. New York: W. W. Norton, 1993.

Rich, Adrienne. "When We Dead Awaken: Writing as Re-vision." *College English* 34, no. 1 (October 1972): 18–30. doi:10.2307/375215.

Rich, B. Ruby. *New Queer Cinema: The Director's Cut*. Durham, NC: Duke University Press, 2013.

Richardson, Elsa. "Refusing the Unconscious? Second Wave Feminism and Psychoanalysis." Talk presented at Psychoanalysis and History seminar series, Institute of Historical Studies, University of London, 2015.

Richmond, Susan. "'From Stone to Cloud': Mary Kelly's *Love Songs* and Feminist Intergenerationality." *Feminist Theory* 11, no. 1 (2010): 57–78. doi:10.1177/1464700109355214.

Ridout, Nicholas. *Passionate Amateurs: Theatre, Communism, and Love*. Ann Arbor: University of Michigan Press, 2013.

Ridout, Nicholas. *Theatre and Ethics*. New York: Palgrave Macmillan, 2009.

Robinson, Hilary. "The Early Work of Griselda Pollock in the Context of Developing Feminist Thinking in Art History and Criticism." Edited by Raluca Bibiri. *Images, Imagini, Images*, no. 7 (2017): 19–50.

Roe, Alex Martinis. *Two Voices*. Berlin: Universität der Künste Berlin, 2014.

Rohy, Valerie. *Anachronism and Its Others: Sexuality, Race, Temporality*. Albany: State University of New York Press, 2009.

Roseneil, Sasha. *Common Women, Uncommon Practices: The Queer Feminism of Greenham*. London: Cassell, 2000.

Ross, Christine. *The Past Is the Present; It's the Future Too: The Temporal Turn in Contemporary Art*. New York: Continuum, 2012.

Rowbotham, Sheila. *The Past Is before Us: Feminism in Action since the 1960s.* Harmondsworth, UK: Penguin, 1990.

Rowe, Dorothy. "Retrieving, Remapping, and Rewriting Histories of British Art: Lubaina Himid's 'Revenge.'" In *A Companion to British Art: 1600 to the Present,* edited by Dana Arnold and David Peters Corbett, 289–314. Chichester, UK: Wiley-Blackwell, 2013.

Roysdon, Emily, and Joseph Henry. "'What Instruments Have We?': A Conversation with Emily Roysdon." *Momus* (blog), accessed July 6, 2015. http://momus.ca/what-instruments-have-we-a-conversation-with-emily-roysdon.

Russ, Joanna. *Magic Mommas, Trembling Sisters, Puritans and Perverts: Feminist Essays.* Trumansburg, NY: Crossing, 1985.

Sandvoss, Cornel. *Fans: The Mirror of Consumption.* Oxford: Polity, 2005.

Sarachild, Kathie. "A Program for Feminist 'Consciousness Raising.'" In *Notes from the Second Year: Women's Liberation,* 78–80. New York: Radical Feminism, 1970. https://library.duke.edu/digitalcollections/wlmpc_wlmms01039.

Schaffner, Ingrid, ed. *Queer Voice: Laurie Anderson, Harry Dodge and Stanya Kahn, Sharon Hayes, John Kelly, Kalup Linzy, Jack Smith, Ryan Trecartin, Andy Warhol.* Philadelphia: Institute of Contemporary Art, University of Pennsylvania, 2010. Exhibition catalog.

Schneider, Rebecca. "Performance Remains." *Performance Research* 6, no. 2 (January 2001): 100–108. doi:10.1080/13528165.2001.10871792.

Schneider, Rebecca. *Performing Remains: Art and War in Times of Theatrical Reenactment.* London: Routledge, 2011.

Schneider, Rebecca. "Remembering Feminist Remimesis: A Riddle in Three Parts." *TDR/The Drama Review* 58, no. 2 (2014): 14–32. doi:10.1162/DRAM_a_00344.

Schneider, Rebecca. *Theatre and History.* Houndmills, UK: Palgrave Macmillan, 2014.

Scott, Joan Wallach. *The Fantasy of Feminist History.* Durham, NC: Duke University Press, 2011.

Sedgwick, Eve Kosofsky. *Tendencies.* London: Routledge, 1994.

Setch, Eve. "The Face of Metropolitan Feminism: The London Women's Liberation Workshop, 1969–79." *Twentieth Century British History* 13, no. 2 (January 1, 2002): 171–90. doi:10.1093/tcbh/13.2.171.

Sharpe, Christina. *In the Wake: On Blackness and Being.* Durham, NC: Duke University Press, 2016.

Sharpe, Christina. "The Wake." In *In the Wake: On Blackness and Being,* 1–24. Durham, NC: Duke University Press, 2016.

Siegel, Katy. *Since '45: America and the Making of Contemporary Art.* London: Reaktion, 2010.

Singerman, Howard. *Art Subjects: Making Artists in the American University.* Berkeley: University of California Press, 1999.

Smith, Barbara, ed. *Home Girls: A Black Feminist Anthology.* New York: Kitchen Table: Women of Color Press, 1983.

Smith, Terry. "Contemporaneity in the History of Art." *Contemporaneity: Historical Presence in Visual Culture* 1 (2011): 3–34. doi:10.5195/CONTEMP.2011.32.

Smith, Terry. "Contemporary Art and Contemporaneity." *Critical Inquiry* 32, no. 4 (2006): 681–707. doi:10.1086/508087.

Smith, Terry. *What Is Contemporary Art?* Chicago: University of Chicago Press, 2009.

Smith, Vanessa. "Abundant Evidence: Black Women Artists of the 1960s and 70s." In *WACK! Art and the Feminist Revolution*, edited by Cornelia H. Butler and Lisa Gabrielle Mark, 400–413. Los Angeles: Museum of Contemporary Art, 2007. Exhibition catalog.

Sørensen, Trine Friis. "Judith Shakespeare—Undead or Alive? On Kajsa Dahlberg's Artist Book *A Room of One's Own/A Thousand Libraries*." In *Notes on Location*. Copenhagen: Frie Udstillingsbygning, 2015. https://www.notesonlocation.dk/#section8.

Sorkin, Jenni. "Social Construction." *Frieze*, no. 105 (March 2007): 35–36.

Spivak, Gayatri Chakravorty. *A Critique of Postcolonial Reason: Toward a History of the Vanishing Present*. Cambridge, MA: Harvard University Press, 1999.

Spivak, Gayatri Chakravorty. *In Other Worlds: Essays in Cultural Politics*. London: Routledge, 2014.

Spivak, Gayatri Chakravorty and Steve Paulson. "Critical Intimacy: An Interview with Gayatri Chakravorty Spivak." *Los Angeles Review of Books*, June 29, 2016. https://lareviewofbooks.org/article/critical-intimacy-interview-gayatri-chakravorty-spivak.

Staple, Polly. "Ah, Feminism." *Frieze*, no. 105 (March 2007): 23.

Steedman, Carolyn. *Dust*. Manchester, UK: Manchester University Press, 2001.

Stein, Gertrude. *How Writing Is Written*. Edited by Robert Bartlett Haas. Los Angeles: Black Sparrow, 1974.

Steinweg, Reiner. "Two Chapters from 'Learning Play and Epic Theatre.'" In *Lehrstück und Episches Theater: Brechts Theorie und die Theaterpädagogische Praxis*, translated by Sruti Bala, 17–21, 23–31. Frankfurt am Main: Brandes and Apsel, 1995. http://bgxmag.com/steinweg2chapters.aspx.

Sulter, Maud. *Jeanne Duval: A Melodrama*. Edinburgh: National Galleries of Scotland, 2003. Exhibition catalog.

Sulter, Maud. "Maud Sulter on Negotiating the Muse." In *Jeanne Duval: A Melodrama*, 13–15. Edinburgh: National Galleries of Scotland, 2003. Exhibition catalog.

Sulter, Maud, ed. *Passion: Discourses on Blackwomen's Creativity*. Hebden Bridge, UK: Urban Fox, 1990.

Sulter, Maud. "Without Tides, No Maps." In *Lubaina Himid: Revenge*, by Jill Morgan and Lubaina Himd, 26–35. Rochdale, UK: Rochdale Art Gallery, 1992. Exhibition catalog.

Taubin, Amy. "And What Is a Fact Anyway? (On a Tape by Martha Rosler)." *Millennium Film Journal*, nos. 4–5 (Summer 1979): 59–63.

Taylor, Diana. *The Archive and the Repertoire: Performing Cultural Memory in the Americas*. Durham, NC: Duke University Press, 2003.

Thomson, Peter, and Glendyr Sacks, eds. *The Cambridge Companion to Brecht*. Cambridge Companions to Literature. Cambridge: Cambridge University Press, 1994.

Tickner, Lisa. "Mediating Generation: The Mother-Daughter Plot." In *Women Artists at the Millennium*, edited by Carol M. Armstrong and M. Catherine de Zegher, 82–120. Cambridge, MA: MIT Press, 2006.

Tobin, Amy. "I'll Show You Mine, If You Show Me Yours: Collaboration, Consciousness-Raising and Feminist-Influenced Art in the 1970s." *Tate Papers* 25 (Spring 2016). http://www.tate.org.uk/research/publications/tate-papers/25/i-show-you-mine-if-you-show-me-yours-2.

Tobin, Amy. "Moving Pictures: Intersections between Art, Film and Feminism in the 1970s." *MIRAJ/Moving Image Review and Art Journal* 4, no. 1 (December 2015): 118–34. doi:10.1386/miraj.4.1-2.118_1.

Tobin, Amy. "Working Together, Working Apart: Feminism, Art, and Collaboration in Britain and the United States, 1970–81." PhD diss., University of York, 2016. http://etheses.whiterose.ac.uk/16445.

Wagner, Gretchen L. "Riot on the Page: Thirty Years of Zines by Women." In *Modern Women Artists at the Museum of Modern Art*, edited by Cornelia H. Butler and Alexandra Schwartz, 444–61. New York: Museum of Modern Art, 2010. Exhibition catalog.

Walker, Alice. "In Search of Our Mothers' Gardens" (1972). In *Within the Circle: An Anthology of African American Literary Criticism from the Harlem Renaissance to the Present*, edited by Angelyn Mitchell, 401–9. Durham, NC: Duke University Press, 1994.

Walker, Alice. "One Child of One's Own: A Meaningful Digression within the Work(s)." In *In Search of Our Mothers' Gardens: Womanist Prose*, 361–83. 1983; repr., London: Women's Press, 1984.

Ware, Syrus Marcus. "All Power to All People? Black LGBTTI2QQ Activism, Remembrance, and Archiving in Toronto." *TSQ: Transgender Studies Quarterly* 4, no. 2 (May 2017): 170–80. doi:10.1215/23289252-3814961.

Warner, Michael. *Publics and Counterpublics*. New York: Zone, 2002.

Warner, Michael. "Queer and Then?" *Chronicle of Higher Education*, January 1, 2012. https://www.chronicle.com/article/QueerThen-/130161.

Wazana Tompkins, Kyla. "Ball Busters and the Recurring Trauma of Intergenerational Queer/Feminist Life." *Bully Bloggers* (blog), February 20, 2016. https://bullybloggers.wordpress.com/2016/02/20/ball-busters-and-the-recurring-trauma-of-intergenerational-queerfeminist-life.

Weeks, Kathi. *The Problem with Work: Feminism, Marxism, Antiwork Politics, and Postwork Imaginaries*. Durham, NC: Duke University Press, 2011.

Werckmeister, O. "Walter Benjamin's Angel of History, or the Transfiguration of the Revolutionary into the Historian." *Critical Inquiry* 22, no. 2 (1996): 239–67. doi:10.1086/448790.

West-East Coast Bag (WEB). "Consciousness-Raising Rules" (1972). In *Feminism—Art—Theory: An Anthology, 1968–2000*, edited by Hilary Robinson, 85–86. Oxford: Blackwell, 2001.

Whiteley, Sheila. *Sexing the Groove: Popular Music and Gender*. London: Routledge, 1997.

Wilson, Siona. *Art Labor, Sex Politics: Feminist Effects in 1970s British Art and Performance*. Minneapolis: University of Minnesota Press, 2015.

Winterson, Jeanette. *Why Be Happy When You Could Be Normal?* London: Jonathan Cape, 2011.

Wirth, Andrzej. "The Lehrstück as Performance." Translated by Marta Ulvaeus. *TDR/The Drama Review* 43, no. 4 (1999): 113–21. doi:10.1162/105420499760263570.

Wood, Catherine. *Yvonne Rainer: The Mind Is a Muscle*. London: Afterall, 2007.

Woolf, Virginia. *The Pargiters: The Novel-Essay Portion of "The Years."* Edited by Mitchell Alexander Leaska. London: Hogarth, 1978.

Woolf, Virginia. *A Room of One's Own.* 1929; repr., Harmondsworth, UK: Penguin, 1972.

Woolf, Virginia. *Three Guineas* (1938). Edited by Morag Shiach. In *A Room of One's Own and Three Guineas.* Oxford: Oxford University Press, 2008.

Woolf, Virginia. *A Writer's Diary.* Edited by Leonard Woolf. London: Hogarth, 1953.

X Marks the Spot, Joan Anim-Addo, and Althea Greenan, eds. *Human Endeavour: A Creative Finding Aid for the Women of Colour Index.* London: Women's Art Library, Goldsmiths, University of London, 2015. http://research.gold.ac.uk/id/eprint/19685.

Zanish-Belcher, Tanya, and Anke Voss, eds. *Perspectives on Women's Archives.* Chicago: Society of American Archivists, 2013.

Zapperi, Giovanna. "Woman's Reappearance: Rethinking the Archive in Contemporary Art—Feminist Perspectives." *Feminist Review* 105, no. 1 (2013): 21–47. doi:10.1057/fr.2013.22.

Zarifi, Yana. "Chorus and Dance in the Ancient World." In *The Cambridge Companion to Greek and Roman Theatre*, edited by Marianne Macdonald and J. Michael Walton, 227–46. Cambridge: Cambridge University Press, 2007.

Zegher, M. Catherine de. *Inside the Visible: An Elliptical Traverse of 20th Century Art in, of, and from the Feminine.* Cambridge, MA: MIT Press, 1996. Exhibition catalog.

Zegher, M. Catherine de, ed. *Martha Rosler: Positions in the Life World.* Cambridge, MA: MIT Press, 1998. Exhibition catalog.

Zolghadr, Tirdad. "Tough Love." *Frieze*, no. 105 (March 2007): 33.

Black feminist histories, 9, 10, 103; British lesbian and feminist organizations in *Killjoy's Kastle*, 48, 50–53, 54–59, 61–65; Henderson's "The Black Lesbian," 12; importance of archiving histories in Britain, 55–59, 62–63, 65, 103, 122; Walker on mother's creative life, 136, 137; and whiteness of feminism, 111, 112; and women artists of color, 120, 122; women of color and challenges as writers, 137–39. *See also* Women of Colour Index (woci)

Black Lesbian and Gay Centre, London, 62

Black Lives Matter movement, 12, 105, 173n32

Black Woman Time Now exhibition (London, 1983), 117, 120, 122

Blocker, Jane, 17

Bodek, Richard, 96, 97

body. *See* embodiment

"Book Bloc" protests, 59–60

books and reading: Brecht's comparison with rehearsal, 59, 72, 78; and feminist chorus, 88, 89–92, *91*, 94, 95, 97, 102–5, 107–8; and feminist experience, 59, 67, 69–70, 80, 84; Gender Studies Dance Party in *Killjoy's Kastle*, 59–60, *60*; reading groups, 10, 57, 88, 103–5, 108; reading Woolf and creativity, 79–80; "recitation" and feminist literature, 88–89, 95, 97; Winterson's embodiment of texts, 149–50. *See also* libraries; writing and rewriting

Boudry, Pauline, 130; *Salomania* (film with Renate Lorenz), 69, 72–78, *73–75*, *77*, 84, 85

Brecht, Bertolt, 57, 78, 81, 86; and chorus, 88, 95–97; epic theater, 60–61, 72, 96; radio works, 95–96; "Theatre for Learning," 60, 95, 96–97. *See also* learning-play (Brecht's *Lehrstück*)

Breuer, Josef, 84

Britain. *See* United Kingdom

British Film Institute (bfi), 47, 48, 53

British Library, London: Sisterhood and After: The Women's Liberation Oral History Project, 163n51, 174n49

Brooklyn Museum, New York: Elizabeth Sackler Feminist Art Center, 21, 105; *We Wanted a Revolution: Black Radical Women 1965–85* (2007), 105–6

Bryan-Wilson, Julia, 19, 139, 159–60n55

Buelow, Erin. *See* Green: NOT TO DISCOU[RAGE] YOU

Burin, Yula, 55, 57, 59, 162n32

Burns, A. K., 33–34

Butler, Judith, 30, 59, 89

capitalism and women's subjugation, 134

Carolyn, Louise, 51

Castagner, Lisa, 142

"Chain Reactions" lesbian fetish night, 163n51

Cherry, Deborah, 119, 172n11

Chester, Gail, 63–64, 65

Chicago, Judy: *The Dinner Party*, 21; *Womanhouse* (with Miriam Shapiro), 101

chorus. *See* feminist chorus; Greek chorus

Chrysalis (feminist journal), 10

cinema: Hollywood films and male gaze, 42

Cinenova collection of women's film, 159n55

Circa 1968 exhibition (2004), 127

collaborative working: community and creativity, 79–80, 135, 148; and feminist chorus, 101–2; and *Killjoy's Castle* installation, 48, 51, 53–54

colonial history and Himid's *Revenge* series, 116

common land and women, 134

consciousness-raising: argument and managing conflict, 116–17; and feminist chorus, 87, 88, 100–102, 108; and learning-play, 80, 86, 100

constellations motif, 9; feminist communities across time, 11, 20, 64, 70, 118–19, 120, 122–25, 137, 146–47, 148; feminist histories and contemporary art, 8, 16, 20, 118, 129–30, 131–32; Himid's maps and constellations of women artists of color, 117–18, 118–19, 120, 122, 131; queer lineages and constellations of influences, 124–25; and temporalities, 11, 16, 20, 64, 70, 81, 122–25; viewer's perspective, 122–24

contemporary: meanings and discussions of, 16–18, 122–24

contemporary art: challenges of defining, 17–18. *See also* art history

conversations and feminist communities,

109–32, 148; Himid's *Five* (*Revenge* series)
as conversation, 113–16, 117, 125; student–
teacher conversations, 124–25, 127, 129–30,
142
Cooper, Dennis, 158n26
Craig, Lauren, 162n28
creativity: common ground for women's creativity, 134–50; community and creativity,
79–80, 135, 148; fans' generation of new
texts, 25, 27, 41; need for time to create,
8–9, 11, 68–69, 78–81, 141. *See also* writing
and rewriting
Cruikshank, Margaret, 59
Cubitt Gallery, London, *2*
curation and installation of art: feminist perspectives, 19–20; Himid's work as curator,
108–9, 117
Cvetkovich, Ann, 140–41, 152n6, 152n17

Dahlberg, Kajsa, 97; *A Room of One's Own/
A Thousand Libraries*, 69, 80, 81, *81*, 85
dance: Boudry and Lorenz's *Salomania*, 69,
72–78, *73–75*, *77*, 84, 85; and Greek chorus,
94; Green's *NOT TO DISCOU[RAGE] YOU*,
69, 82–86, *82–83*
Davis, Angela, 59
Debord, Guy, 174n48
"Deep Lez" concept, 54
de Lauretis, Teresa, 9, 16, 137
depression and creative life, 140, 141
Deutsche, Rosalyn, 30, 70, 146, 159n44
DeWitt, Helen, 51
Diamond, Elin, 57, 71
Didi-Huberman, Georges, 152n7
di Franco, Karen, 101
digital platforms and art, 25
Dinshaw, Carolyn, 15–16, 70, 123, 152n6
Disobedient Objects exhibition (London,
2014–15), 59–60
do-it-yourself (DIY) production methods, 3,
7, 25, 43
Dworkin, Andrea, 67

education and learning: learning from history
and reenactment, 10–11, 13–15, 18, 40–41,
44, 46; Women's Liberation Movement,
177n35; Woolf's "poor," "new" college

concept, 135, 139, 142–43, 146, 147. *See also*
group practices and learning; learning-
play (Brecht's *Lehrstück*); universities and
academia
e-flux journal: *What Is Contemporary Art?*,
17
Eichhorn, Kate, 85–86
Eisenman, Nicole. *See* Ridykeulous
Elsie Piddock Skips in Her Sleep (Eleanor
Farjeon), 133–34
embodiment: dancing and Greek chorus, 94;
embodied communities, 102; embodied
reading and feminist chorus, 88, 89, 92,
107–8; and feminist art history, 19; hysteria
and women's bodies, 84; rehearsal and reenactment, 69, 71, 72–78; rehearsal process
as art, 71, 81–86; time in the body, 15–16;
Winterson's embodiment of books,
149–50
enslaved people and Himid's *Revenge* series,
116
epic theater, 60–61, 72, 96
Every Ocean Hughes (*formerly* Emily Roysdon), 7, 28, 38, *38–39*, 129, 153; *Ecstatic
Resistance* exhibition, 44; *Untitled (David
Wojnarowicz Project)*, 1, *3*, 31–32

FAG Feminist Art Gallery, 54
fans and feminism, 6–10, 9, 19, 21–46, 84,
140–41; contemporary art and histories
of feminism, 4, 21–22, 40–41, 44, 46;
diversity of fans and models of fandom,
23–28; dynamic relationship across time,
6, 28–29, 146; fandom as deviant behavior,
27–28; intensity of interaction and creative
production, 25, 27, 41; reenactment and
activism, 40–41, 44, 46; reenactment and
rehearsal, 74, 76
Farjeon, Eleanor. *See Elsie Piddock Skips in
Her Sleep*
Federici, Silvia, 134
feminism: as "longest revolution," 5, 135; as ongoing project, 142
Feminist Activist Forum (FAF), 61
feminist art and art history, 19–20
Feminist Art Center. *See* Brooklyn Museum
feminist chorus, 8, 9, 10, 67, 87–108, 147; and
Hamid's *Five*, 113–16

medes's "SCUB Manifesto," 30–31, *31*; "reviews procedure" and responses to, 33–34

The L Word (TV series), 118

Making Black Waves: Lesbians Talk (Mason-John and Khambatta), 61–62, 63, 65

Making Histories Visible archive, 110, 117, 130

male gaze and Hollywood cinema, 42

Malik, Samia, 101, 103, 105

maps and Himid's work, 106–7, *107*, 110, 117–18, 120, 122, 131

Martin, Rosy, 56

masculinity: gay masculinity and queer feminist art, 32–33

Mason-John, Valerie. See *Making Black Waves*

Meyer, Richard, 17

Milan Women's Bookstore Collective, 11, 136–37, 139

Mills, Ella, 119, 172n24

Mirza, Heidi Safia, 59

Miss World Contest, 160n58

Mitchell, Allyson and Deirdre Logue: *Her's Is Still a Dank Cave*, 54. See also *Killjoy's Kastle*

Mitchell, Juliet, 5, 100, 135, 138, 177n35

Modleski, Tania, 136

Molesworth, Helen, 19–20, 146

Moraga, Cherríe, 138

Morris, Olive, 56–57

Moten, Fred, 9, 143, 147–48

mother-daughter metaphor and feminism, 29

Move, Richard, 166n52

Ms Understood exhibition (London, 2009–10), 160n60

Mueller, Roswitha, 72, 97, 101

Müller, Ulrike, 28, 29–30, 34, 44, 152n18

Mulvey, Laura: *Riddles of the Sphinx* (film with Peter Wollen), 44, *45*; "Visual Pleasure and Narrative Cinema" film, 42–44, *43*, *45*, 46

music: and queer and feminist communities, 3, 153n18; rock-and-roll and fandom, 40

Nazimova, Alla: *Salomé* (film), 72–73, 74, 76, 78

Nembhard, Gina, 162n28

networks. See constellations motif

Nixon, Mignon, 19

non-binary identities, 77

Oakley, Ann, 177n35

October (journal): questionnaire on "The Contemporary," 17, 139

Orbach, Susie, 90

organizations and groups: defunct organizations in *Killjoy's Kastle*, 48, 50–53, 54–59, 61–65; and feminist chorus, 87–108; small groups and feminism in 1970s, 100–101, 108. See also fans and feminism

Organization of Women of African and Asian Descent (OWAAD), 62

Osborne, Peter, 17, 18, 156n59

Out of the Archives exhibition (London, 2010), 160n60

Parker, Rianna Jade. See Thick/er Black Lines collective

Parker, Rozsika: *Framing Feminism* (with Pollock), 111, 112

performance studies, 18, 19. See also reenactment; re-performance and art

performativity, 30, 89, 125

Perry, Sondra: *Typhoon Coming On*, 172n15

Pethick, Emily, *2*

The Place is Here exhibition (London, 2017), 106, 117, 122

Plath, Sylvia: "Love Letter," 40–41

poetry: feminism and new possibilities, 9–10

A Political Feeling, I Hope So exhibition (2004), 46; "separatist curtain," 67–68, *68*

politics and activism: archival material, 44; "Book Bloc" protests, 59–60; continuities and similarities in lesbian activism over time, 44; fans and reenactment, 40–41, 44, 46; interest of contemporary art in feminism, 22, *24–25*, 25; Kelly's *Love Songs* and multi-generational views on, 35–42; Leonard's "I Want a President" project, 88, 97–99, 108; *LTTR* and demand for political activism, 34; workers' choruses in Weimar Germany, 96, 97. See also consciousness-raising; Women's Liberation Movement (WLM)

universities and academia: precariousness of academic life, 141–42; as space for writing and creativity, 139–42, *144–45*, 148–49; teacher–student interactions and influences, 124–25, 127, 129–30, 142; and undercommons, 147–48; Woolf's alternative college for women, 142–43, 146, 147, 148

Virago Classics series, 67, 88

WACK! Art and the Feminist Revolution exhibition (2007), 6, 21, 44, 106
Walker, Alice, 136, 137, 139
Walsh, Susan, 110
Weimar Germany and chorus, 88, 96–97
We Wanted a Revolution: Black Radical Women 1965–85 (Brooklyn Museum, 2007), 105–6
"Where We At" artists' collective, 106
Whitney Independent Study Program (ISP), 152–53n18; Kelly as tutor, 127, 129, 130
willful women, 134, 149
Williams Gamaker, Michelle, 101, 103, 104–5
Wilson, Siona, 101
Winterson, Jeanette, 149–50
WITCH collective, 102
Wittig, Monique, 89
Wojnarowicz, David, 1, 3; *Rimbaud in New York*, 31–32
Wollen, Peter, 174n48; *Riddles of the Sphinx* (film with Laura Mulvey), 44, *45*
women artists, 94, 109–32, 146–47; constellation of influences, 124–25; conversations on race and women artists, 9, 111, 112–13, 117, 125; and discovery of feminist art, 19–20; Himid's maps and constellations of women artists of color, 117–18, 118–19, 120, 122, 131; marginalization of women artists of color, 88, 104–5, 106–7, 112, 115
women of color and feminism, 9, 10, 103, 106, 111; challenges as writers, 137–39. *See also* Black feminist histories; Women of Colour Index (WOCI)

Women of Colour Index (WOCI), 101, 103; Reading Group, 10, 57, 88, 101, 103–5, 108
Women's Art Library, 23, 57, 101, 103; and Gasson's *The River*, 92
Women's Liberation Movement (WLM), 46, 135; and consciousness-raising, 100–101, 102; Kelly's involvement in London, 127; Kelly's *WLM Demo Remix*, 38, *38–39*, 40–41, 129; women educating women, 177n35
Women's Library, London, 160n60
women's suffrage and suffragettes, 40, 64, *64*
Woolf, Virginia, 8–9, 134–35, 156n70; *A Room of One's Own*, 8, 11, 68, 69, 78–81, 83, 85, 86, 134, 141, 142; *A Room of One's Own* reimagined by writers and artists, 135–39; *Three Guineas*, 9, 139, 142–43, 146, 147, 150, 176n23
workers' choruses in Weimar Germany, 96, 97
writing and rewriting: common ground for women's creativity, 134–35; creativity of fans, 27, 41; feminist chorus and embodied reading, 88; reworkings of Woolf's *A Room of One's Own*, 135–50; women of color and challenges as writers, 137–39; writing as privileged occupation, 137–38, 138–39. *See also* books and reading

X Marks the Spot (art and archive research collective), 56, 57, 101

"Year of Feminism" (Brooklyn Museum, 2007), 105
Yussuf, Aurella. *See* Thick/er Black Lines collective

Zaman, Rehana, 101, 103, 104
Zami I conference, 63
Zamimass, 63
Zegher, Catherine de, 151n3, 173n40
zines, 2–3, 28, 38; participatory format and historical material, 2–3; on Salome, 74, 76. *See also LTTR* (zine)
Zong (slave ship), 116